ARTPOWER

≠Blank

Copyright © by Artpower International Publishing Co.,Ltd

Address: 21/F, Skyline Commercial Centre, 71-77 Wing Lok Street,
         SheungWan, Hong Kong

Website: www.artpower.com.cn
E-mail: artpower@artpower.com.cn

Edited and produced by Artpower International Publishing Co.,Ltd

Chief Editor: Vivian Lei   info@artpower.com.cn
Copy Editor: Evelyn Wu   evelyn@artpower.com.cn
Designer: Vivian Lei   vivian@artpower.com.cn

ISBN: 978-988-18893-5-5

Printed and bound in China

In the late 1990s, David Carson published his first book—*The End of Print*, which seemed to announce the end of the print media. Irrevocably, in the 1980s, since the invention of the Personal Computer and the insertion of the use of such computers into the print media industry's workflow, these computers have made a significant impact in the industry. Not only is the Print Industry affected, but the pre-print production and workflow pipeline received a whole new makeover. Modern print designers cannot easily fathom the workflow of a print designer 20 years ago, especially the pre-print preparation part, as the original companies that handled this area have all but vanished one after another.

Perhaps the traditional means of conferring information by means of print and books cannot compare with modern day emails and the internet, or even the foundation may have had a whole shift in structure, but if not for the printed works' ability to transfer information, what else is left of the print industry? This is what a modern day print designer has to think about.

Preface

Written by **Ken-tsai Lee**

Creative Director of Ken-tsai Lee Image Design Company.
Visiting Associate Professor of Taiwan University of Arts.
Taiwan (China) Representative of Art Directors Club NY
Great China region Representative of Type Directors Club NY.

Marshall McLuhan once said—I think of art, at its most significant, as a DEW line, a Distant Early Warning system that can always be relied on to tell the old culture what is beginning to happen to it.

Thus besides the original ability of print, what else is left of it? The touch of paper? The smell of ink? Between the over emphasis on transmitting information, and the strengthening of artistic value, will be what the future direction is. Whether there will be a future third direction beyond the mass produced cheap print works and print works of collector's value, is left for all to observe and wonder.

I once saw an article, mentioning the beginning of the computer and paperless environment in an office setting, but even after 20 years of development, the need for paper is only increasing instead of decreasing, which means the need for paper is something that modern day computers cannot replace.

And then, what a designer has to also consider is the effect of print on the environment, as environmental protection is a topic that designers of the 21st century will have to face eventually.

I am very pleased to be invited by ARTPOWER Publishing to write the preface of this book, *#Blank—a book on printing*, and is hopeful that many designers all over the world are persevering over the creation of excellent masterpieces in print.

Special Mention: David Carson
Marshall McLuhan

Contents

Preface

004-005

Branding Identity

010-132

011	Ken-tsai Lee
020	Lundgren+Lindqvist
029	James Kape
032	LEAP Design
036	Brown & White Creative
039	Edwin Tan
042	Research Studios
048	Thorbjørn Ankerstjerne
057	Stas Sipovich
060	Tuukka Koivisto
064	Bart van Delft
068	Daniel Dittmar
069	The Creative Method
070	VONSUNG
080	G-MAN
090	Homework
094	La caja de tipos
108	Yomesubo
109	&Larry
110	Ministry of Design
116	Kai Zan
127	Tadas Karpavičius

Publication

133–232

134   Ken-tsai Lee
142   Kai Zan
144   Dario Verrengia
148   KentLyons
158   Purpose
164   Mind Design
168   Fuse
170   Coppens Alberts
176   KreativeHouse
182   Tadas Karpavičius
186   Patricio Murphy
190   Yomesubo
196   Demian Conrad
200   Moshik Nadav
206   Tuukka Koivisto
210   Daniel Dittmar
212   Saffron Brand Consultants
218   G-MAN/Nick Rhodes
220   Mammal
224   Thompson Brand Partners

Package

233–304

234   Anagrama
240   &Larry
256   Si Maclennan
262   Stas Sipovich
265   Yasuko Ikeda
276   Moshik Nadav
288   Fluotype
290   Ken-tsai Lee
291   Scott Lambert
296   The Creative Method

Directory

305–320

We Are Graphic Designers

Branding
Identity

Design
Ken-tsai Lee, Cheng Chung Yi
Illustrator
Robert Lin
Project
ADC NY, Young Guns 6 in Taiwan (China)

Ken-tsai Lee took charge of the whole identity design of the ADC Young Guns Show 6.

He asked Robert Lin to draw 50 creatures in different shapes so as to represent the 50 young designers on the finalists in the competition.

Each unique shape of the creature represents the exceptional talent of each designer on the finalist.

Illustrator
Robert Lin

YG613

ERIC ELMS

+ was born and raised in San Diego, then moved to New York to attend Pratt Institute
+ now runs a small design studio in Brooklyn
+ shares his free time with his wife, friends and books

YG6

DANIEL ESKILS

+ was born in the middle of nowhere in Sweden, now lives in Stockholm
+ founded a production company with producer Johan Junker
+ has since worked with Sony Ericsson, Acne Jeans, Caribou, and Those Dancing Days

YG645

ALEX TROCHUT

+ was born in Barcelona, studied in Elisava and briefly worked in Berlin
+ spent two years employed at Toormix and two more at Vasava
+ now works freelance for clients, studios and agencies around the world

YG615

+ co-founded Studio Anybody in Australia, then worked for Fabio Ongarato Design
+ moved to New York in 2006 where he started at Lloyd & Co as Senior Art Director
+ has worked with Jil Sander, Nike, Ryan McGinley, Tina Barney and Willy Vanderperre

JASON EVANS

Design

Ken-tsai Lee, Cheng Chung Yi

Project

ADC NY, Young Guns 6 in Taiwan (China)

Design

Ken-tsai Lee, Cheng Chung Yi

Illustrator

Robert Lin

Project

ADC NY, Young Guns 6 in Taiwan (China)

Since these 50 young designers surpassed many other designers in the competition, it showed their brilliance.

By bringing recognisable characteristics to each designer on the finalist, each unique shape of the creature represents each designer with exceptional talent.

These fascinating and distinctive illustrations made the show more charming.

Design

Ken-tsai Lee, David Weng

Interactive design

Victor Tsai

Project

Visual Identity for Taiwan Designers' Week 2009

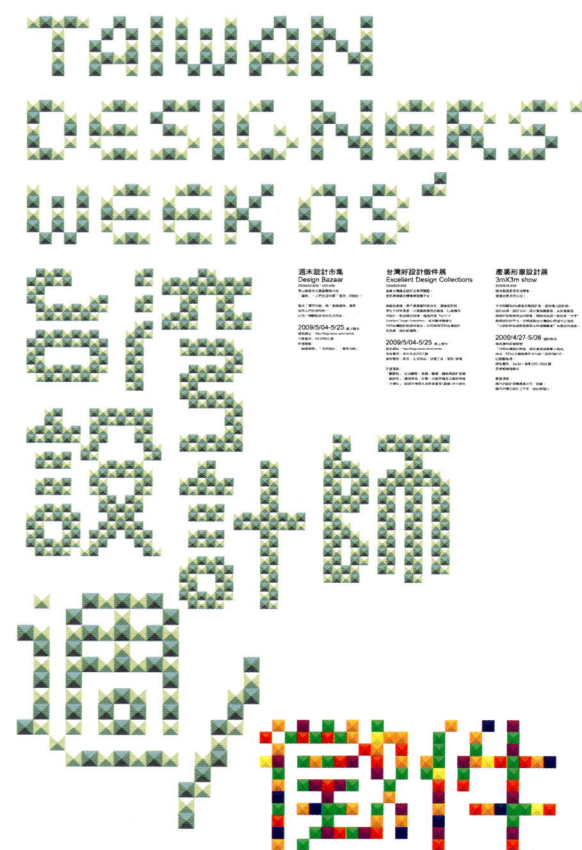

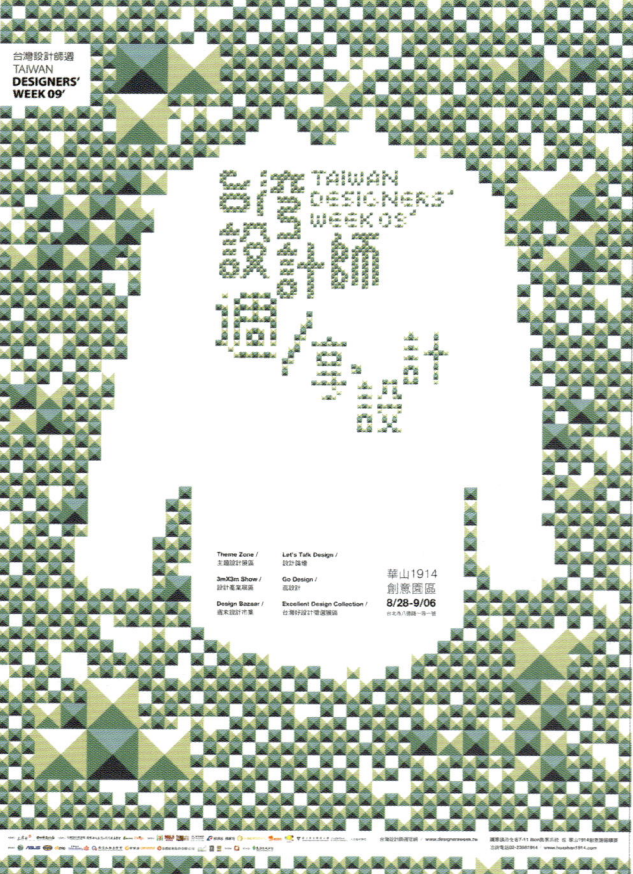

TAIWAN DESIGNERS' WEEK 09'
台灣設計師週/享設計
GUIDE BOOK/導覽手冊 8/28-9/06

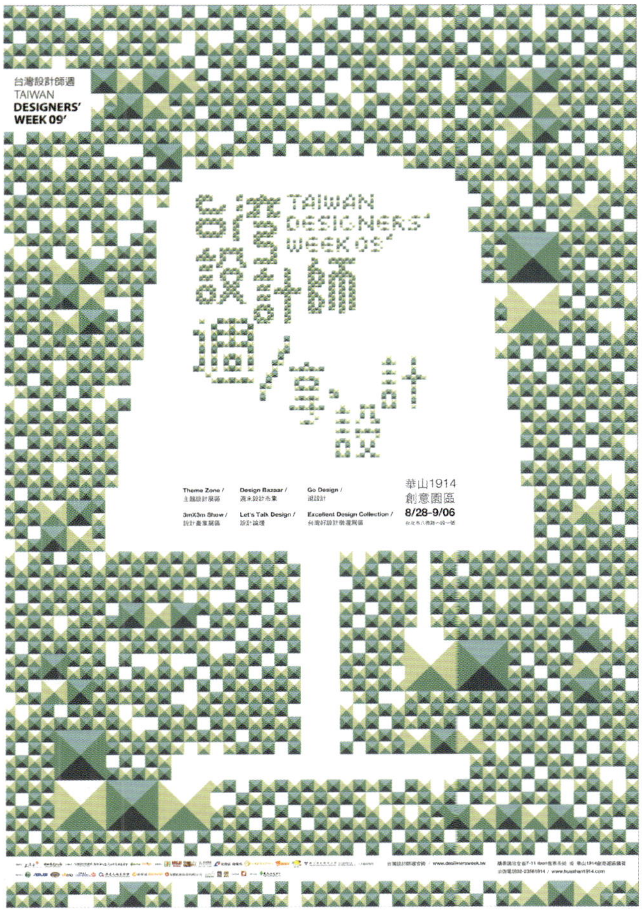

台灣設計師週
TAIWAN
DESIGNERS'
WEEK 09'
TAIWAN DESIGNERS' WEEK 09'
台灣設計師週/享設計
Theme Zone /
主題設計展區
Design Bazaar /
週末設計市集
Go Design /
逛設計
3mX3m Show /
設計產業展區
Let's Talk Design /
設計論壇
Excellent Design Collection /
台灣好設計徵選展區
華山1914
創意園區
8/28-9/06
台北市八德路一段一號

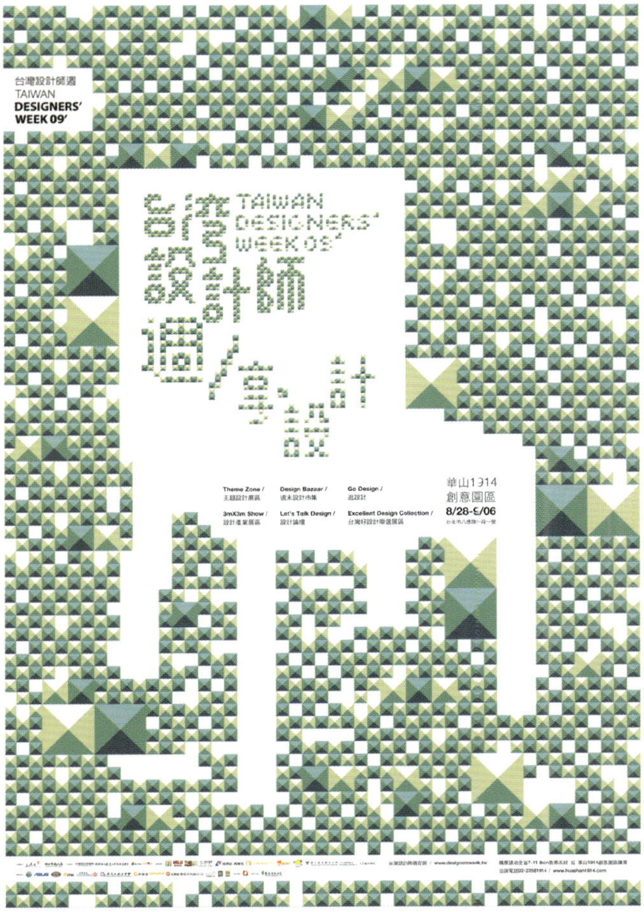

台灣設計師週
TAIWAN
DESIGNERS'
WEEK 09'
TAIWAN DESIGNERS' WEEK 09'
台灣設計師週/享設計
Theme Zone /
主題設計展區
Design Bazaar /
週末設計市集
Go Design /
逛設計
3mX3m Show /
設計產業展區
Let's Talk Design /
設計論壇
Excellent Design Collection /
台灣好設計徵選展區
華山1914
創意園區
8/28-9/06

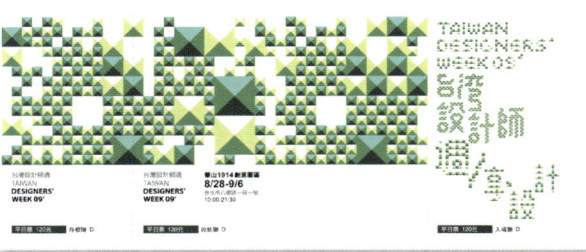

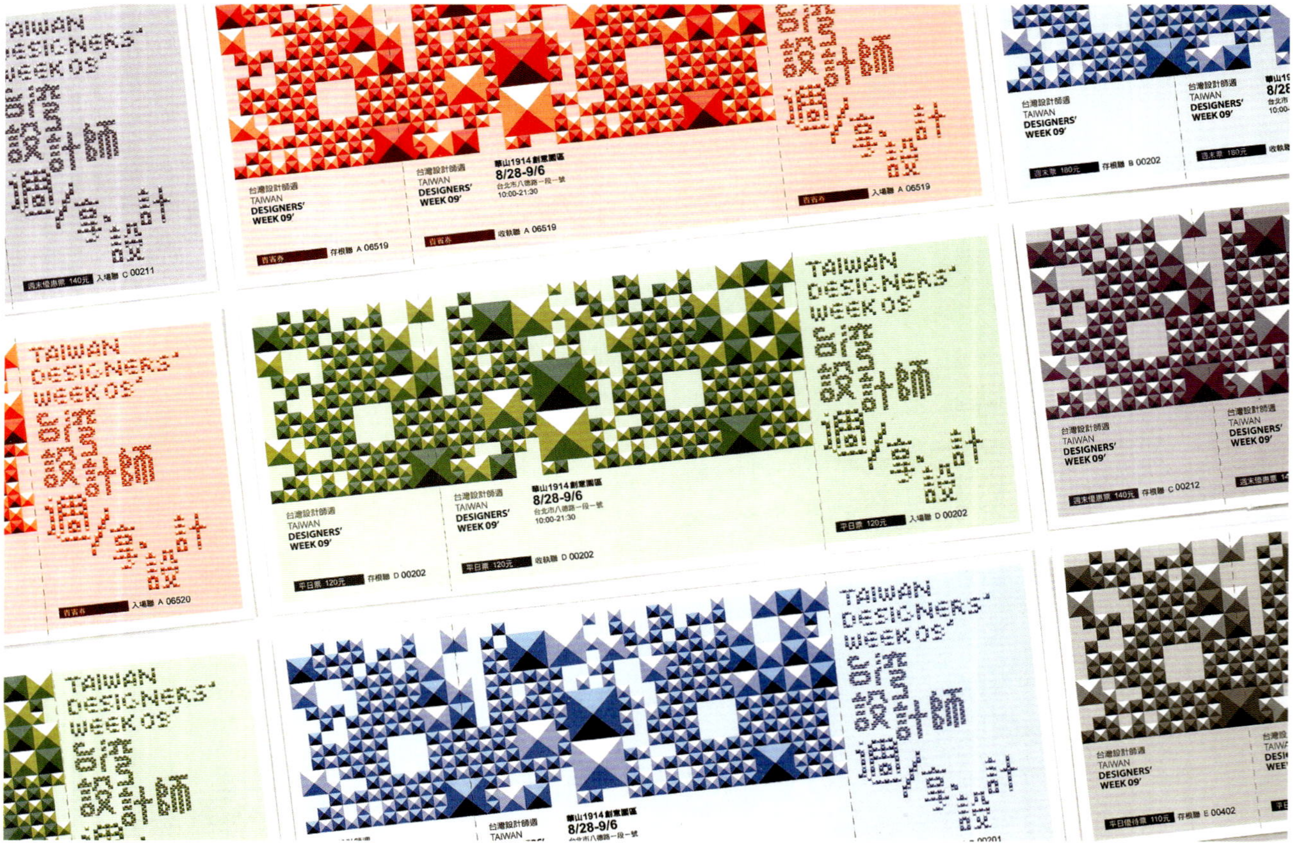

TAIWAN DESIGNERS' WEEK 09'
台灣設計師週/徵件

8/28-9/06
@華山1914創意園區

台灣好設計徵件展
Excellent Design Collections
只要腦袋裡有好創意、口袋裡有好設計，
無論是不是專業科班出生、
學生不用等畢業，歡迎報名投稿，
有機會成為2009的經典設計！

週末設計市集
Design Bazaar
徵求潛藏於台灣各大公司行號、校園中，
公司或個人自行努力設計開發的獨特設計商品，
有機會正式向消費者發聲。

台灣好設計 / 設計市集 徵件日期
2009/5/04-5/25
線上報名：http://blog.roodo.com/nanhai

2009台灣設計師週
熱烈招募中！

3mX3m產業展 / 逛設計 招募日期
2009/5/04-5/29
詳情請上活動官網：
http://www.designersweek.tw

產業形象設計展
3mX3m show
徵求獨立設計師、設計品牌、公司，
或強調設計美學相關企業組織參展，
以3mX3m為單位發表最新概念設計、品牌形象。

逛設計
Go Design
徵求台灣各地設計主題相關之商業或展演空間，
一同串聯呈現台灣設計師週氛圍，
讓更多民眾知道，原來設計就圍繞在我們身邊。

贊助．合作
SPONSOR
共襄2009台灣設計師週。

洽詢電子郵件信箱：
twdw.works@gmail.com
或電洽華山創意園區02-2358-1914

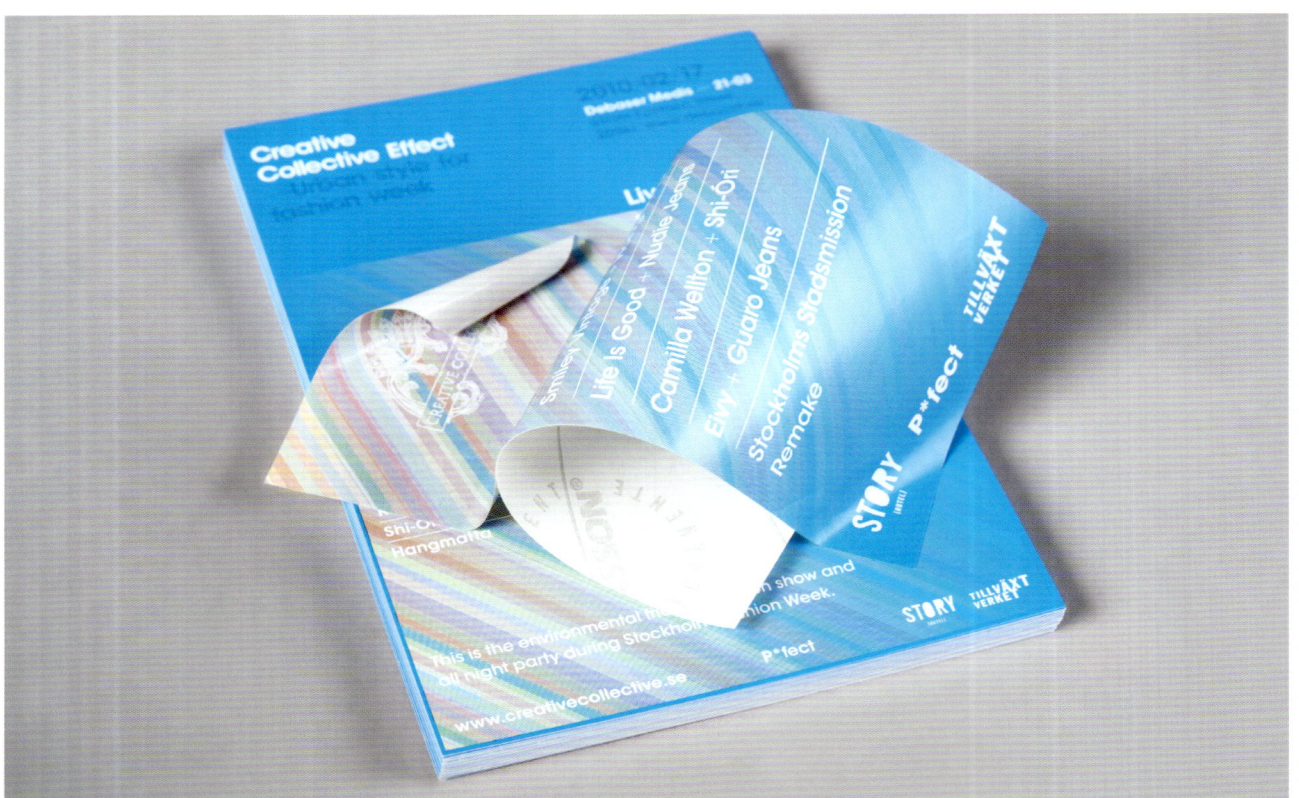

Creative Collective Effect is a fashion show focusing on eco conscious clothing. Initiated by Creative Collective, the show featuring well-known brands such as Nudie Jeans, took place during Stockholm Fashion Week.

Lundgren+Lindqvist designed the identity for the show comprising a WordPress blog, a logotype, posters and flyers plus a set of stickers. The key words of the identity was *recycling*, *collaboration*, *engagement* and *creativity*. This was emphasized on the poster by cropping the logotype to six different pieces and mixing them to create a graphical pattern.

Along the lines of each piece, the paper was perforated so that the pieces could easily be ripped out and fit together to form the logotype. This calls for the previously mentioned creativity and symbolizes the act of collaboration and recycling. The perforation lines were set to resemble stitches on garments.

Design
Lundgrer+Lindqvist
Project
Creative Collective Effect
Client
Creative Collective

Creative
Collective Effect
—Urban style for
fashion week

2010/02/17

Live: Movits — Dans: P'fect
www.creativecollective.se
www.pfect.se
Debaser Medis — 21.00–03.00
Stockholm fashion week | 230:– (dörren)
200:– (förköp)

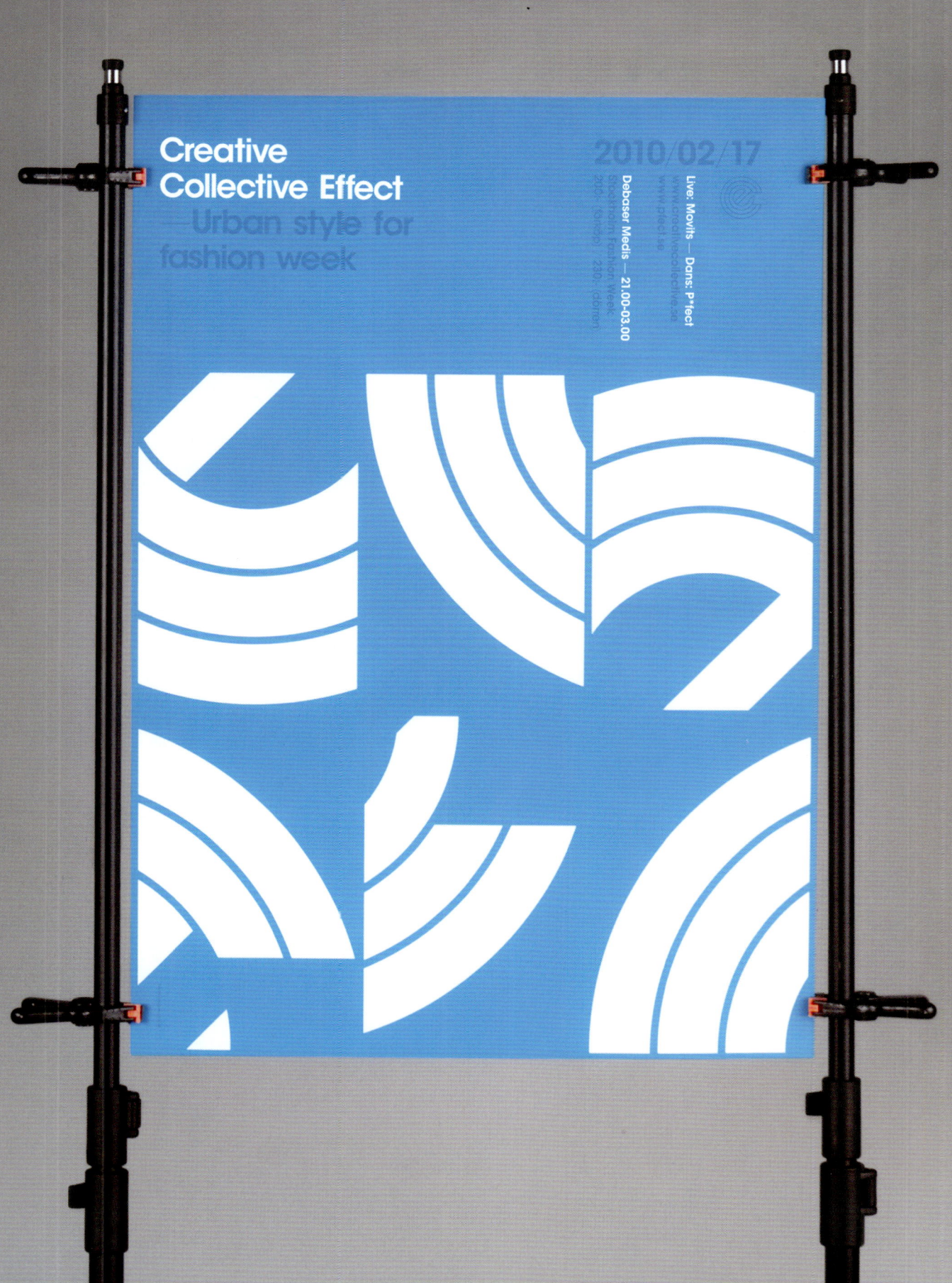

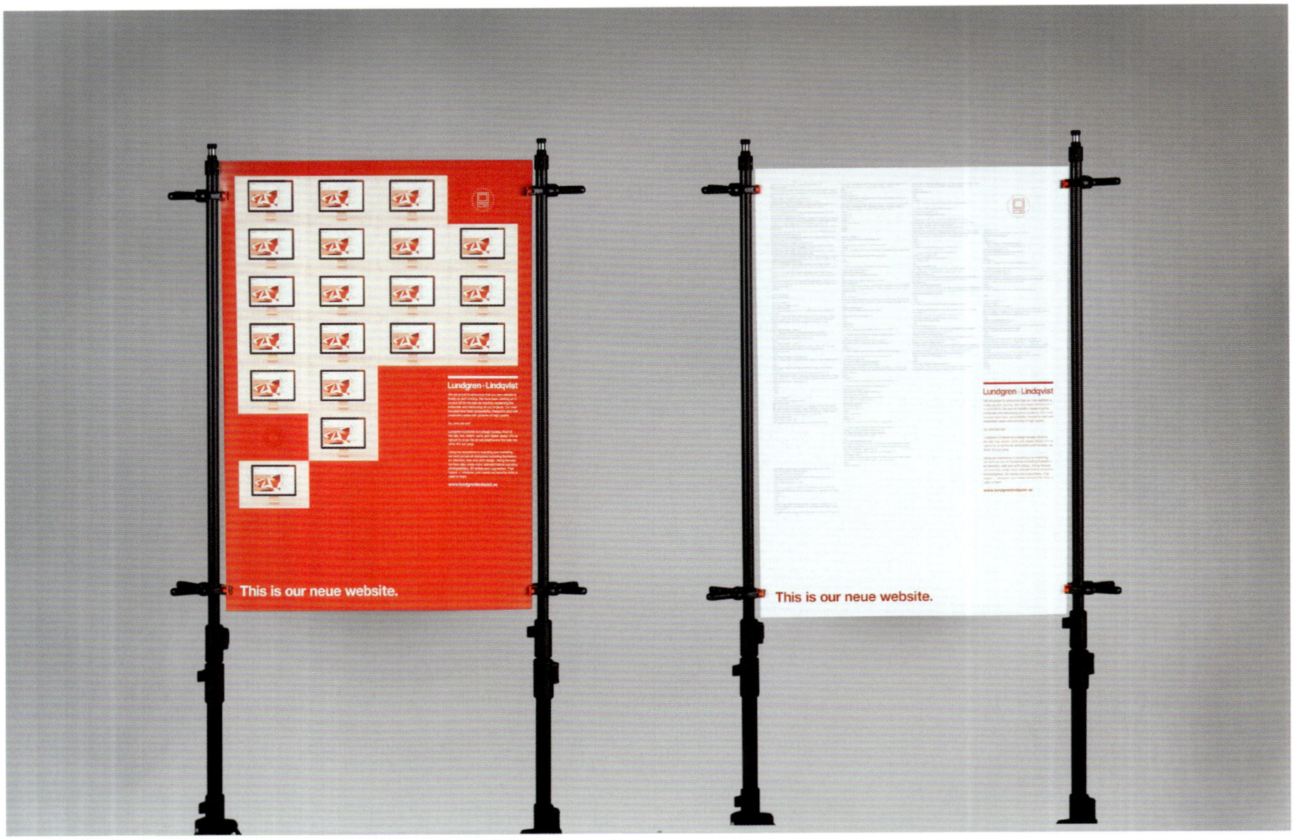

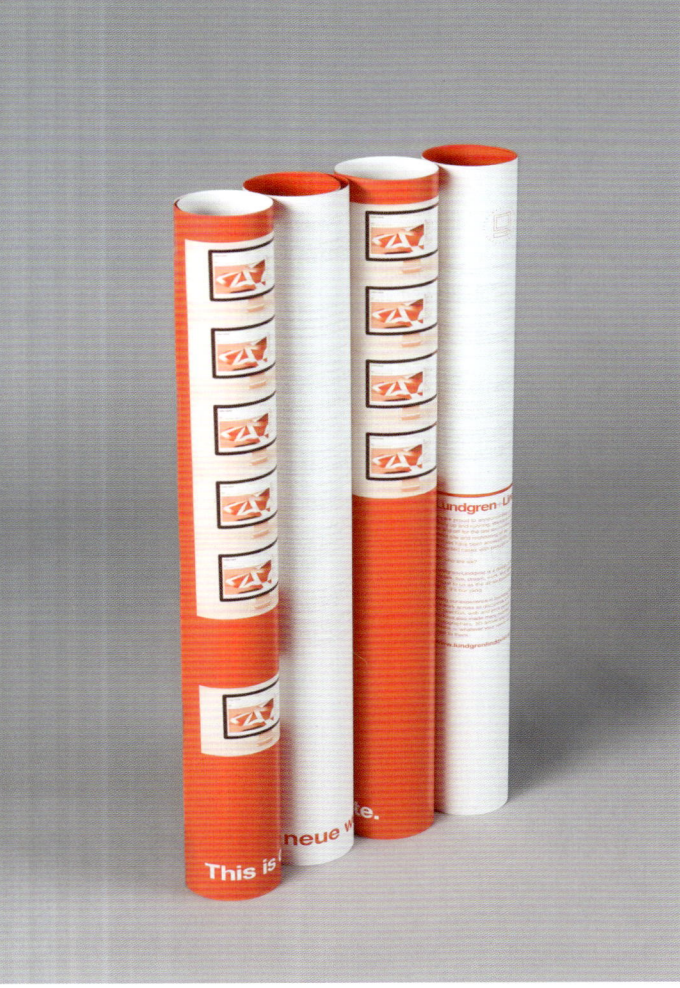

Design
Lundgren+Lindqvist
Project
Lundgren+Lindqvist
Client
Self initiated

Redesign of Lundgren+Lindqvist's identity, website and stationary.

The business cards are triplexed GF Smith Colorplan (Cool Grey, Bright Red and Pristine White) and have negative embossing, foil blocking and UV-varnish.

The letter paper is Colorplan Pristine White with negative embossing and the S65 window envelopes are made out of Colorplan Cool Grey.

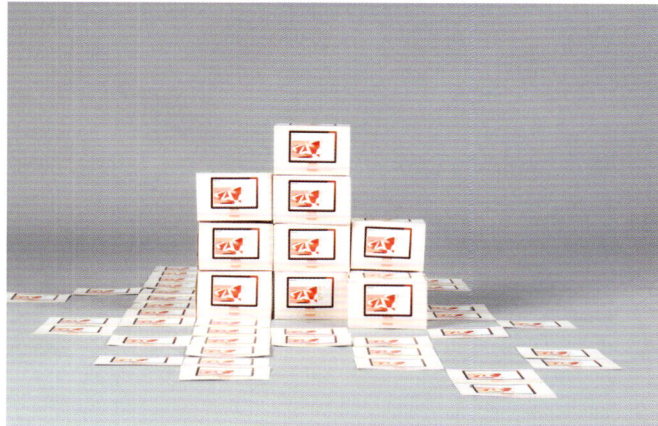

Design
Lundgren+Lindqvist

Project
Lundgren+Lindqvist

Client
Self initiated

The promotional poster is printed on both sides on MultiArt Silk paper with partial UV-varnish and water-varnish finishing.

One side displays our website and the other its underlying code, two sides of our business.

The intentional typo in the headline (neue instead of new) hints of the use of the Helvetica Neue typeface throughout the identity.

Design
Lundgren+Lindqvist
Project
Philip Ljungström

Philip Ljungström is a very talented photographer based in Gothenburg, Sweden. He works in several different fields including fashion and extreme sports.

Lundgren+Lindqvist was approached for designing Philip Ljungström`s business cards and for a collaborative project designing a promotional poster for Victor Västernäs, a top sailor aiming for the London Olympics 2012.

The business cards were printed with 2 PMS colours and white foil blocking with an embossing used to highlight the most important information.

Design
James Kaɔe

Project
Göteborg University

Every year, Göteborg University (HDK) has a Christmas market for students to sell their designs and I was asked to design the poster for this event.

It was decided to screen print the design with a limited run of 100 copies to be used in shops around Göteɔorg. Every copy was signed so the shop owner had something memorable to keep and left over copies sold out at the Christmas market.

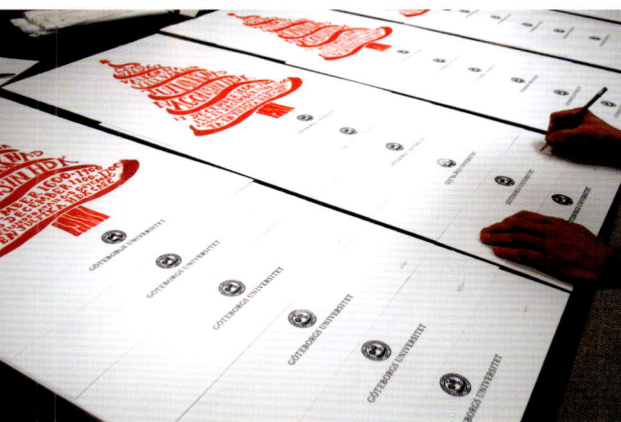

Nikki Mumford
Director..
use my mind pr

603 Elizabeth Street
Surry Hills NSW 2010
M 0410 424 769
T 02 8399 0411
nikki@usemymind.co
www.usemymind.co

umm..

umm..

MEETING
AT 12PM

use my mind pr
603 Elizabeth Street
Surry Hills NSW 2010
02 8399 0411
www.usemymind.com.au
usemymind@usemymind.com.au

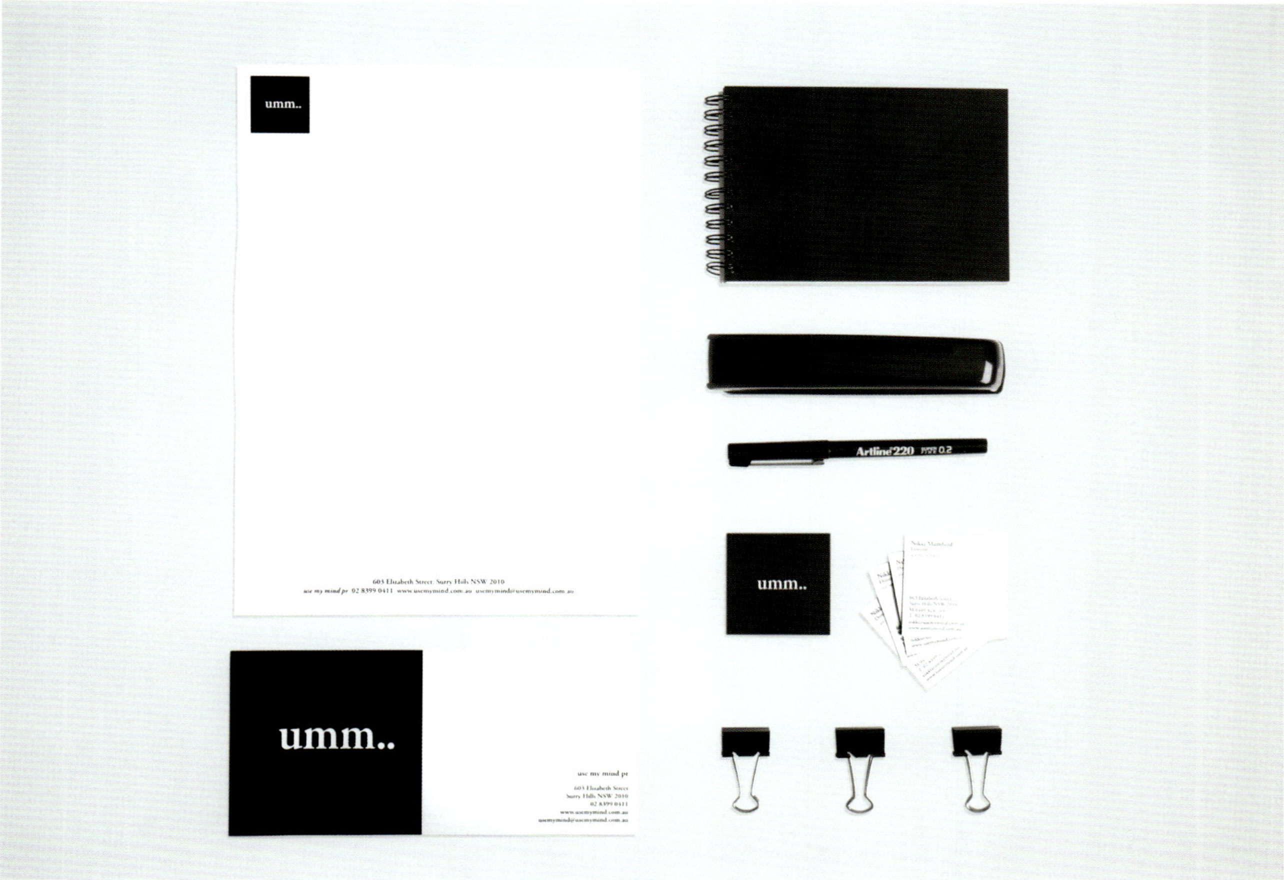

Design

James Kape

Project

Use my mind

'Use My Mind' is a publicity company, based in Sydney, Australia. Recently I was commissioned to create an entire update of both their logo design and associated identity.

The emphasis of this project was in creating a new logo, for use on a series of business cards, complimentary slips and letterheads.

When designing the logo, I decided to shorten the name 'Use my mind' to its acronym 'umm' to create a more thought-provoking representation and in doing so, it became representative of a common speech pattern within public relations.

Design
LEAP Design
Project
Apus
Client
Apus Investment Limited, HONG KONG

LEAP helped start-up hedge fund company Apus Investment develop its visual corporate identity.

As the company is an investment manager, we created a conservative-looking logo for Apus.

We used typography and the colours blue and white, to come up with a simple and elegant logo design that conveys the company's professional image.

Design
LEAP Design

Project
Belhams

Client
Belhams, Australia

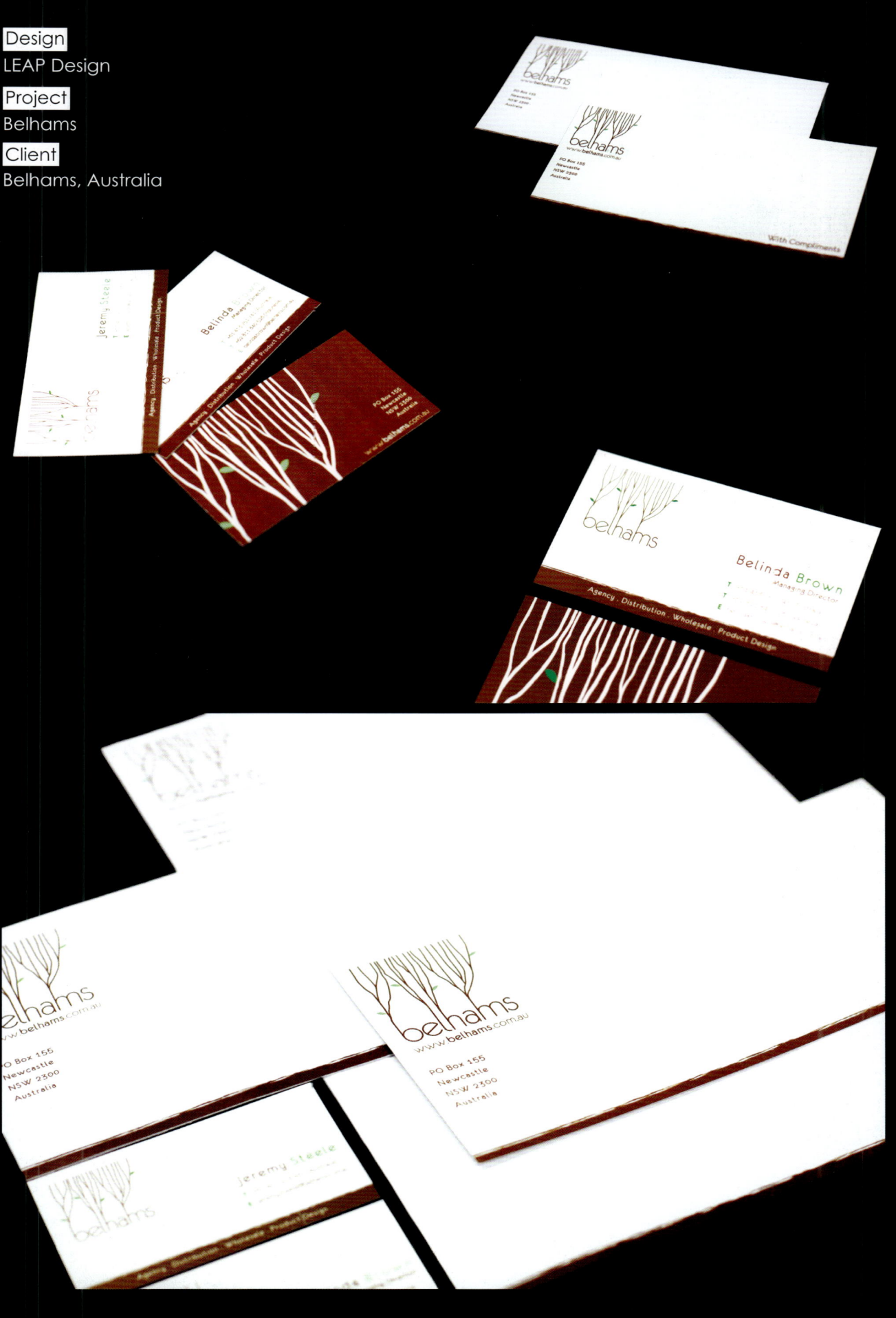

Design
LEAP Design

Project
Quadros International

Client
Quadros International, United Arab Emirates

LEAP created a new corporate logo for Quadros International, one of Dubai's largest interior outfitting companies.

Quadros has a solid presence in the construction and interior design industry, hence we designed a bold Q-shaped logo to truly represent its leading stature.

Design
Brown & White Creative

Project
Brown & White Creative

Client
Self initiated

The business cards were designed by Susannah White and Rich Brown, directors of Brown & White Creative. Both card designs were printed on 625gsm Dutch Grey Board, with debossed foil block lettering.

pauline.ning

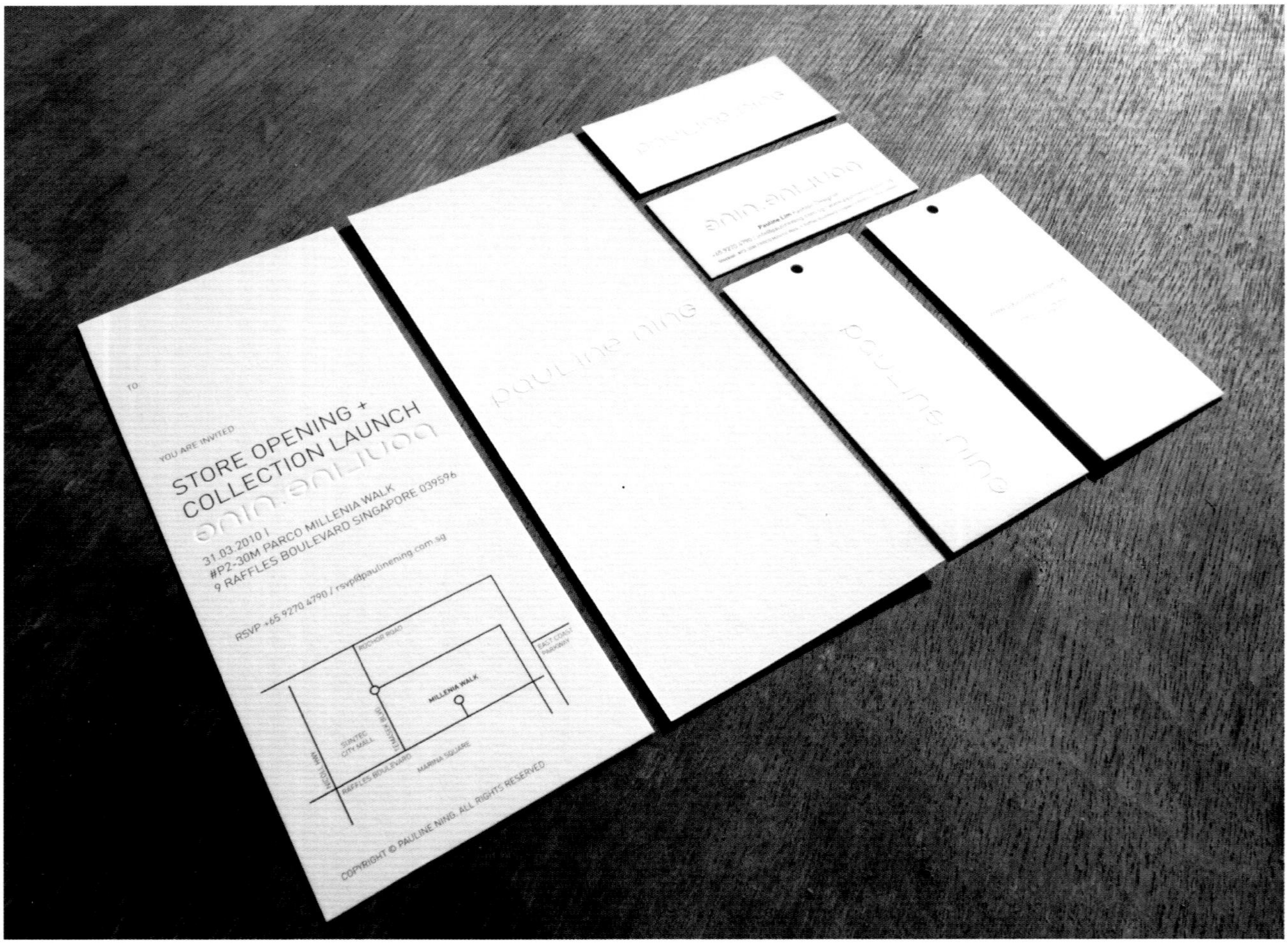
TO:
YOU ARE INVITED
STORE OPENING +
COLLECTION LAUNCH
31.03.2010 |
#P2-30M PARCO MILLENIA WALK
9 RAFFLES BOULEVARD SINGAPORE 039596
RSVP +65 9270 4790 / rsvp@paulinening.com.sg
MILLENIA WALK
EAST COAST PARKWAY
RAFFLES BOULEVARD
MARINA SQUARE
COPYRIGHT © PAULINE NING. ALL RIGHTS RESERVED

STORE OPENING +
COLLECTION LAUNCH

Design
Edwin Tan
Project
Pauline.ning

Pauline.ning is a branding exercise for a new fashion label based in Singapore.

We wanted the design to be subtle enough to not grab attention from the garments, but strong enough to express the brand's fundamental image.

To keep production cost within budget, the embossing mould is reused for all their collaterals.

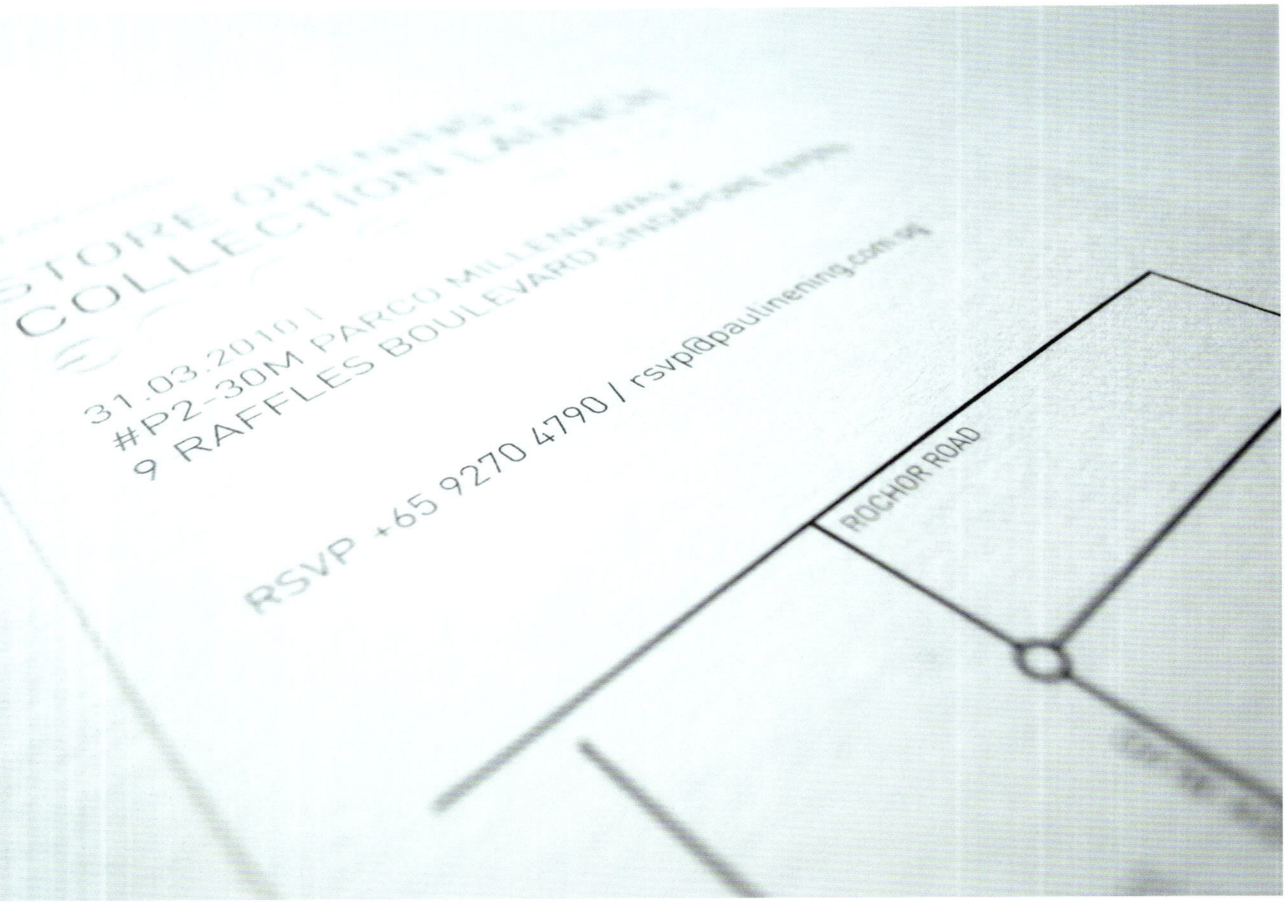

STORE OPENING
COLLECTION LAUNCH

31.03.2010 |
#P2-30M PARCO MILLENIA WALK
9 RAFFLES BOULEVARD SINGAPORE 039596

RSVP +65 9270 4790 / rsvp@paulinening.com.sg

ROCHOR ROAD

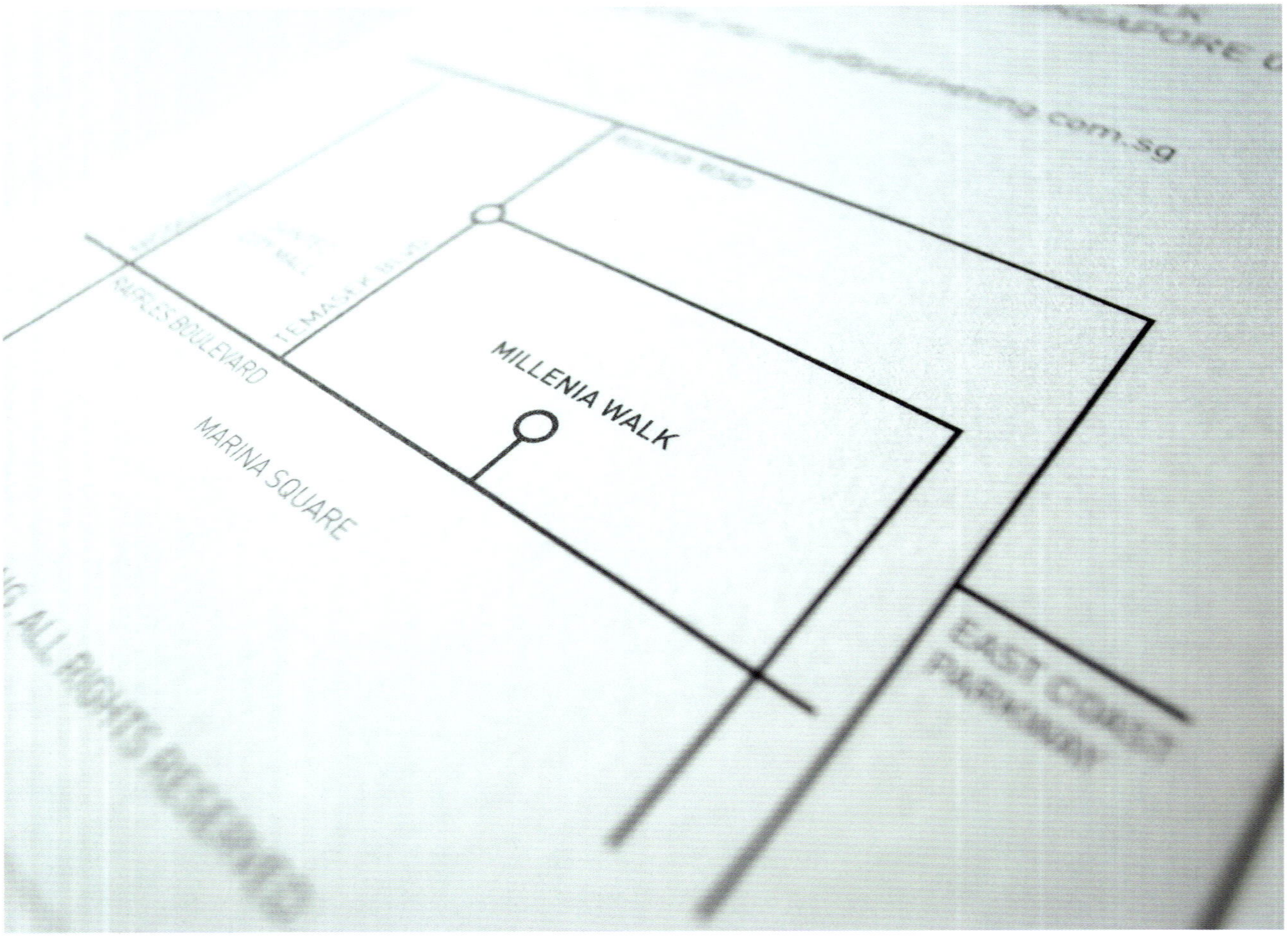

RAFFLES BOULEVARD

MARINA SQUARE

MILLENIA WALK

EAST COAST
PARKWAY

Pauline Lim Fashion Designer
info@paulinening.com.sg | www.paulinening.com.sg
1 Raffles Boulevard Singapore

pauline.nine

Research Studios created the material for the 2010 D&AD Student Awards. The infographic theme has been applied to both print and digital materials as the call for entries to both tutors and students.

Core to the campaign are the poster call for entries and a new approach to engaging both tutors and students with a striking double-sided poster 'calling tutors with extra oomph' for the academic audience and 'wanted students with excess talent' developed on the client side.

Research Studios also created an 80 page nominations newspaper, and all the graphics for the awards ceremony, which took place at Spitalfields Mark, London.

Design
Research Studios
Project
D&AD Student Awards 2010

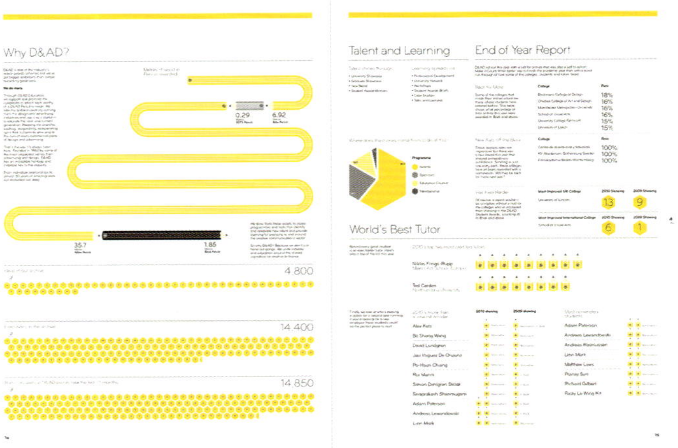

Calling all...

Pencil Pushers

D&AD Student
Awards 2010

Launch Date: Monday 21 September 2009
Deadline: Friday 19 March 2010
studentawards.dandad.org/2010

Your step-by-step guide

The first 10 briefs are online now.

The full set of 27 industry briefs and your tutor pack will be available on 21 September 2009.

1 > Log-on to the Student Awards site

2 > View the 2009 Annual with feedback from the judges

3 > Download the 2010 briefs

4 > Register your students for 2010

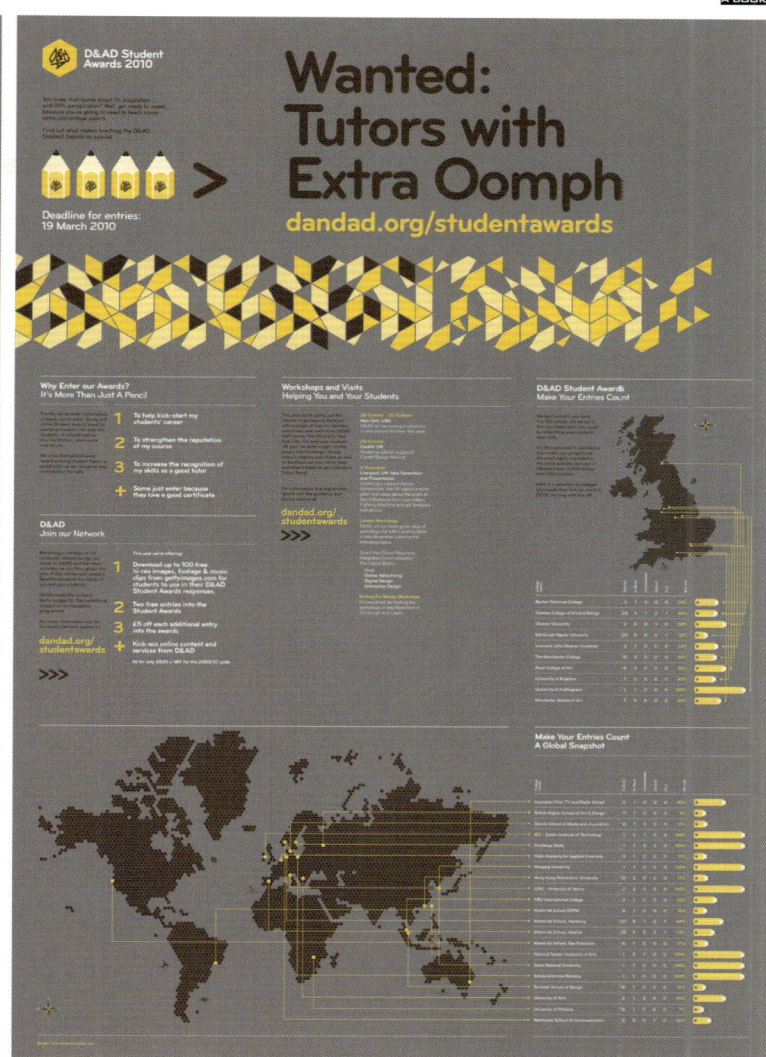

Wanted: Tutors with Extra Oomph

dandad.org/studentawards

D&AD Student Awards 2010

Deadline for entries: 19 March 2010

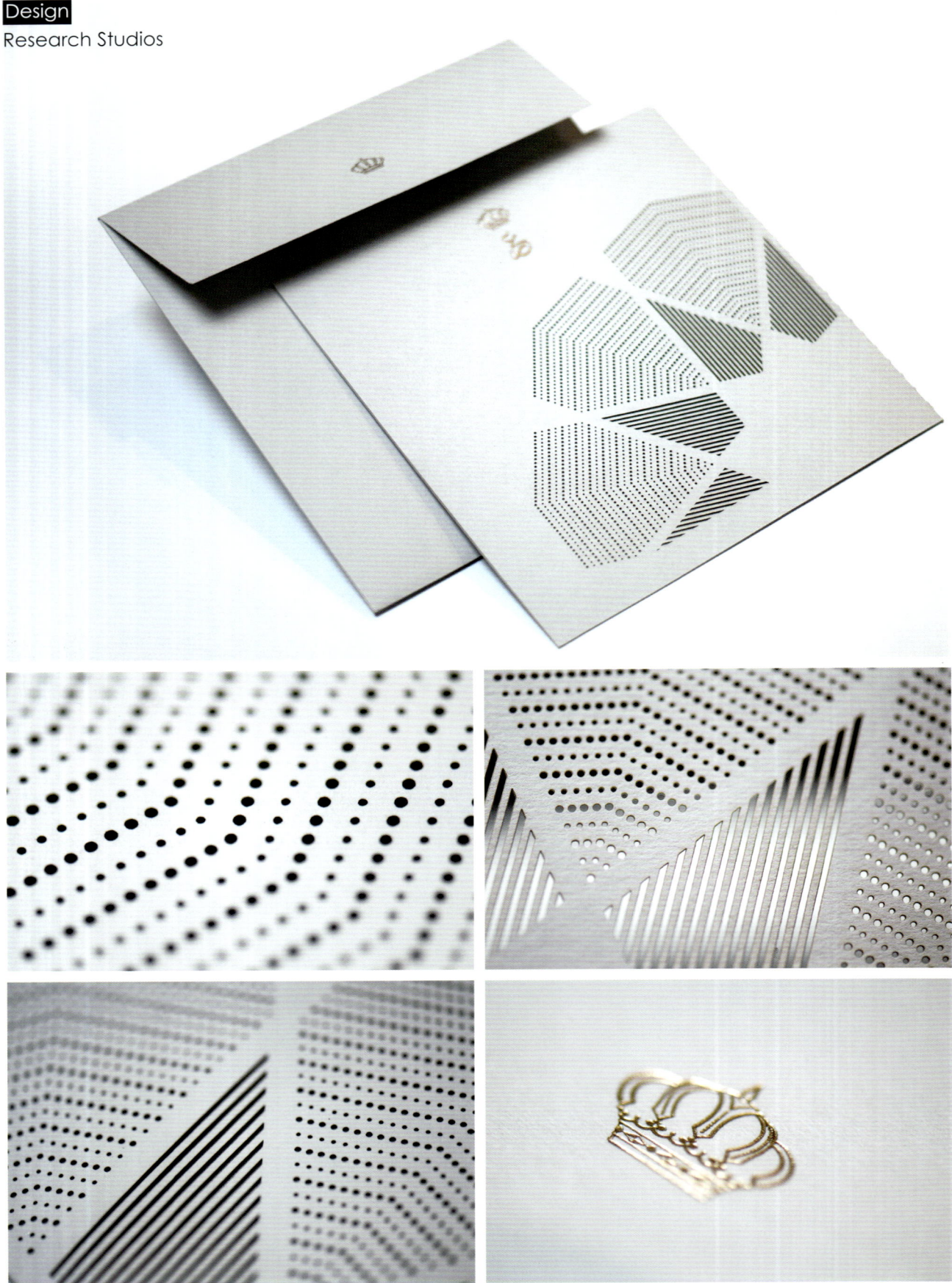

Research Studios has been part of a unique collaboration with the Royal Family of Jordan and their End of Year card 2009. The result has married together the modern and the traditional to complement a very forward looking and inspirational monarchy.

The Royal Family of Jordan – New Year Card

The final designs combined a modern neutral colour palette, lazer cutting, detailed print and finishing techniques with Their Majesties royal cypher, caligraphy and traditional graphic elements required, by protocol, in such a project.

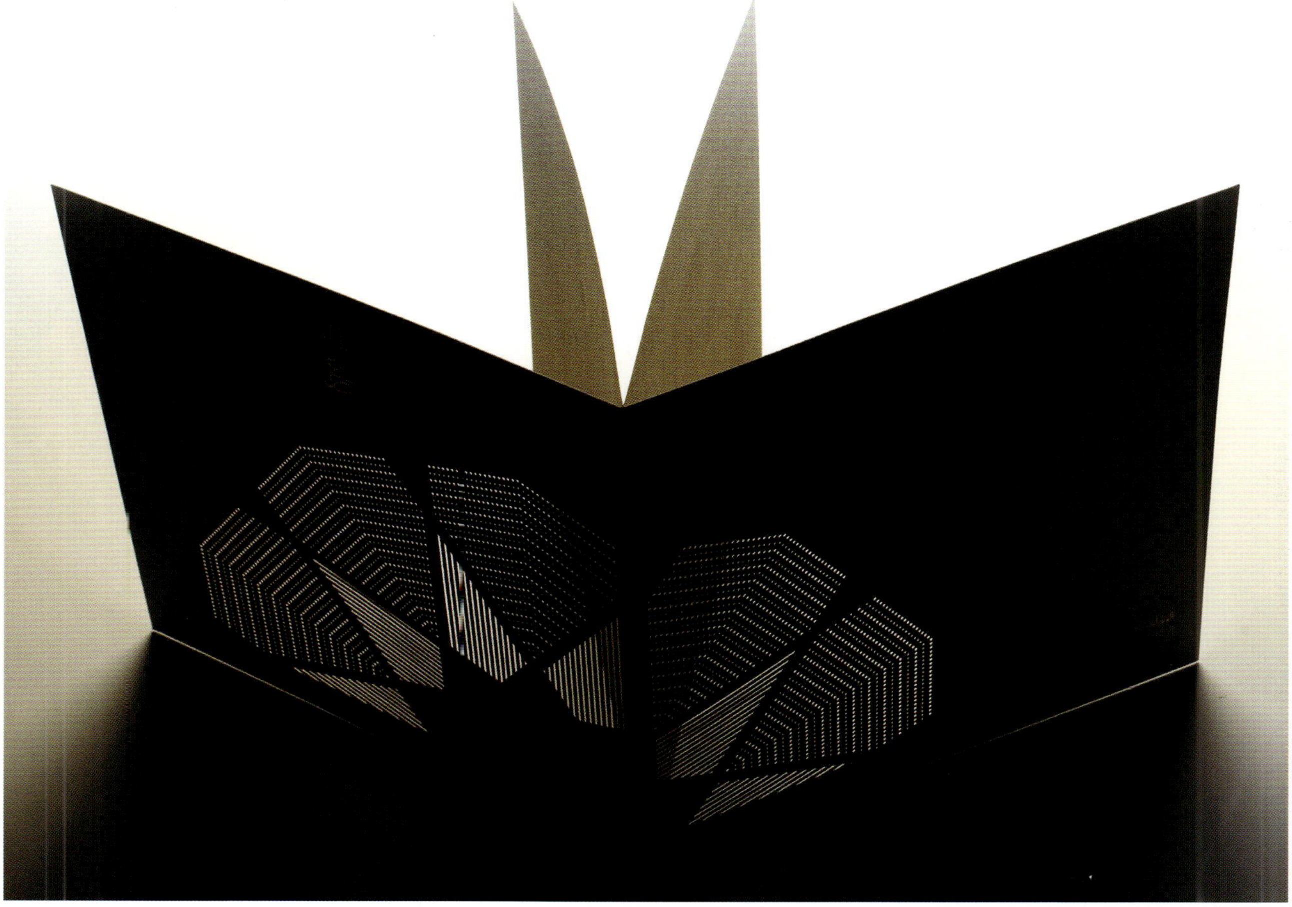

Design
Thorbjørn
Ankerstjerne

Project
Qasimi Identity

Design and art
direction for
London based
fashion label Qasimi.
With Fabio
Sebastianelli.

Logo, stationary,
website and logo
animation.

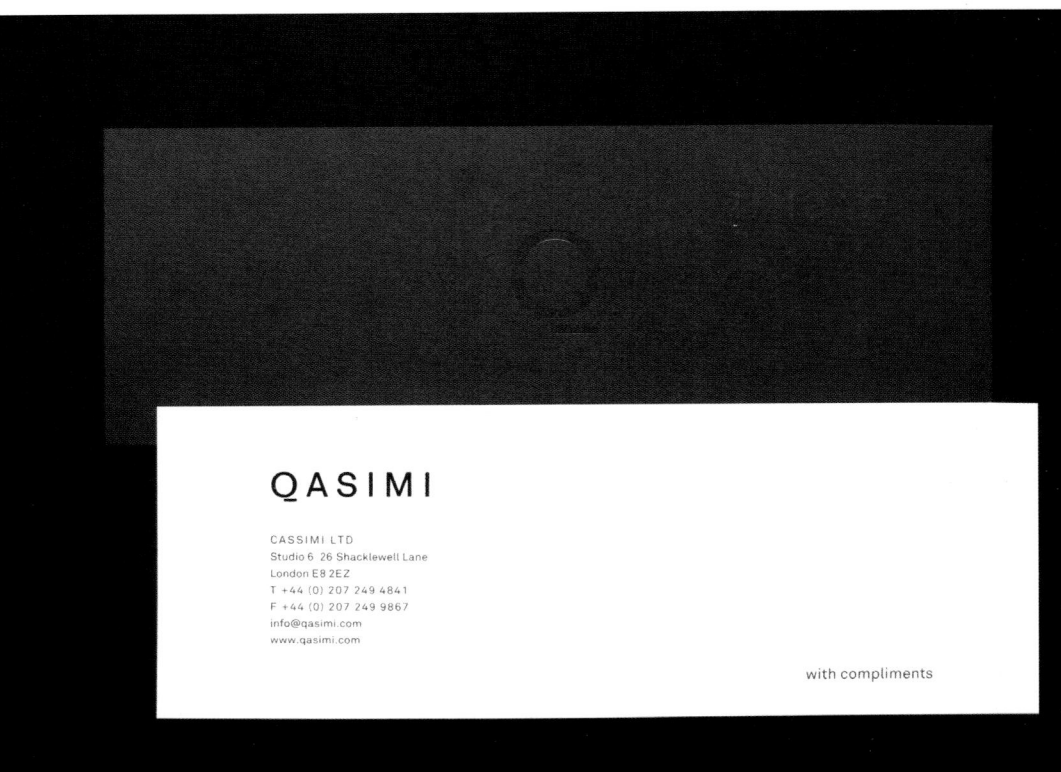

QASIMI

CASSIMI LTD
Studio 6 26 Shacklewell Lane
London E8 2EZ
T +44 (0) 207 249 4841
F +44 (0) 207 249 9867
info@qasimi.com
www.qasimi.com

with compliments

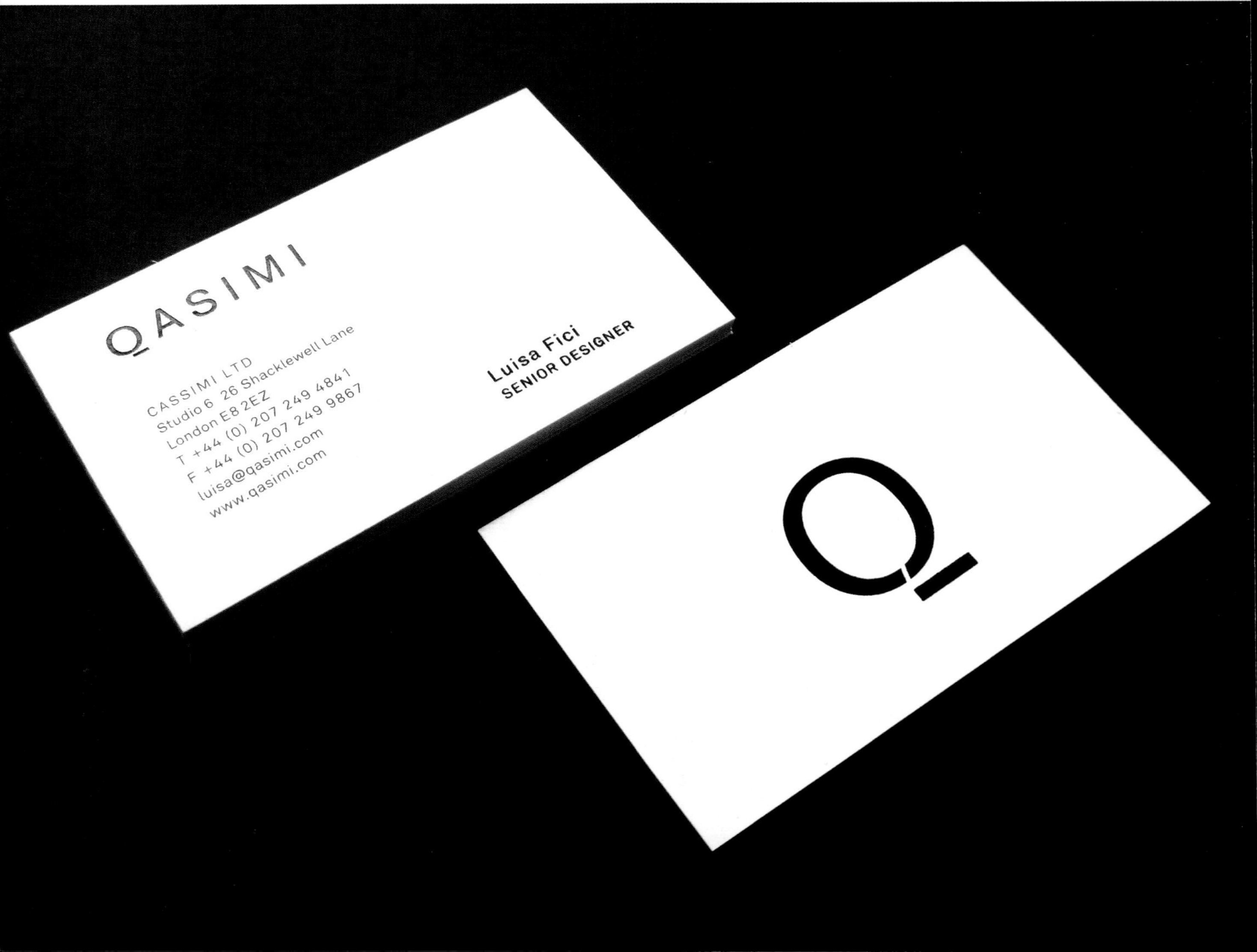

QASIMI

CASSIMI LTD
Studio 6 26 Shacklewell Lane
London E8 2EZ
T +44 (0) 207 249 4841
F +44 (0) 207 249 9867
luisa@qasimi.com
www.qasimi.com

Luisa Fici
SENIOR DESIGNER

Q

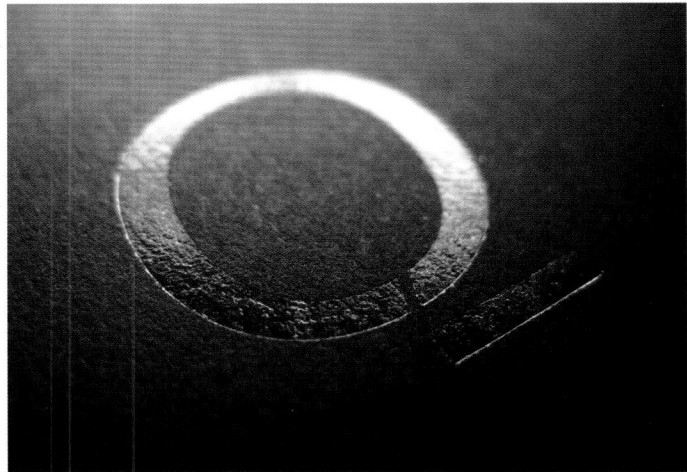

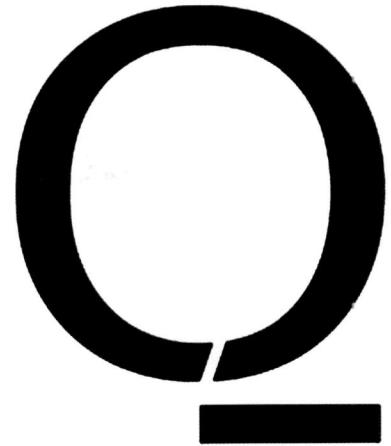

QASIMI

CASSIMI LTD
Studio 6 26 Shacklewell Lane
London E8 2EZ
T +44 (0) 207 249 4841
F +44 (0) 207 249 9867
info@qasimi.com
www.qasimi.com

QASIMI

CASSIMI LTD
Studio 6 26 Shacklewell Lane
London E8 2EZ
T +44 (0) 207 249 4841
F +44 (0) 207 249 9867
info@qasimi.com
www.qasimi.com

Dear Sir / Madam   London 19.05.09

VAT number: 922146057
CASSIMI LTD trading as QASIMI
Company No 6432869
Registered in England and Wales
20–22 Bedford Row, London WC1R 4JS

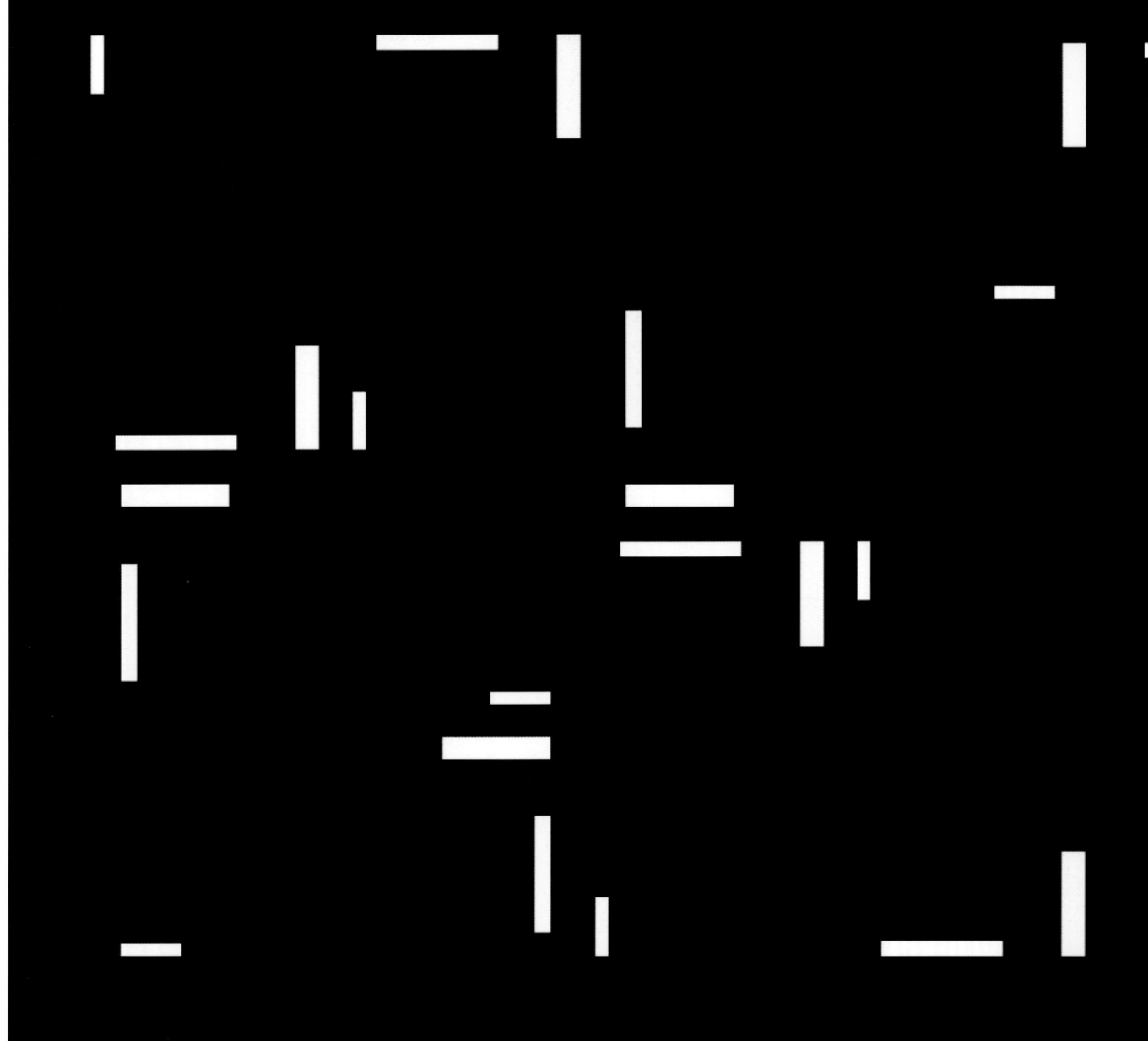

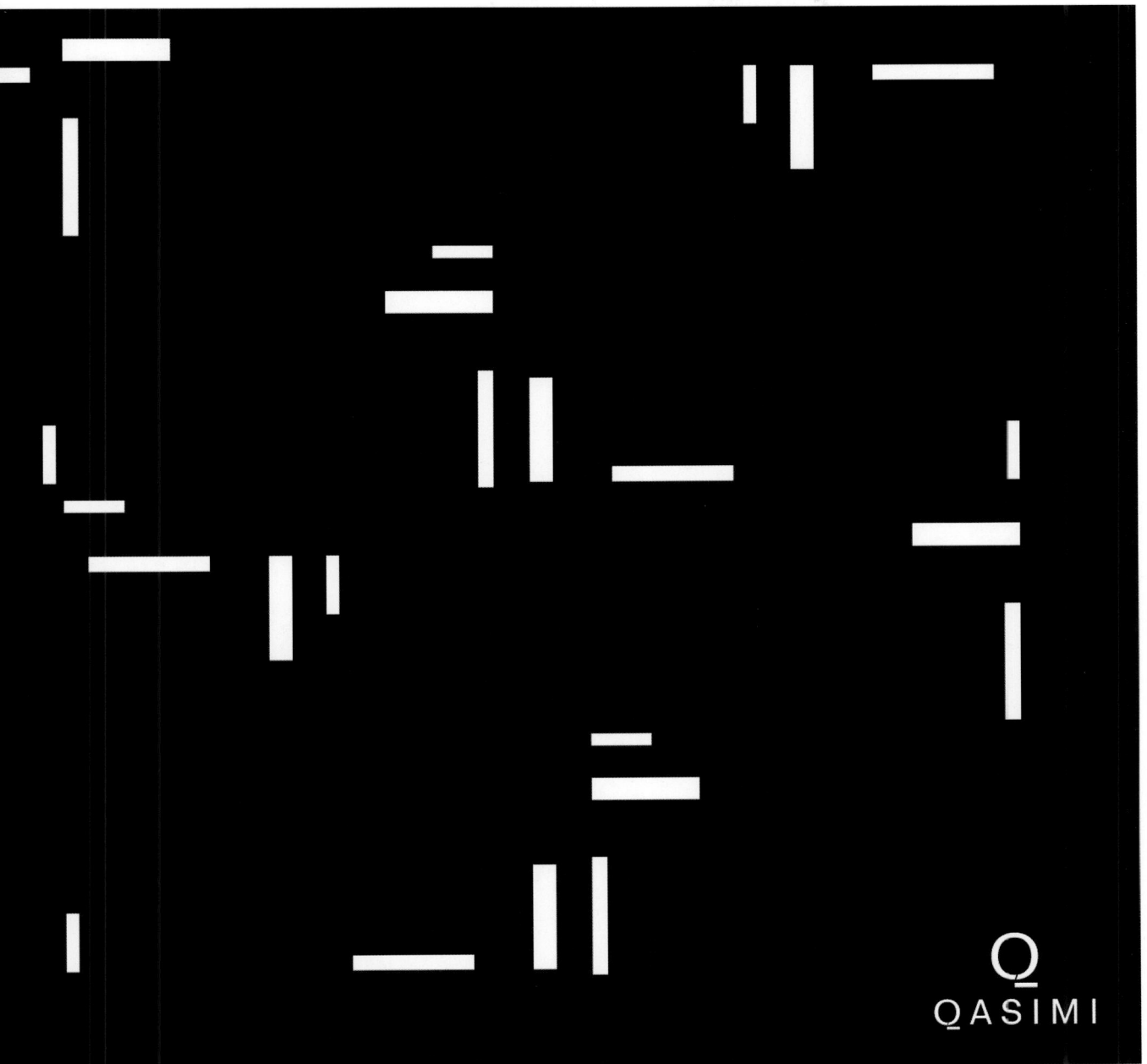

Design
Thorbjørn Ankerstjerne

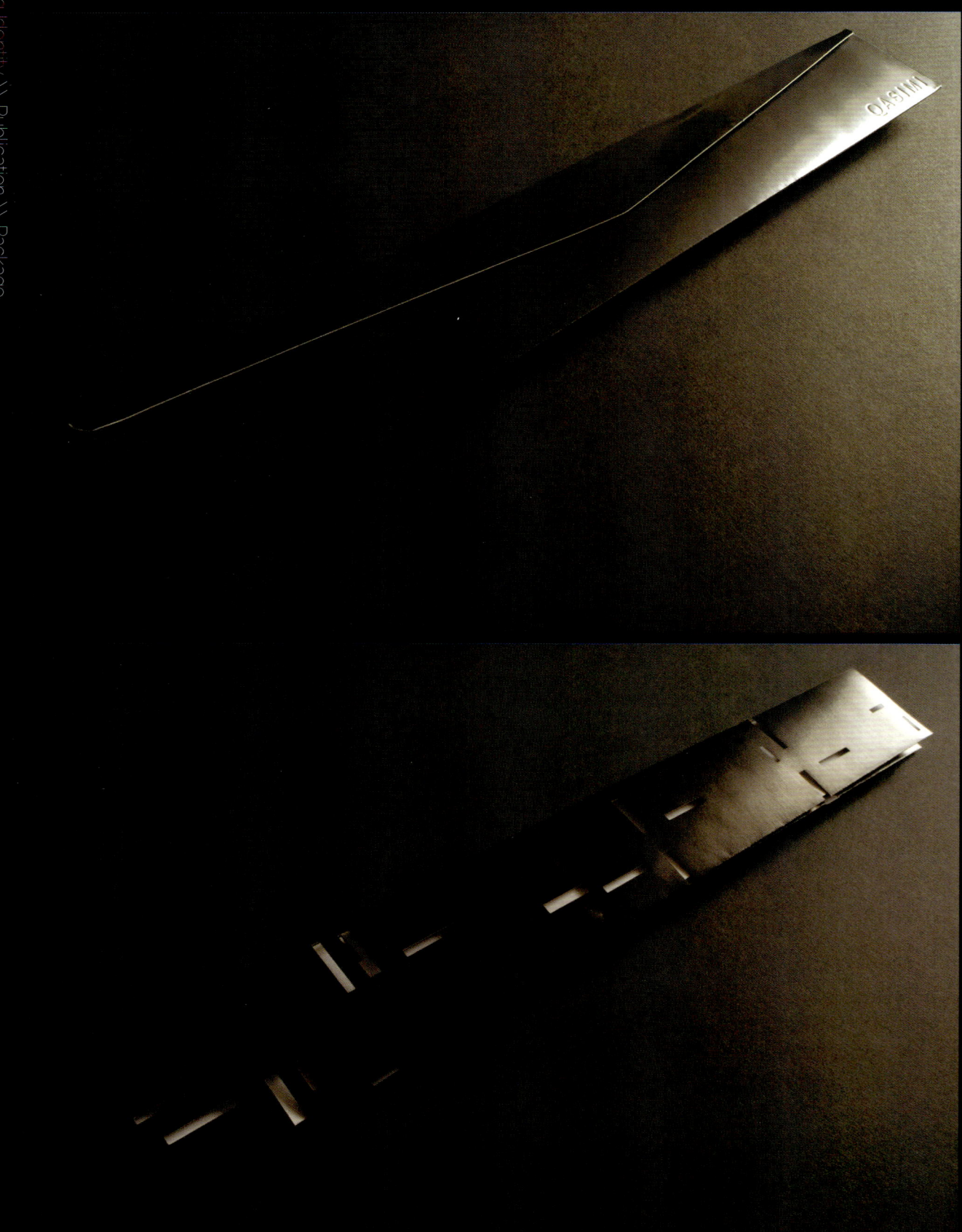

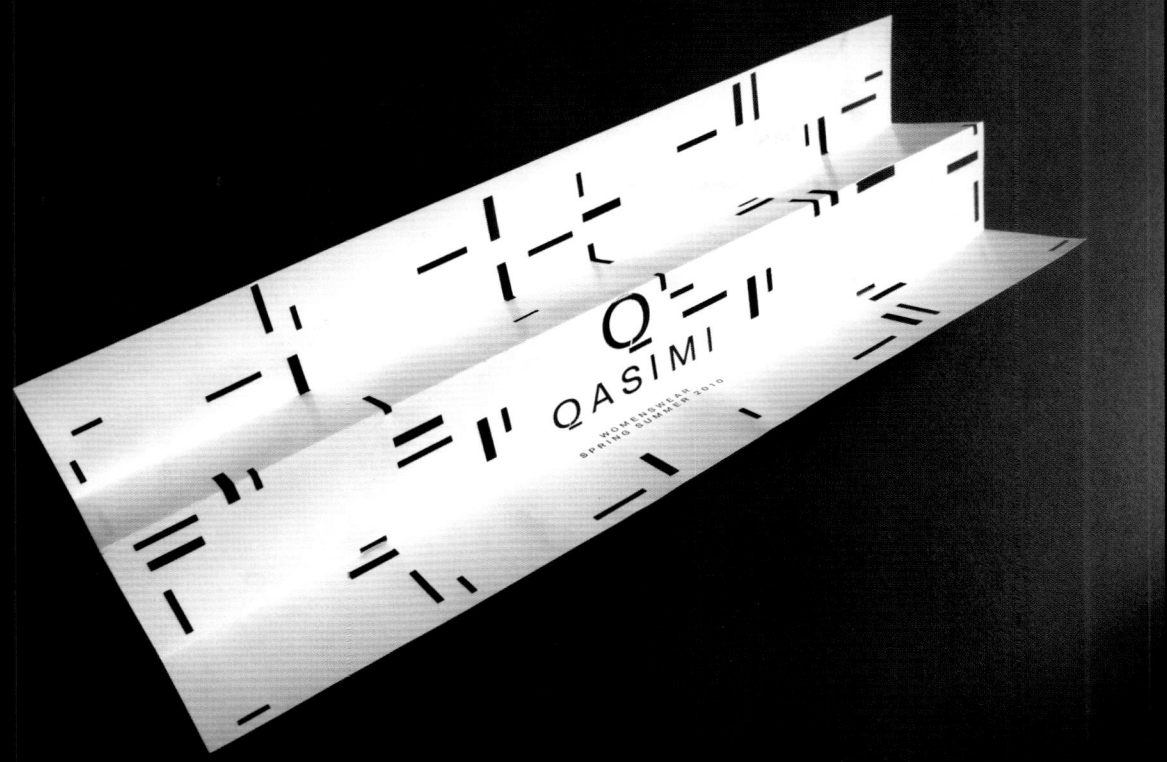

Invite for Womenswear SS10, London Fashion
Week 2009.

Bespoke envelope, 4 x 31 cm
Laser cut invites.

Carrier bag

Design
Thorbjørn Ankerstjerne

Project
Menswear SS10

Gold foiled bible paper.

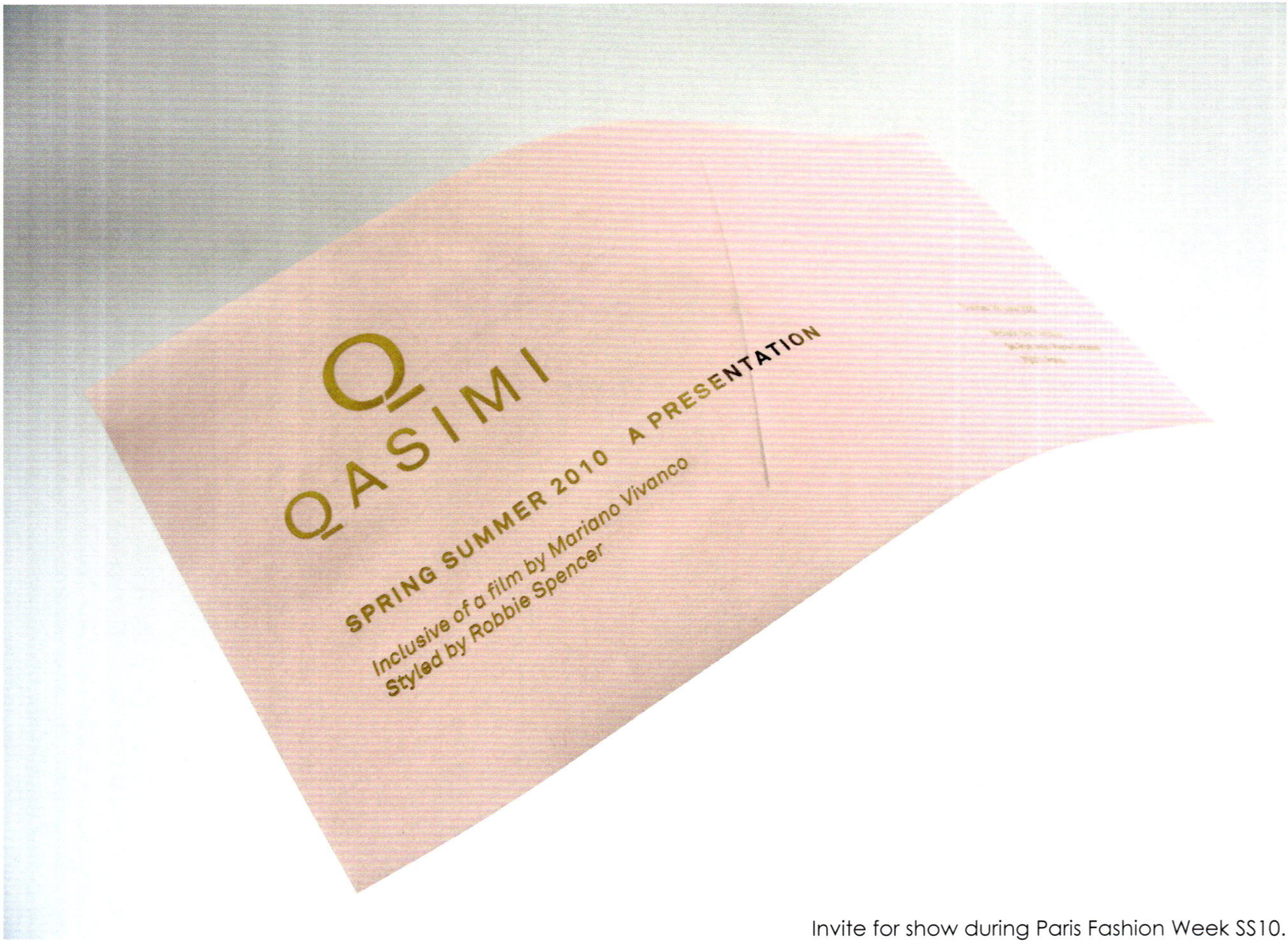

Invite for show during Paris Fashion Week SS10.

Коурустанович
Андрей Анатольевич
коммерческий директор

г. Краснодар
ул. Коммунаров, 268
(БЦ «Кавказ»)
тел.: 210-20-10
8-918-346-16-4
e-mail :kap@
www.rest

РЕСТАВРАЦИЯ

Design

Stas Sipovich

Project

Restauracia

Brand identity, logo and stationery for the premium finishing materials producer.

Design

Stas Sipovich

Project

IDOL

IDOL is a glossy magazine for and about people who are ahead of their time. Music, fashion, nightlife and society gossips are the main publication topics. It's a reference book of each progressive. It's the Bible of our time.

Design
Stas Sipovich

Project
CRA

Brand identity, logo and stationery for the advertising agency with the name Regional Marketing Center.

Design
Stas Sipovich

Project
Shag

Photographer aka ШАГ (Cyrillic) logo, stationery.

058

Design

Stas Sipovich

Project

VV identity

Brand identity, logo and stationery for the company with specialization: carrying out of research and development, and as development and manufacture of new types of gauges in the field of vector's vibromeasurement.

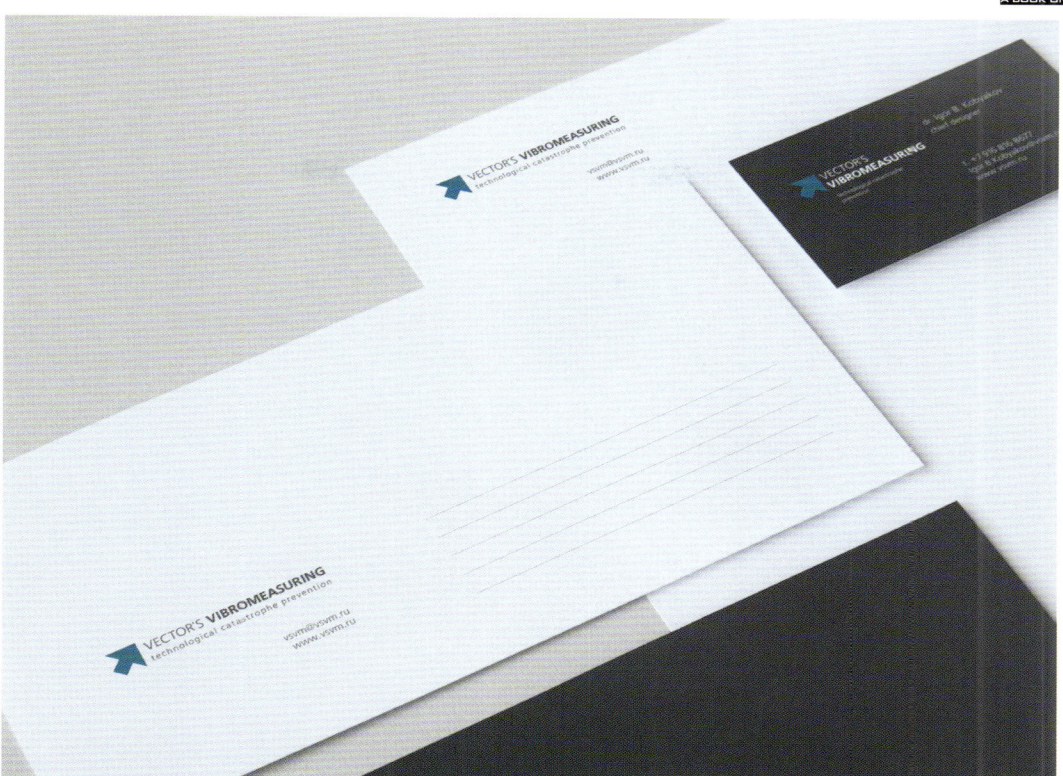

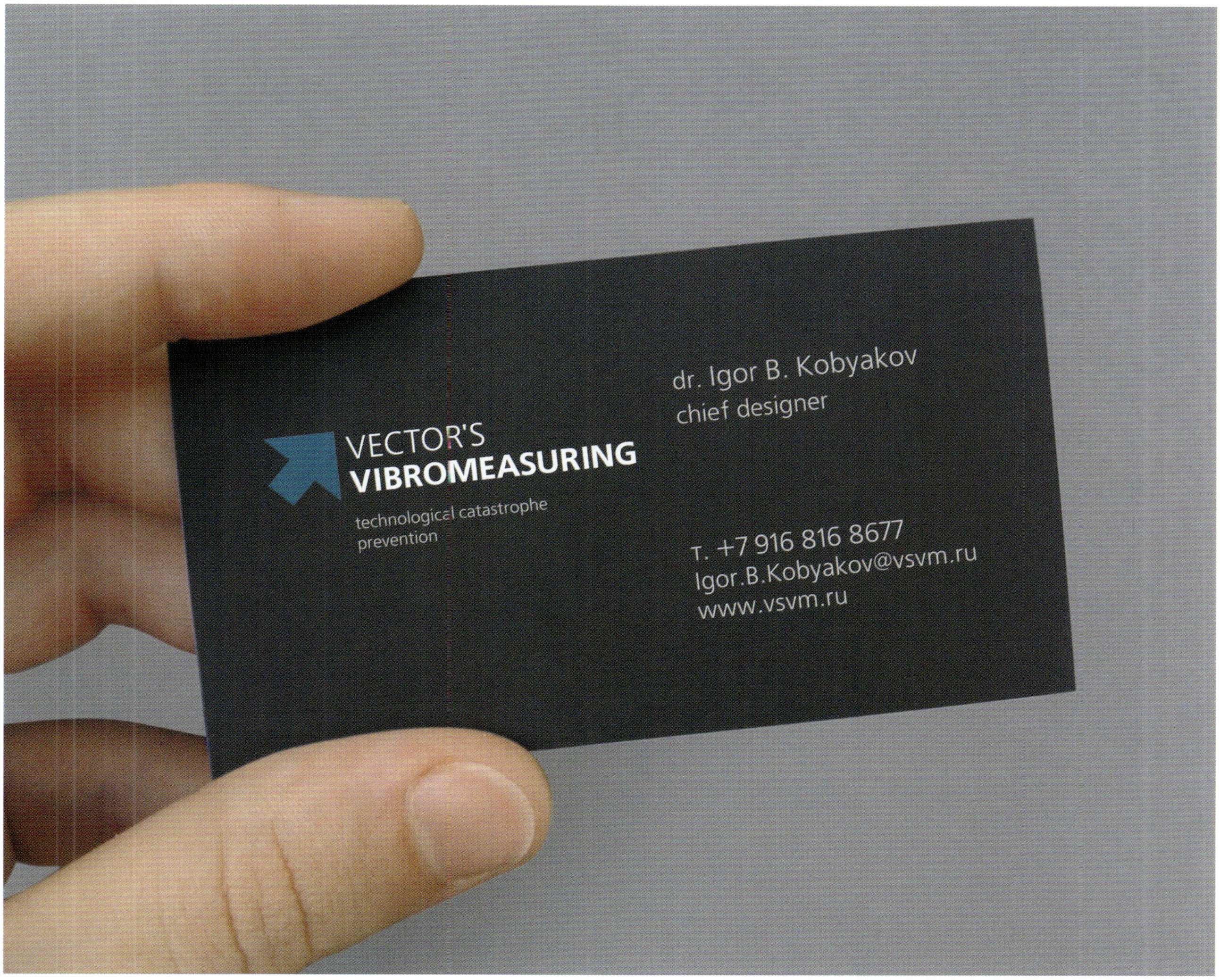

VECTOR'S
VIBROMEASURING
technological catastrophe prevention

dr. Igor B. Kobyakov
chief designer

т. +7 916 816 8677
Igor.B.Kobyakov@vsvm.ru
www.vsvm.ru

Design
Tuukka Koivisto

Project
Helsinki Day Invitation

Design
Tuukka Koivisto
Project
Helsinki Day Invitation

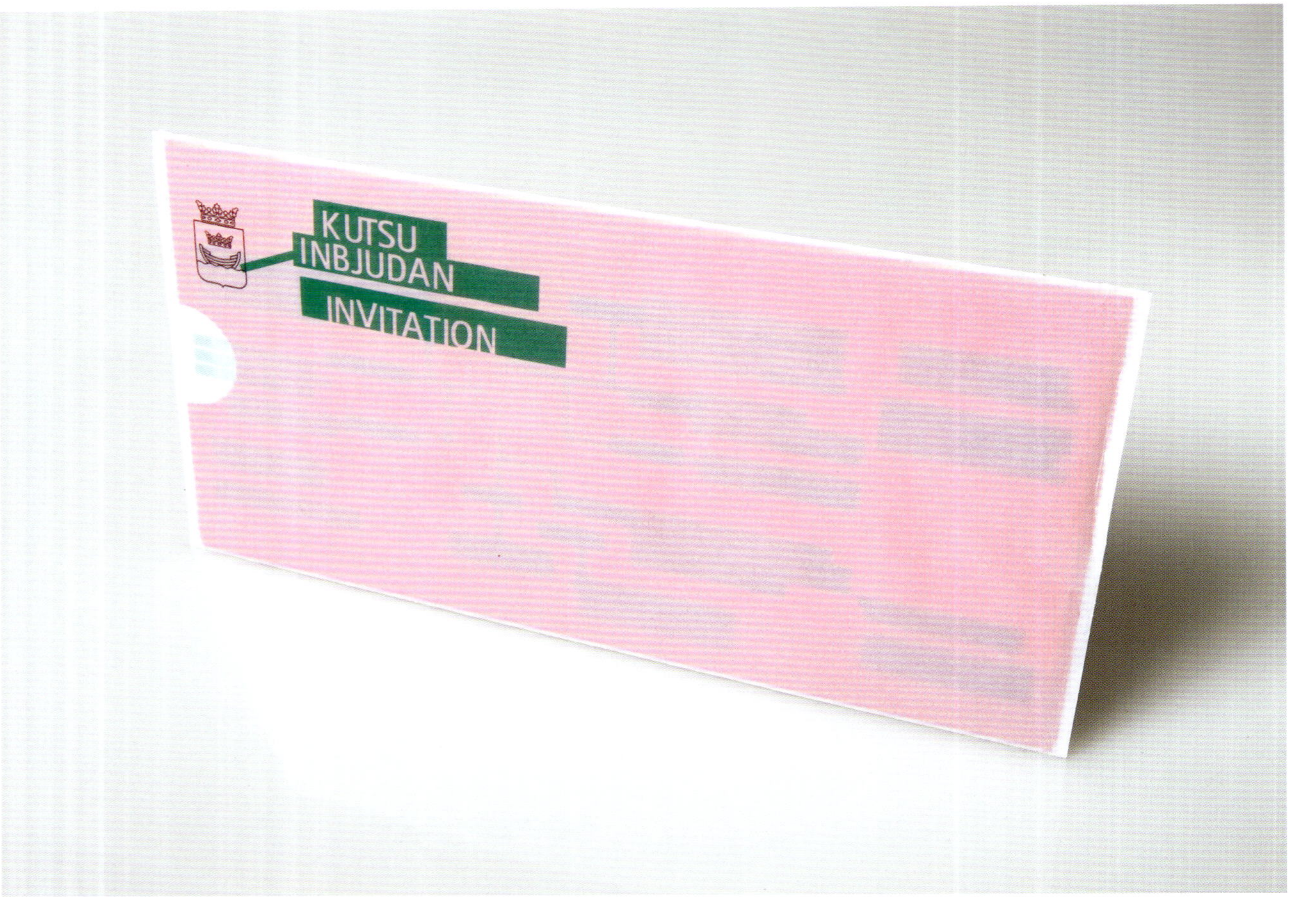
KUTSU
INBJUDAN
INVITATION

Stadshuset
Norra esplanaden 11-13
Helsingfors
NÄR
Fredagen den 12/06/09
kl.19.00-21.30
Anmälan om förhinder
senast 5.6.2009
helsinki2009@hel.fi
Inbjudan är personlig.
Var vänlig och
uppvisa detta
inbjudningskort vid dörren.
Regrets only by June 5
helsinki2009@hel.fi
The invitation is personal.
Please present this card
at the entrance.
KUTSU
INBJUDAN
INVITATION

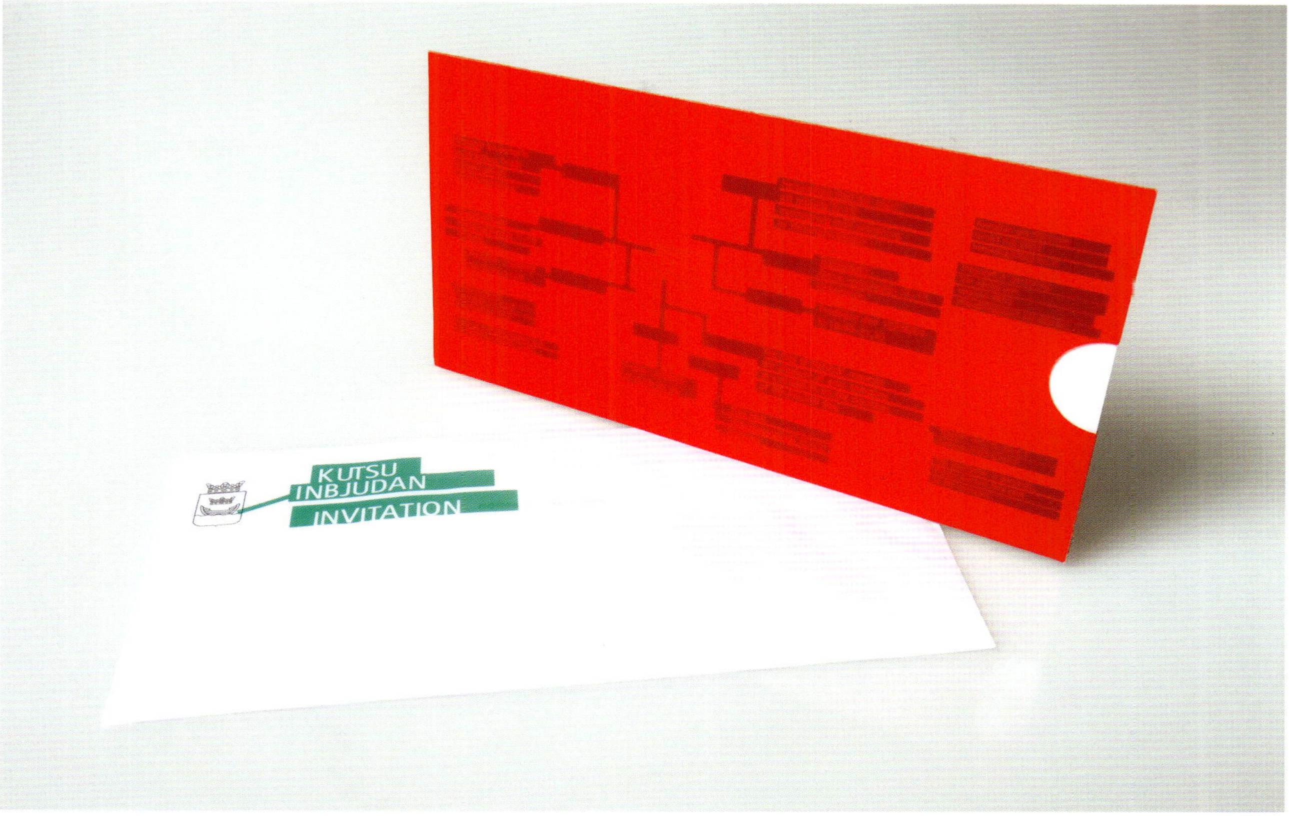

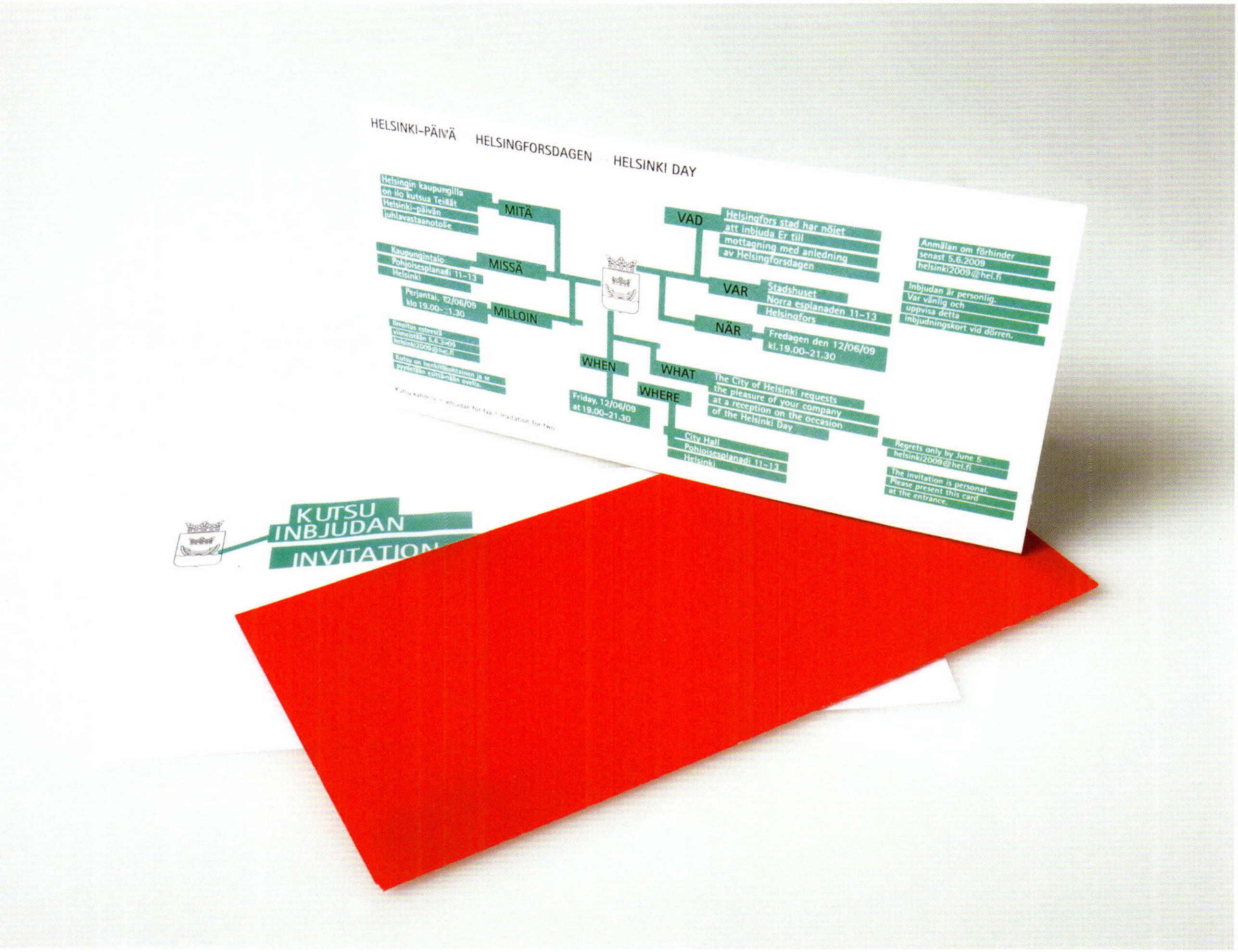

Design

Bart van Delft

Project

Stander Stroopwafels

These business cards are one of the many items that are created for this original Dutch Waffles baker. The style reflects the traditional and fresh side of the product.

These were printed on 400 grams paper with a matt laminate.

Coen Stander
tel nr: 06 - 48 27 27 11
email: coenstander@gmail.com

Design
Bart van Delft

Project
Stander Stroopwafels

For this Nails and Manicure stylist I've made a complete style and these business cards are the first item that is printed. The decorative style symbolizes the art of Nail Design, with a female flavor.

It is printed on 400 grams paper with a matt laminate.

NEWEST NAILS

Torenstraat 11a [pand Hair Maxx]
4901 EG Oosterhout

T: 0162-420420
M: 06-20558091

W: www.newestnails.nl
E: info@newestnails.nl

Openingstijden:

Ma: 11:00 - 16:00 uur
Di: 09:00 - 17:30 uur
Wo: 09:00 - 17:30 uur
Do: 09:00 - 17:30 uur
Vr: 09:00 - 21:00 uur
Za: 09:00 - 16:00 uur
Zo: Gesloten

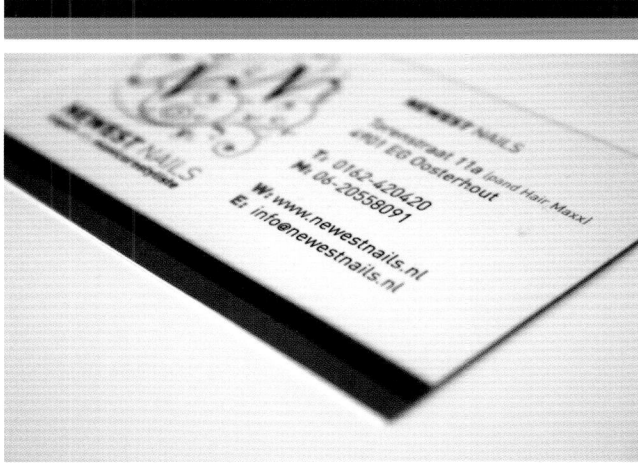

Design

Bart van Delft

Project

Moving Card

This card was used for announcing the move of me and my girlfriend.
The design was inspired by our modern style with a twist of pink.

It is printed on 300 grams matt paper

Design

Daniel Dittmar

Project

Hopshopper

'Hopshopper' is an iPhone application that brings loyalty cards to a digital platform in order to reduce clutter, and minimize hassle. This brief called for a smart and stylish re-brand, whilst still keeping the design playful and androgynous.

The concept looked at the cyclical nature of fashion, and played on the idea of a vintage 'mom & pop' feel, whilst keeping a modern aesthetic to suit. The colours are considered from the different levels in a car-park, and used in parallel to keep a softer feel to the branding.

Design
The Creative Method

Project
New Zealand Cheese School

The aim was to design and develop a stationery suite to communicate the core business of cheese education and making in New Zealand. The stationery needed to be bold, simple, immediate and memorable.

The concept was simple and based on the colour and shape of a block of cheese, the provinence of the brand was further reinforced through die-cut holes in the stationery in the shape of New Zealand.

The Design Museum London commissioned us to design their bookmark for their quarterly DESIGN OVERTIME events. A festive night of shopping, music, and making, the SPARKLE THE DARK UP events aimed at Christmas shopping done early in the Design Museum Shop. We also had to highlight the current museum's showcase, celebrating the love of ceramics at the Design Museum's exhibition Patricia Urquiola – Purely Porcelain. Our(standing up) bookmark was designed to be one-part shopping bag, one-part porcelain mug.

Design
VONSUNG
Project
Design Museum

DESIGN MUSEUM

SPARKLE
THE DARK UP
DESIGN OVERTIME

designmuseumshop.com

FRIDAY 23
JANUARY
18:00 – 22:00

£5 in advance, £8.50 on the door

For the perfect winter interlude, celebrate your love of ceramics at the Design Museum's clay medley. Informal talks and hands on workshops to inspire the pottery enthusiast, and a last chance to see the exhibition Patricia Urquiola · Purely Porcelain.

ARE WE THERE YET, MUM?
Led by the project management team, Podium, London-based branding design studio VONSUNG collaborated with Podium to design for the overall art direction, naming, branding, print, collateral, packaging, uniform, way-finding and website. Many of these design items were used in unusual ways by fresh-thinking VONSUNG to add extra interest to the first show cafe for children.

VONSUNG decided to use a number of the branding products in the cafe, challenging the preconceived uses of the pieces and turning them into idiosyncratic design statements for the patrons. The identity of the cafe was created using Roman alphabet characters to make learning more enjoyable and interactive.

'KIDS CAFE PICCOLO was designed to offer a fairy tale feeling for children with an adult-like atmosphere for their parents to enjoy,' said Joseph Sung, creative director of VONSUNG, the branding design agency responsible for the overall branding design of the complex.

Design
VONSUNG
Project
Kids Cafe Piccolo

'We wanted to reflect this with Podium's interior of the cafe, giving it the wow factor that you'd expect from a premium, design-led coffee shop in Seoul.

With many feature graphic walls in the main dining and play room space it was particularly useful for us to be able to cover the walls using educational graphic— we thought of astrological signs for the children to connect the dots.'

Design
VONSUNG

Project
Viet Hoa Cafe

The restaurant's meal is authentic. So we choose the simple classic font for the identity.
We use a flower as an icon for giving character on the name. 'HOA' means blossoming in Vietnamese.

The main task was to uniformly unify the space in terms of colour and materials—as we set about to acquiring furniture that would have an impact.

The palette was earthy and neutral yet structured with distinct lines, like sculptures, are references to Vietnam's surrounding water and sky.

The furniture finishes amplify the straight lines of the restaurant's wood and strip panelling.

My design sensibility was formed in the 1980s, and many of my inspirations come from that period—'Power Dressing'. The main feature of the restaurant is the 9 meter-long center table which houses the King & Queen chair underneath the David Chipperfield chandelier.

Brown and lime green was chosen as colourways. Brown for Vietnam country mother-ground, lime green from their food which includes plenty of fresh herbs.

We wanted to achieve the feeling of freshness, organic and healthy food.

Appetisers

		£
1	Prawn crackers	1.80
2	Deep fried aubergine/tofu/vegetable	3.90
3	Summer rolls (prawns & crabstick)/tofu *	3.90
4	Spring rolls/Spring rolls with salad	3.30/3.60
5	Banh cuon (steamed rolls) served with mint, bean sprouts, Chinese sausage	4.90
6	Steamed peanuts in shell *	2.70
7	Paper wrapped prawns	4.10
8	Banh xeo - Crispy pancake (prawns & pork)/vegetables	5.90
9	Sesame prawn toast/minced prawn & squid	3.00
10	Grilled tiger (prawn/mussel) with garlic chilli sauce	7.00
11	Salted (fish/prawns/squid/tofu/aubergine/ribs) with chilli & garlic	5.60
12	Salted soft shell crab in garlic dressing	7.00
13	Satay (chicken/prawns/tofu) *	4.10
14	Spare ribs	4.10
15	Grilled beef in betel leaf *	5.50
16	Crispy (duck/mock duck) with pancake, salad & basil	7.10 (1/4) 13.50 (1/2)

Soup

17	Pho - rice noodle soup with (beef/chicken/prawn/tofu)	4.20/5.90
18	Bun - rice vermicelli in spicy soup with (beef/chicken/prawn/tofu)	4.20/5.90
19	Hu Tiu - rice noodles soup with prawns	4.20/5.90
20	Special Pho/Special Bun/Hu tiu with seafood	6.70
21	Wun tun soup/Wun tun soup with egg noodles	3.70/5.90
22	Mi vit - roasted duck sour soup with egg noodles	6.70
23	Canh chua - Hot and sour soup with (fish/prawns/chicken/vegetables)	4.50/6.70
24	(Tofu/Green leaves) soup with (prawns/chicken/pork/vegetables)	4.20/5.90
25	Viet Hoa Hu Tiu - rice vermicelli with assorted meat & prawns served with soup	6.70

Seafood Dishes

26	Stewed fish with chilli & lemon grass	6.95
27	Grilled tilapia fish	11.50
28	Fried tilapia fish (in fish sauce with mango)	9.80
29	Fried catfish (in fish sauce with ginger)	9.80
30	Grilled/steamed sea bass with sweet chilli sauce	14.00
31	Drunken fish (cooked in white wine with 'cloud ear' mushrooms)	7.00
32	Fish in (lemon/tamarind/sweet & sour) sauce	6.50
33	Sizzling salmon	9.90
34	Stewed tiger prawns with chilli lemon grass in coconut sauce	7.90
35	Prawns in (lemon/tamarind/sweet & sour) sauce	6.50
36	Sizzling (prawns/squid) with spring onions	6.70
37	Green ginger prawns with spring onions	6.50
38	(Prawns/Squid) with chilli & blackbean sauce	6.50
39	Mussels with garlic chilli & blackbean sauce	6.50
40	Deep-fried squid (in corn starch)	5.50
41	Stir-fried prawns with (green leaves/broccoli)	6.50
42	Stir-fried (prawns/squid) with pickled greens	6.50
43	Stir-fried seafood with mixed vegetables	7.20

Beef/Lamb Dishes

44	Shaking beef (quick fried beef cubes on a bed of green salad)	7.90
45	Beef dipped in tamarind sauce *	6.90
46	Beef slices in smoked oyster sauce	6.90
47	Sizzling beef with spring onions	6.90
48	Beef with chilli & black bean sauce	6.50
49	Stir-fried beef with (green leaves/broccoli)	6.50
50	Stir-fried beef with pickled green	6.50
51	Shredded beef (in spicy bean sauce)	6.90
52	Lamb with chilli & lemon grass	6.90

Pork Dishes

53	Sweet & Sour (pork/ribs)	5.30
54	Stir-fried pork with onions	5.30
55	Stir-fried pork with chilli & black bean sauce	5.50
56	Stewed pork & duck eggs served with pickled bean sprouts	6.90

Design
G-MAN

Project
MAY68

Designer/Art Director—G-MAN (Graham Jones)

Limited set of 4 artcards for Manchester electro band MAY68. Printed in neon pink Pantone 806 on uncoated card on an old litho press.

These were inserted in the first 7 Inch single release by the band. Illustrations by lead singer Judy Wainwright.

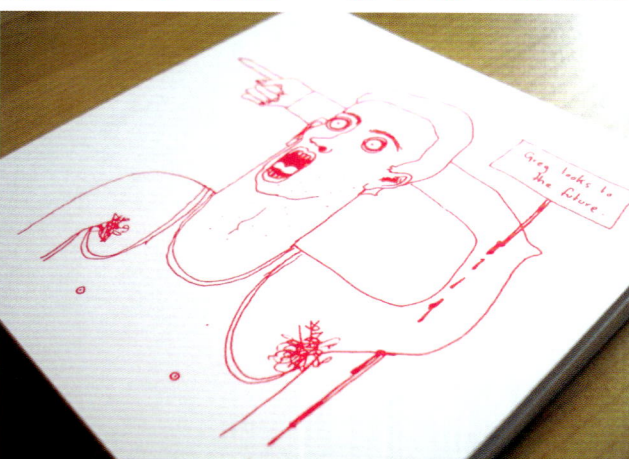

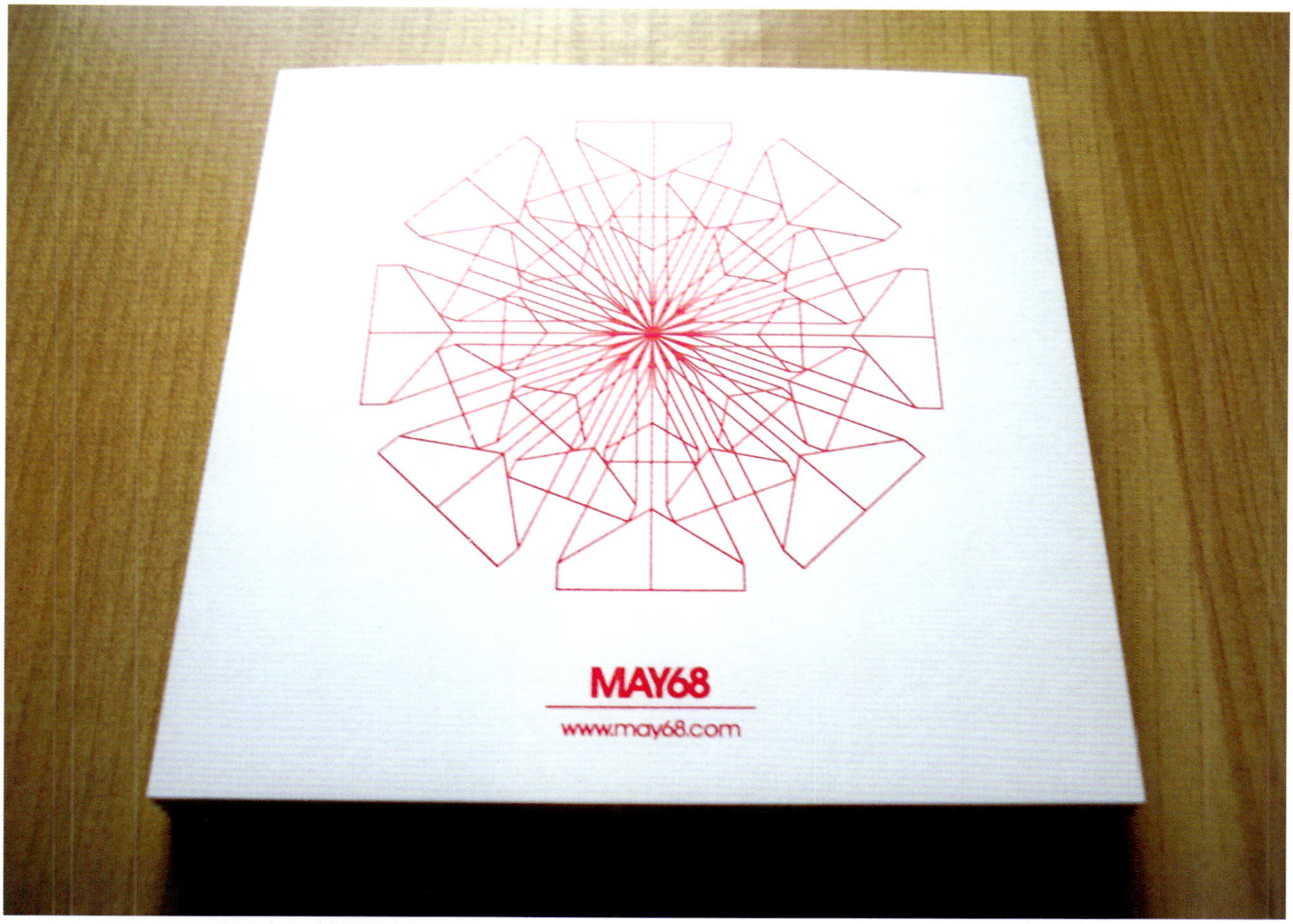
MAY68
www.may68.com

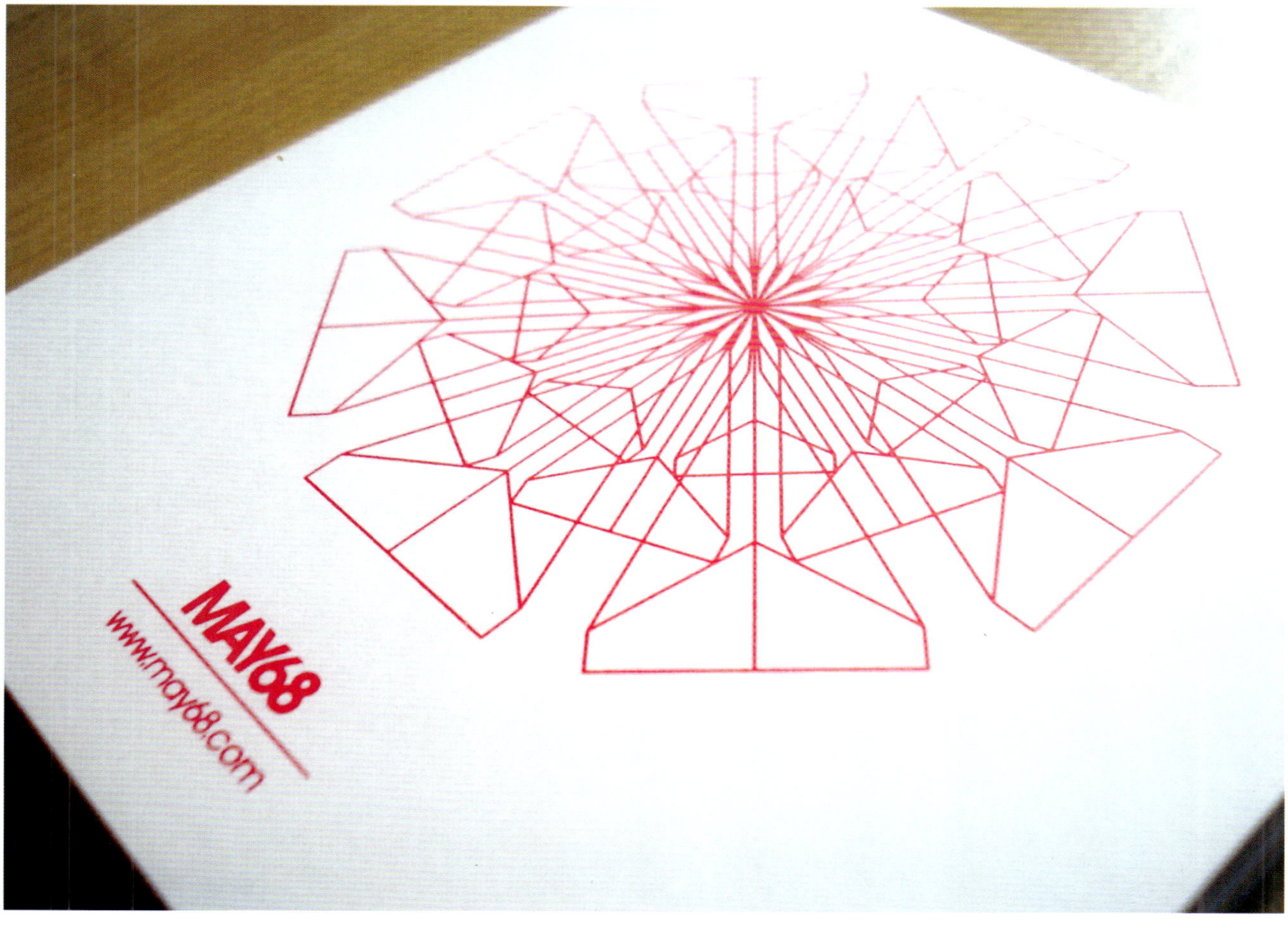
MAY68
www.may68.com

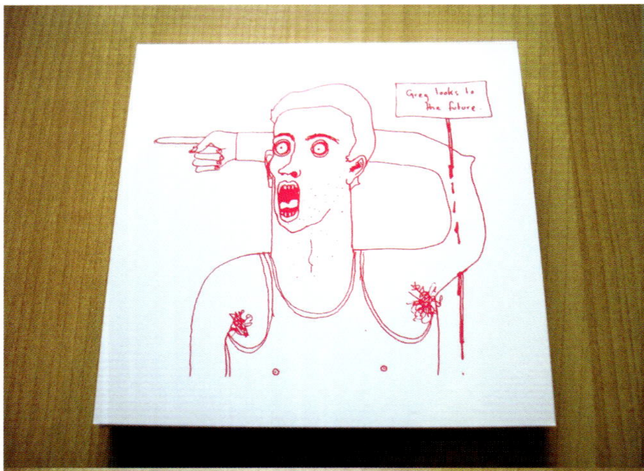
Greg looks to the future.

MAY68
www.may68.com

MAY68
www.may68.com

MAY68
www.may68.com

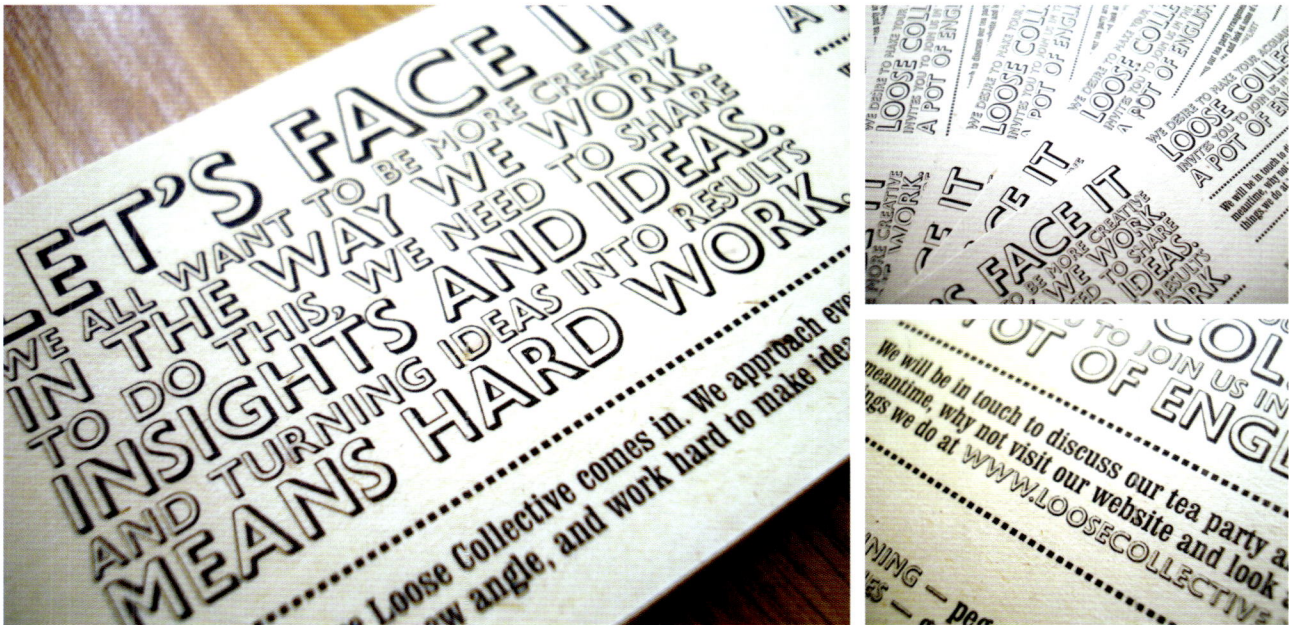

LET'S FACE IT WE ALL WANT TO BE MORE CREATIVE IN THE WAY WE WORK. TO DO THIS, WE NEED TO SHARE **INSIGHTS AND IDEAS.** AND TURNING IDEAS INTO RESULTS **MEANS HARD WORK.**

That's where Loose Collective comes in. We approach every project from a new angle, and work hard to make ideas happen.

WE DESIRE TO MAKE YOUR ACQUAINTANCE. **LOOSE COLLECTIVE** INVITES YOU TO JOIN US IN THE SHARING OF **A POT OF ENGLISH TEA.**

We will be in touch to discuss our tea party arrangements. In the meantime, why not visit our website and look at some of the things we do at WWW.LOOSECOLLECTIVE.NET

PEGGY MANNING — peggy@loosecollective.net
GRAHAM JONES — gman@loosecollective.net

Design

G-MAN

Project

Loose Collective

Designer/Art Director: G-MAN (Graham Jones)

Letterpressed in black on recycled board. These were sent out with Loose Collective posters to a range of friends and potential clients. The idea was to offer potential clients a free pot of English tea in order to have an initial conversation with them about possible work in the future.

LOOSE
COLLECTIVE

"...is one percent inspiration and ninety-n... ...spiration." — THOMAS A. ED...

— XI POT OF EN...

LET'S FACE IT
WE ALL WANT TO BE MORE CREATIVE.
IN THE WAY WE WORK.
TO DO THIS, WE NEED TO SHARE
INSIGHTS AND IDEAS,
AND TURNING IDEAS INTO RESULTS
MEANS HARD WORK.

That's where Loose Collective comes in. We approach every
project from a new angle, and work hard to make ideas happen

LOOSE COLLECTIVE
A POT OF ENGLISH...

A
CONTEMPORARY
VISUAL ART EXHIBITION
SAVE US
PREVIEW OPENING
THURSDAY 17TH JUNE
5–9PM

A
CONTEMPORARY
VISUAL ART EXHIBITION
SAVE US
PREVIEW OPENING
THURSDAY 17TH JUNE
5–9PM

Design
G-MAN

Project
Save Us

Designer/Art Director: G-MAN (Graham Jones)

Letterpressed in warm red on luxury gloss and uncoated boards.
Invite/Flyer for a contemporary visual art exhibition with a local church
being used as actual the exhibition space.

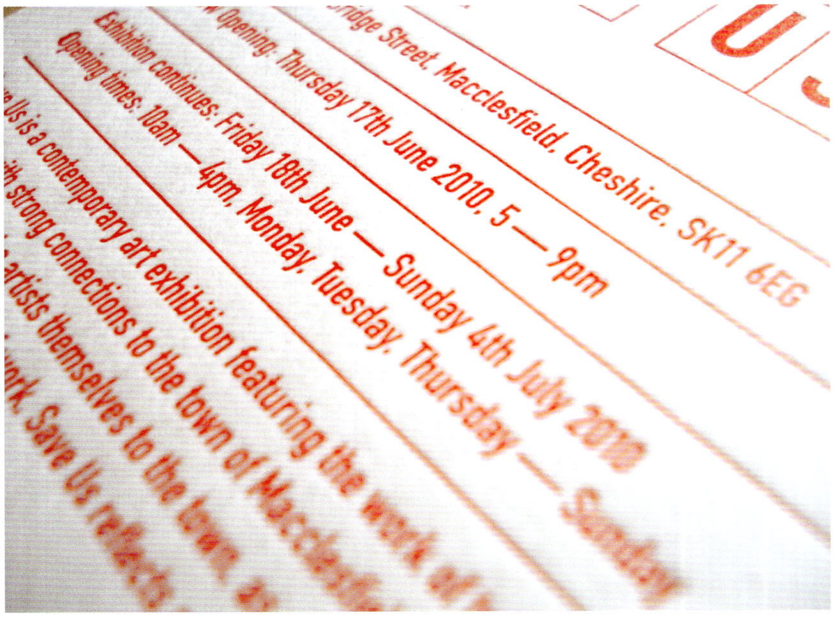

Artists include:
Andrea Booker
Ben Cook
Ian Davenport
Hilary Jack
Ralph McGaul
Ian Rawlinson and Nick Crowe
Mit Senoj
David Shrigley
Jen Southern
Daniel Staincliffe

For more information please contact:
karen@occasionallysomewhere.org
www.barnabyfestival.org.uk

Julie Fagerholt
Requests the pleasure
of your company
to celebrate the new exclusive
Signature Pieces Collection S/S 2007

LONDON
31ST OF AUGUST – 22ND OF SEPTEMBER 2006

AGENT
M & L HARRIS
BEVERLY BARNETT
18 DEVONSHIRE STREET LONDON W1G 7AU
PHONE +44 (0) 207 580 5580

PARIS
5TH OF OCTOBER – 8TH OF OCTOBER 2006

FAIR
TRANOI BOURSE DE COMMERCE
RUE DE VIARMES PARIS 01
TINA LUNDTOFT LARSEN
PHONE +45 26 46 82 00

Design
Homework

Project
Heart Made

Design
Homework

Project
Invitations

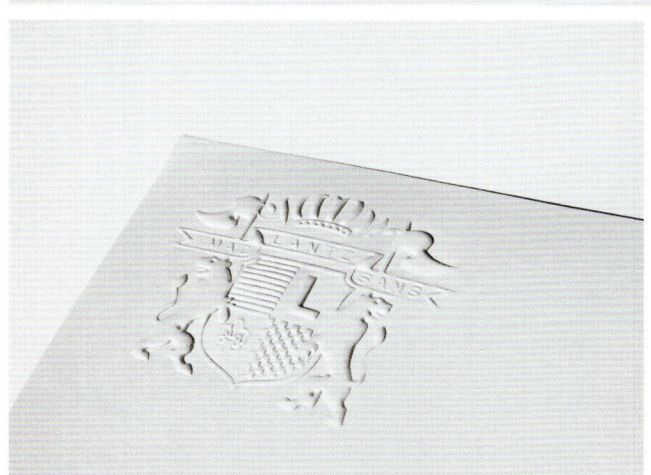

Design
Homework
Project
Invitations

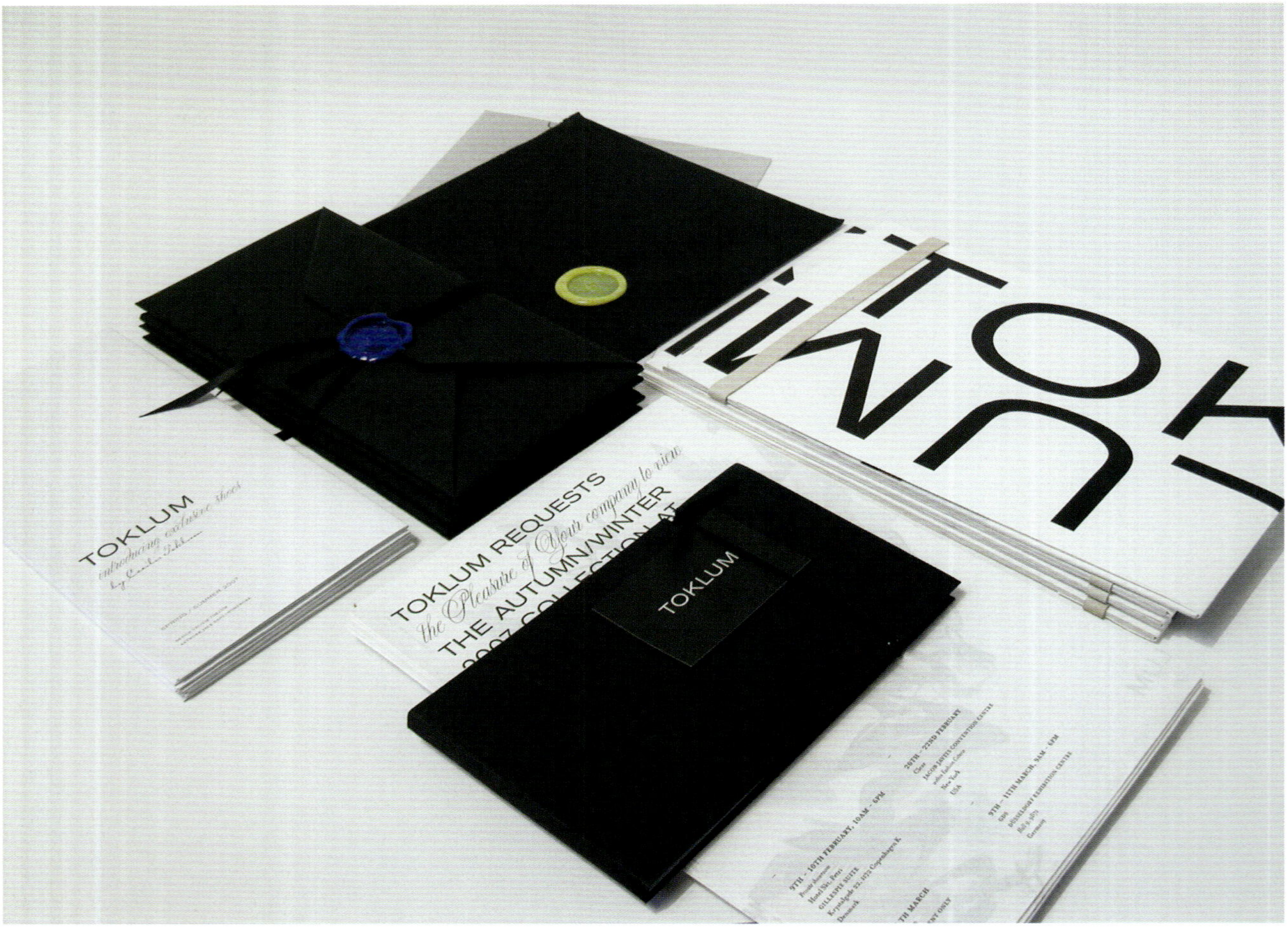

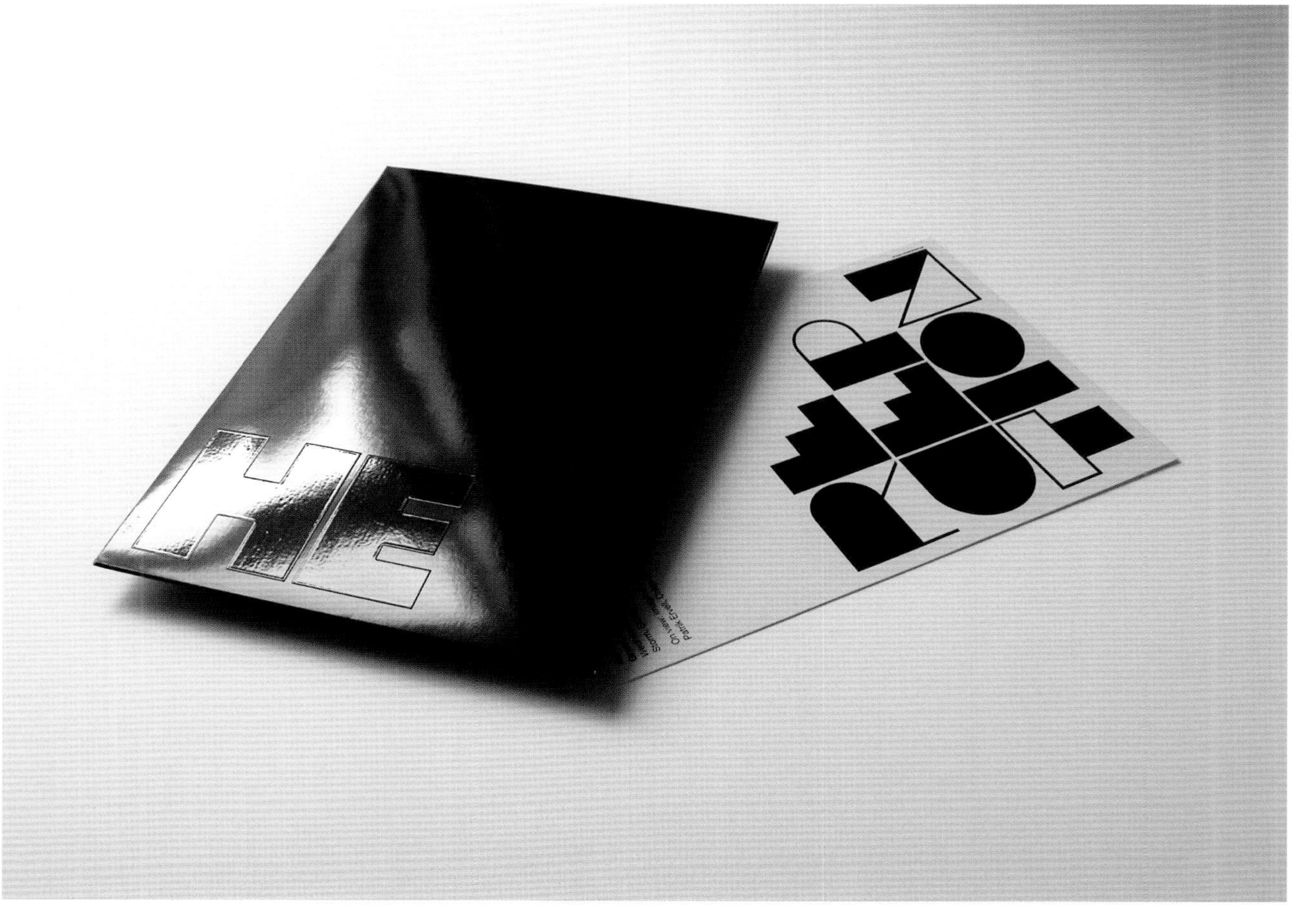

Coro Prieto decided to remodel the commerce where she had worked since many years ago and she thought that was the perfect moment to redesign her identity too.

With this project we started from the idea that when you go to a beauty centre you do it for 'decorate yourself', to become more beautiful. Hence arose the idea of using a calligraphy font decorative style with many ornaments to convert it in the logo.

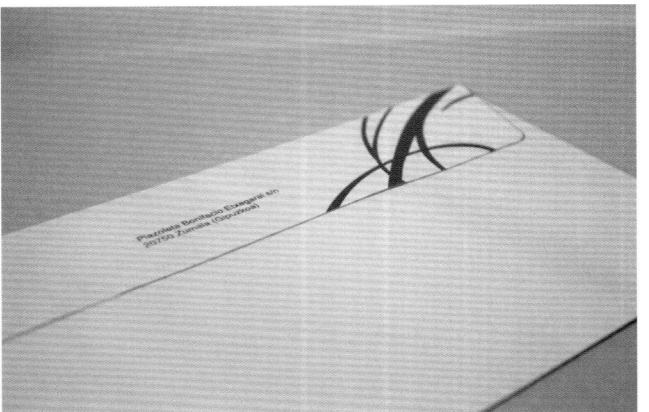

Then we saw that this picture had become a signature, the signature that everyone uses when has to authenticate the content of something or when somebody need to sign a document.

With this logc as an identity sign, Coro Prieto ensures to their customers the good results of her work.

To further emphasize the decorative character of the mark, we added both bags as stationery and exterior signage parts of the logo that can work like ornaments. The result was a coordinated project in all of elements, mainly based in beauty concept.

Aside from the logo, we made personal cards for each one of the workers of the beauty centre, appointment cards to give to customers, envelopes, stickers to customize beauty products, bags and the sign outside the building.

Design
La caja de tipos
Project
Imanol & Arianne—Wedding Invitation

Design

La caja de tipos

Project

Imanol & Arianne—Wedding Invitation

'I want my grandmother who is 80 years to like the invitation' is what the bride told us when she made us the request. On that basis it was clear that we had to do a traditional invitation, but we didn't want typical one.

Nothing to use laid paper neither classic calligraphic typographies. Instead we chose a coated paper and Helvetica for the text inside.

The outside was decorated with a floral pattern that seems the bride's bouquet. Also we decided to print this part only with a UV–varnish to give a special touch to the invitation. With the colour we also wanted to differentiate this work from what is usually done, hence we chose the blue, an unusual colour for these cases.

The end result was a sober and elegant invitation that left delighted the grandmother.

Design
La caja de tipos

Project
Beñat & Ainhoa
Wedding Invitation

Datorren 2008-ko Maiatzak 17-an, eguerdiko 13-etan, Mendaroko Azpilgoetako elizan ezkontzera goaz. Iluntzean Belaustegi jatetxean ospatu nahi dugun festatxora gonbidatu nahi zaituztegu.

Mesedez erantzun.

Beñat: 656 702 959 / Ainhoa: 660 750 805

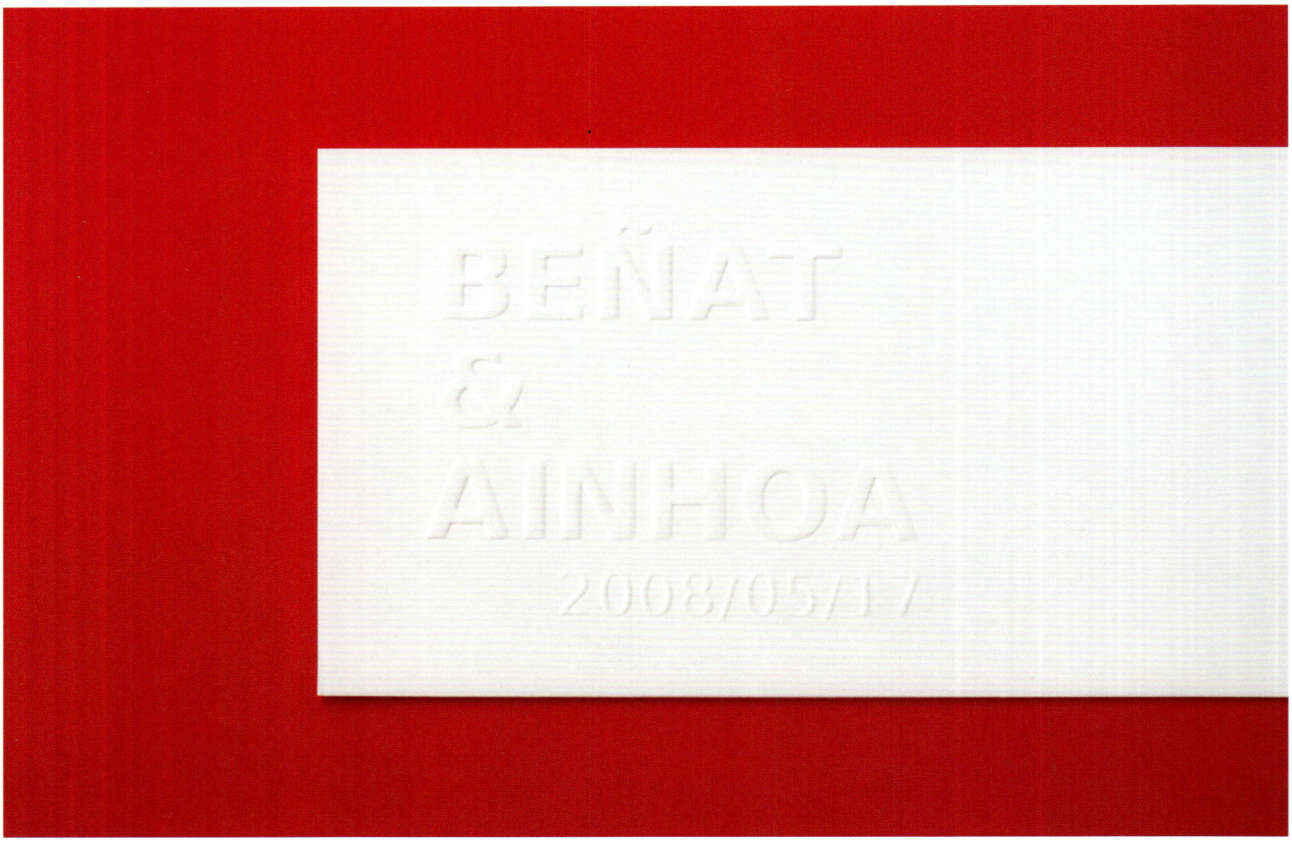

BEÑAT
&
AINHOA
2008/05/17

When Beñat and Ainhoa told us that they were going to get marry they ordered to us to design their wedding invitations. Both the ceremony and the banquet would be familiar, simple and uncrowded. Then their friends would meet with the couple in the evening for the party.

And here we posed a small dilemma. On one side was a quiet and familiar wedding and the other was the carefree in friends' company at the time of the dance. So how to move these concepts to the same invitation? Simple, using both sides of it.

We concluded that the best way to represent the intimate and simple character of the wedding was not to use any item that was not simply the paper. So we put the names of the couple and the date in relief, without a drop of ink that 'stain' the white surface. In fact they were deeply marked on paper but in view were of a very subtle way. To the other side, where was the wedding's explanatory text with all the information, we chose a lively colour in clearly referring to the dance and party's time.

In this case, the couple decided to distribute two types of invitations: one for the family, bigger and presented in its corresponding envelope and another for friends, smaller and manageable, such flyer which functioned like a party's invitation.

Aitor +

07
12

Nagore

20   10   0

Aitor + Nagore—Wedding Invitation

According to the RAE (Spanish language academy) a wedding is a ceremony by which two people unite in marriage and where both parts are indispensable in order for it to carry out.

When we met with Aitor and Nagore to talk about the invitation that we were going to design for them, we commented that it seemed very important that this concept was present in some way because it really is the most important of the ceremony, the fact of uniting two people. They liked the idea so much that we go ahead with it.

We decided that for a project with so much meaning, we had to take risks and use a different material, a clear acetate divided into two parts where each one contained some text of the invitation. To emphasize even more the concept of unity that we wanted to convey, we separated the text by letters scattered randomly on both acetates.

Thus, the only way to read the text and understand the invitation was to bring together these two acetates, as happens in a marriage where two people come together.

102

Design

La caja de tipos

Project

Josu Basterra Gilabert—Communion Card

Josu's parents already knew our work so long as when they commissioned us the design of his Communion card, they imagined we were going to try something different. Looking for documentation on the celebration, we came to the conclusion that the most important thing of the day is that the child receives the Communion at the first time, so that was the idea from which we started working.

What we wanted to do was convert the card in a Sacred Host like Josu would receive in his Communion day. Hence we chose a round format. On one side we embossed the name and surname of Josu as in the Hosts. To the rear where the

data are we wanted something simple and that it wasn't downplay the main part. Looking for documentation images, we realized that many of the real Hosts' borders are decorated with small edgings so we used a calligraphic typeface to try to convert the text into a decorative circle. When we printed it in gray it gave the card the needed touch of colour to differentiate to the background without actually overemphasized. The result was a simple and original job, and both Josu and his parents were delighted.

ETXEPE

Lan
bereziak
**Grandes
mecanizados**

Design

La caja de tipos

Project

Etxepe - Identity

Etxepe is a company with many years of experience in general engineering sector.

It is dedicated to drill and shape metal parts up to 14 meters that later become key parts of the structure of all types of machinery.

When they commissioned us the design of Etxepe's new identity we had clear idea that what they really needed was a redesign of its brand to follow being visually what they had been for many years.

So, referring to the activity performed, we chose a robust and well-constructed font to compose the logo and give it a feeling of heaviness, an impression enhanced by the contrast in size between the name of the company (Etxepe) and the activity that plays (Lan bereziak—Grandes mecanizados that means General engineering in Basque language and Spanish).

ETXEPE

Lan
bereziak
Grandes
mecanizados

Ibaitarte Industrialdea, A2 - 153 Postakutxa
20870 Elgoibar (Gipuzkoa) Spain
T: +34 943 741 297 / +34 943 740 664
F: +34 943 744 321
www.etxepe.com
etxepe@etxepe.com

Then, by separating a part of the "x" of the rest we are able to represent the die cuts that are made in metal pieces.

In addition, this little element also seems like an item produced in Etxepe that later will become part of other machines.

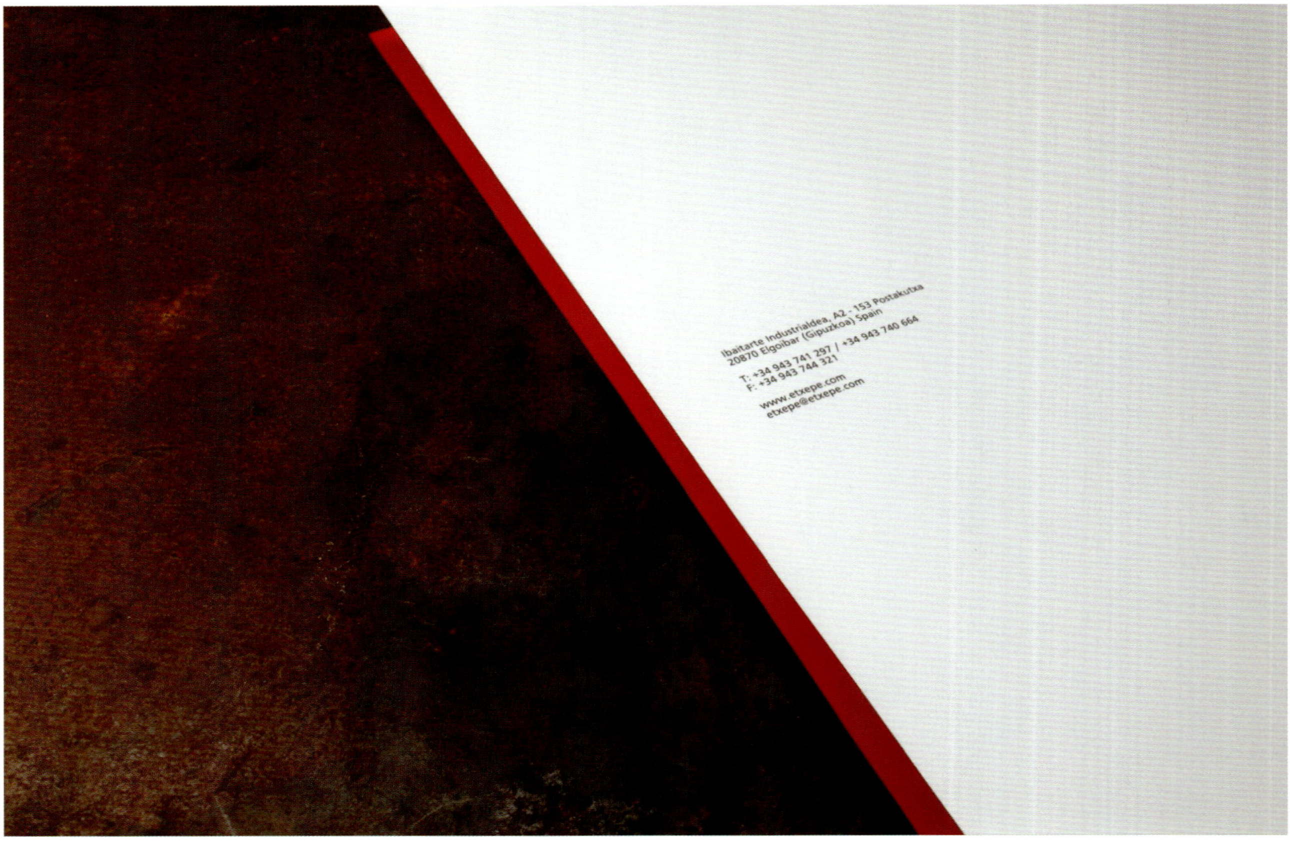

In addition to updating the business card of the company by eliminating all the unnecessary items, we made another custom option for Etxepe's manager as well as the letter sheet, the envelope and a folder to carry documents.

Design
La caja de tipos

Project
Etxepe—Identity

Design
Yomesubo

Project
Yomesubo card

Design
&Larry

Project
General Insurance
Association

Design
Ministry of Design
Project
Prologue

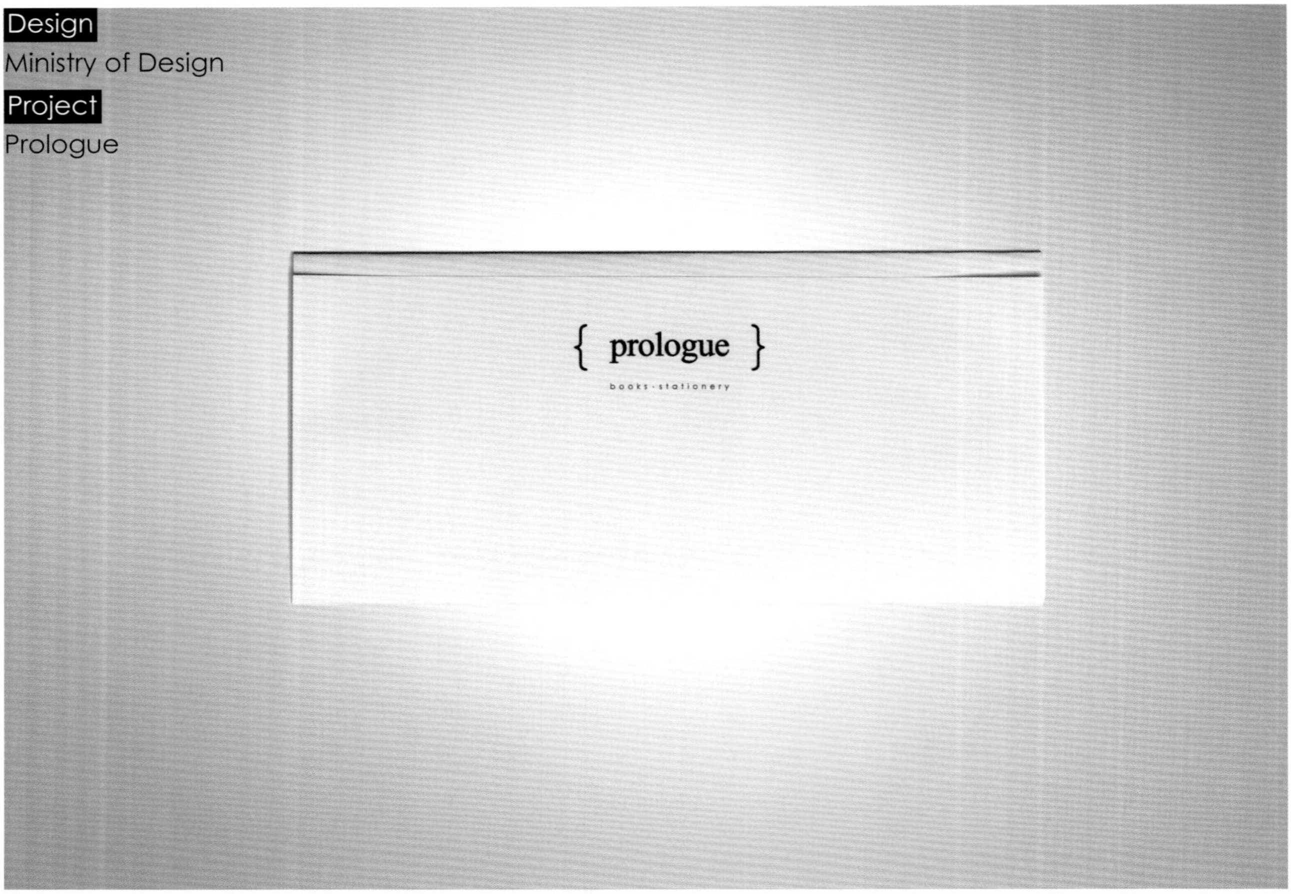

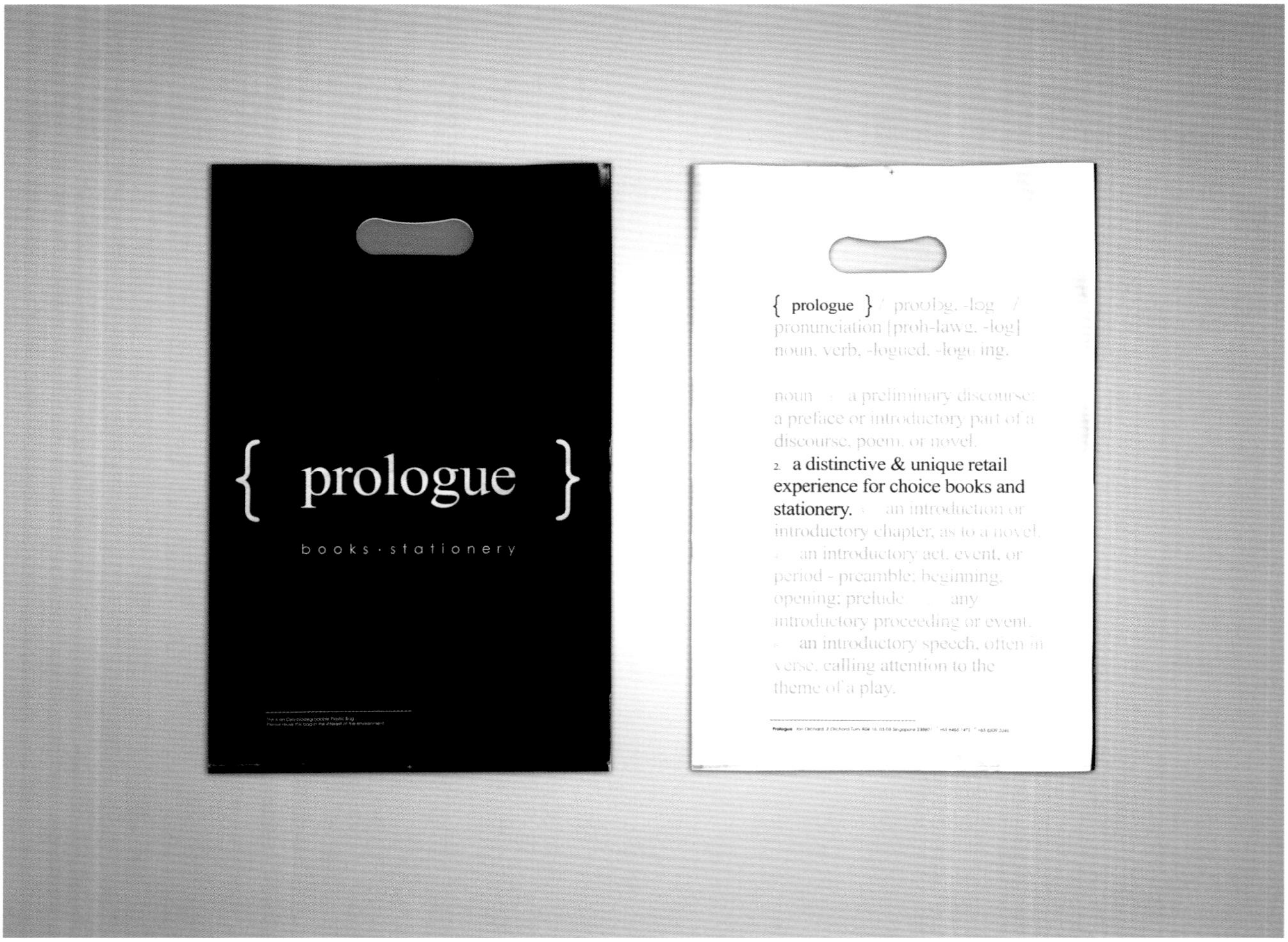

{ prologue } prooˈlɔg, -log /
pronunciation [proh-lawg, -log]
noun, verb, -logued, -logu·ing.

noun   a preliminary discourse;
a preface or introductory part of a
discourse, poem, or novel.
2. a distinctive & unique retail
experience for choice books and
stationery.   an introduction or
introductory chapter, as to a novel.
   an introductory act, event, or
period - preamble; beginning,
opening; prelude.   any
introductory proceeding or event.
   an introductory speech, often in
verse, calling attention to the
theme of a play.

{ prologue }
books · stationery

Design
Ministry of Design

Project
Prologue

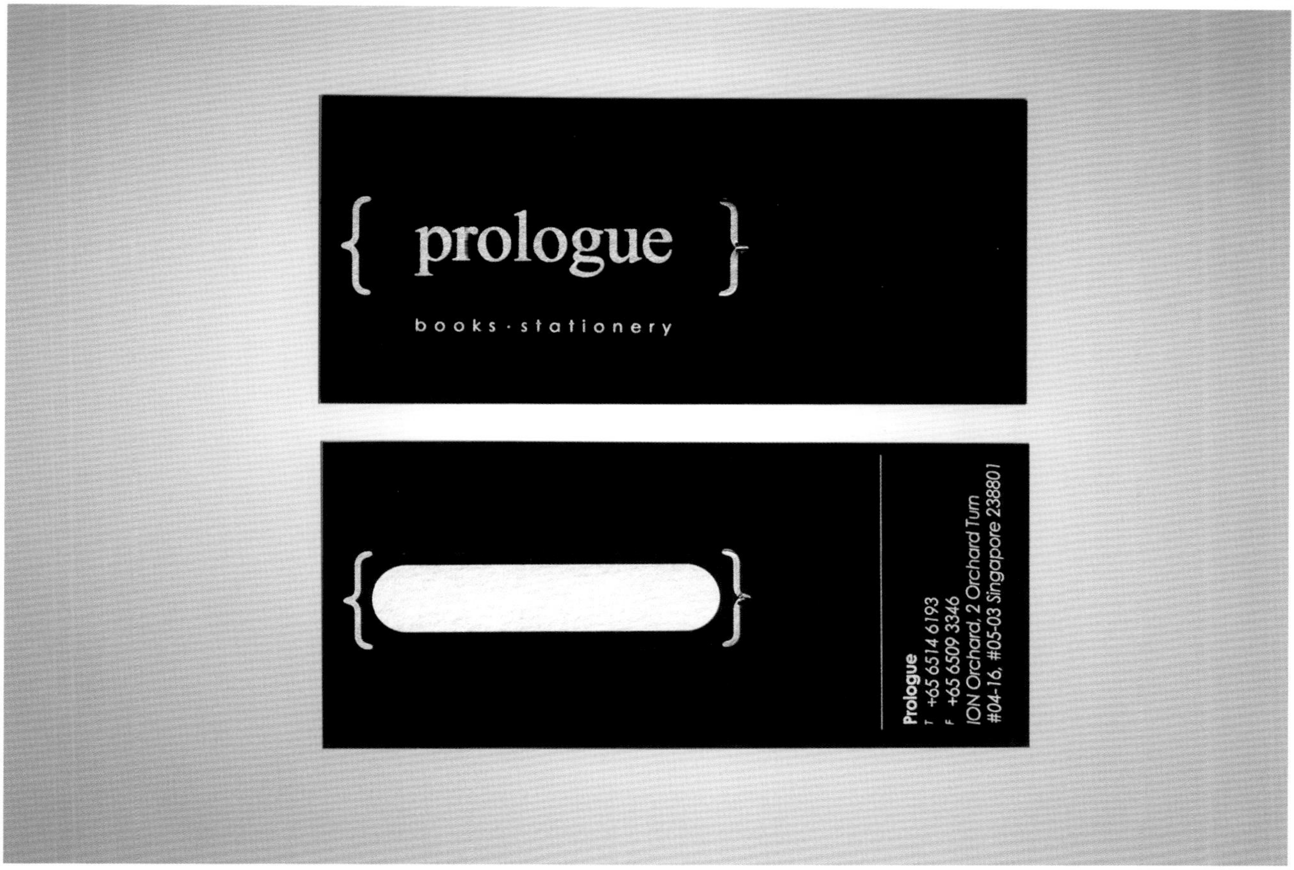

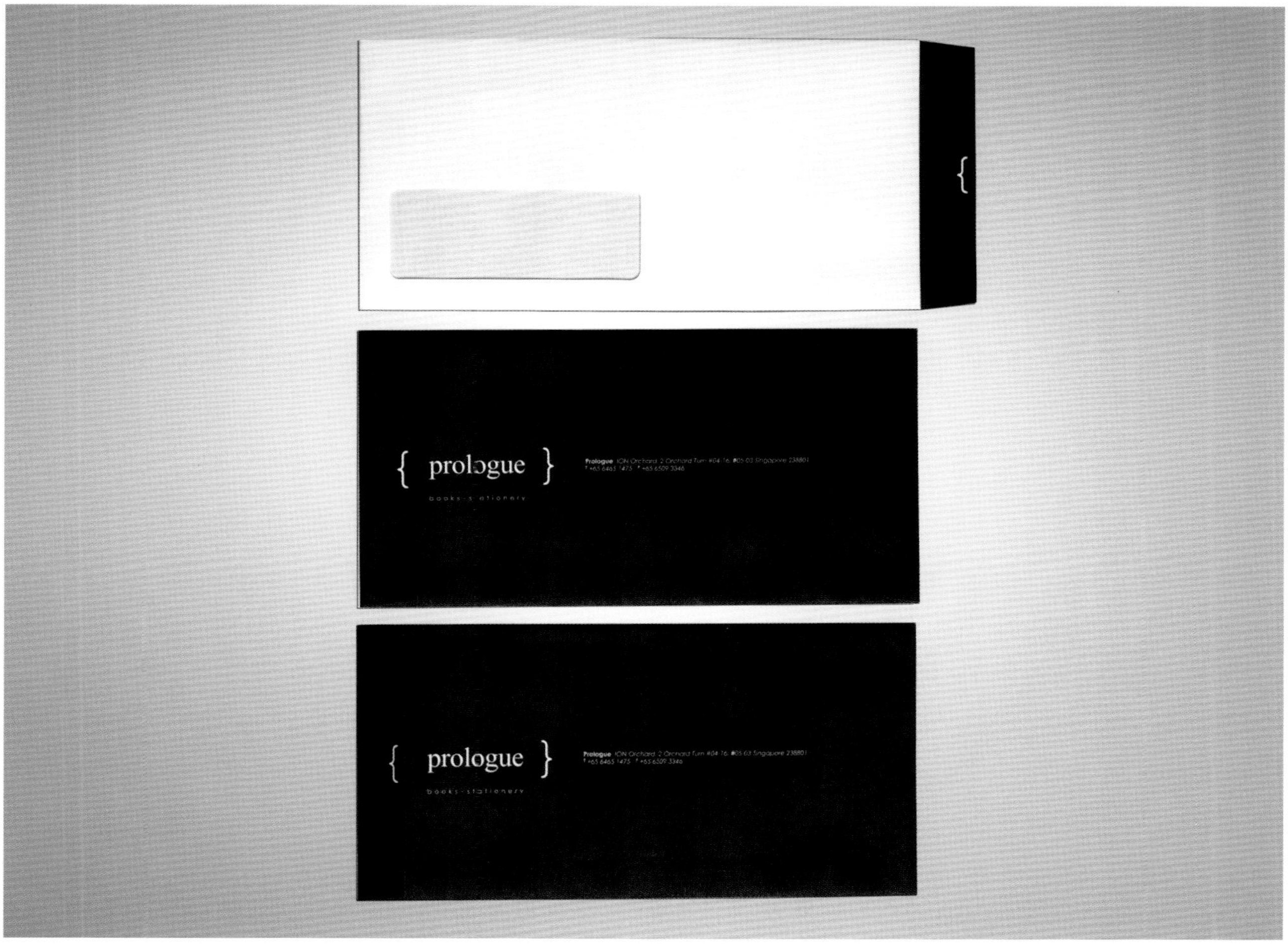

face to face

face to face
face to face
face to face
face to face

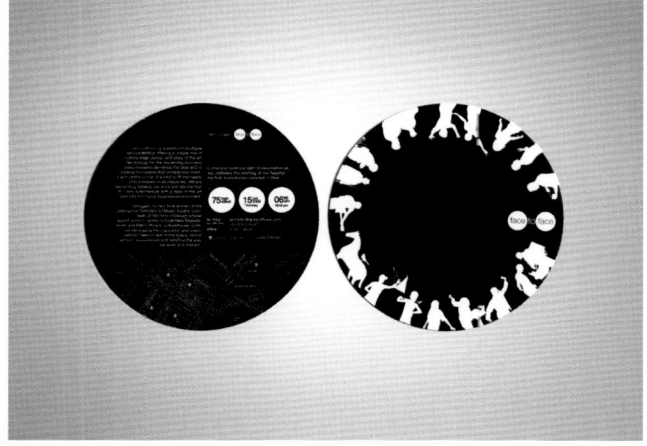

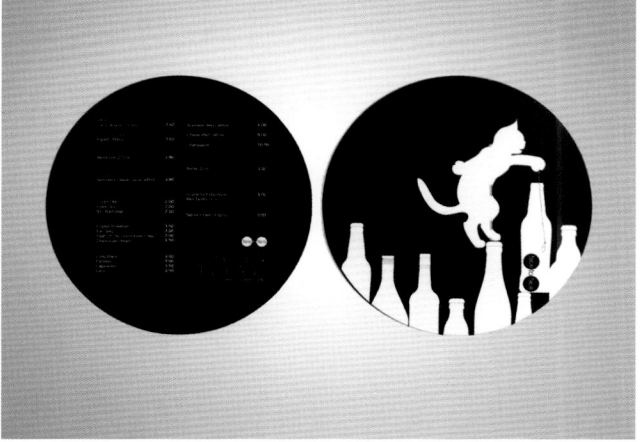

Design
Ministry of Design
Project
Face to Face

無　無

Design
Kai Zan

Project
The Art of Nothingness

Yamauchi Tatsuo Exhibition
Promotion

This work is designed for Japanese
minimalist artist Yamauchi Tatsuo's
exhibition, 'The Art of Nothingness.'

The aim is to create a unique
identity for the event.

The Chinese character, 'Wu,' represents
Nothingness, Emptiness, a Zen mood.

All printed promotional materials featured a
hollowed out image of the character, 'Wu,'
to represent this main theme.

MERRY CHRISTMAS & HAPPY NEW YEAR
ENJOY THE SPIRIT OF THE SEASON
2008

Flat Glass (Low-E / Reflective / Silkscreen / Tempered / Laminated / Insulating / Mirror),
Fabric Glass, Fiber Glass, Glassware

LUKANG FACTORY
Fabric Glass
Float Glass

TAICHUNG FACTORY
Float Glass
Processed Glass

TAOYUAN FACTORY
Fabric & Fiber Glass

HSINCHU FACTORY
Glassware
Rolled Glass

TAICHIA GLASS FIBER CO.
Fabric Glass

TG CHENGDU GLASS CO.
Float Glass
Processed Glass

Design
Kai Zan
Project

Taiwan Glass Christmas Celebration Cards

This is a Christmas card designed for Taiwan Glass Industry
Corporation to be sent to their customers.

The design of this card converted the abstract blueprints of
each Taiwan Glass factory into a Christmas decoration.

**TG DONGHAI
GLASS CO.**
Float Glass

TG TIANJIN GLASS CO.
Float Glass

**QINGDAO FLOAT
GLASS CO.**
Float Glass
Processed Glass

**QINGDAO ROLLED
GLASS CO.**
Rolled Glass

**TG HUANAN
GLASS CO.**
Float Glass
Mirror Glass

**TG CHANGJIANG
GLASS CO.**
Float Glass
Processed Glass

TAIWAN GLASS GROUP
台玻集團

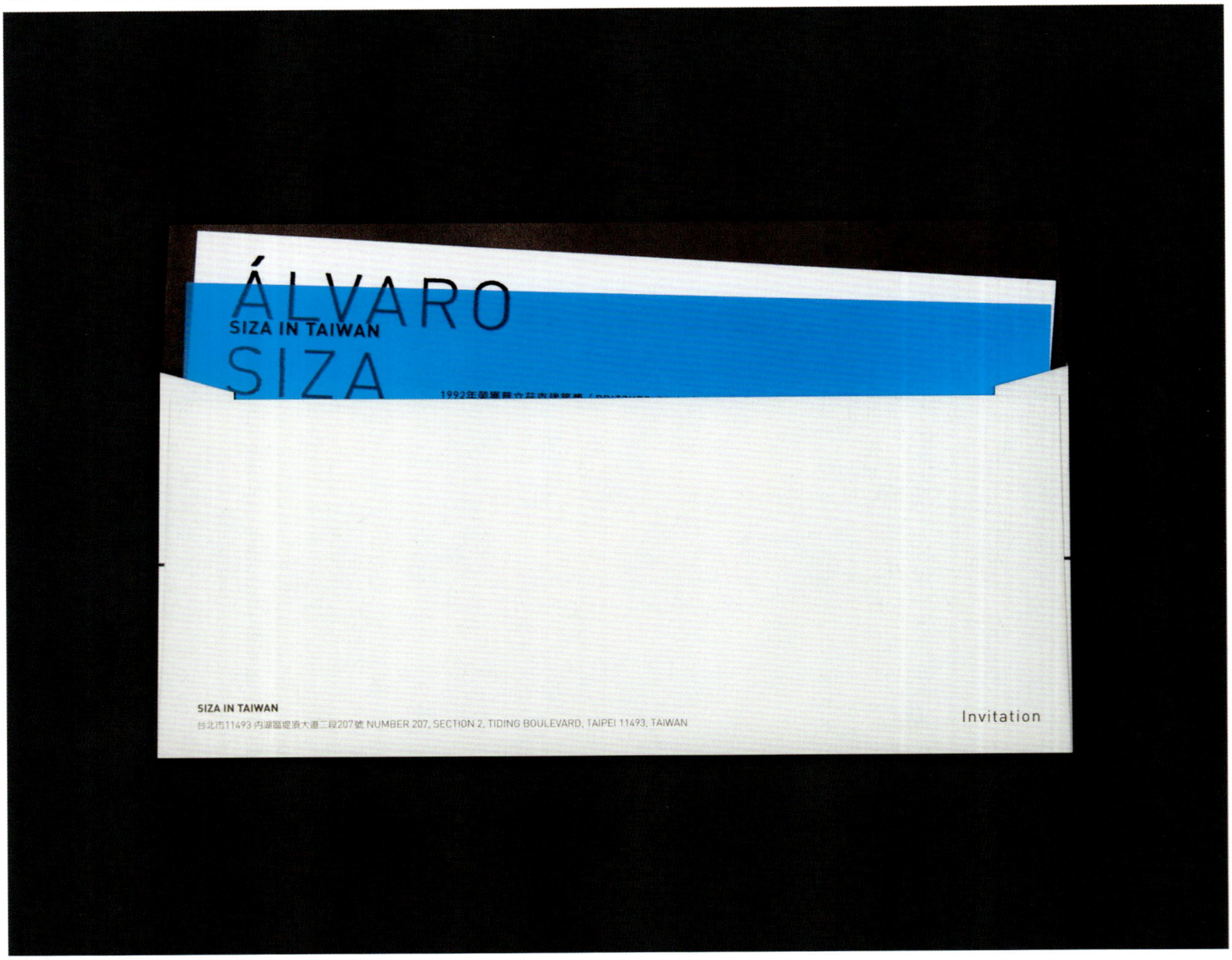

ÁLVARO
SIZA IN TAIWAN
SIZA

1992年建築界立茲內建築獎／ARCHITECT

SIZA IN TAIWAN
台北市11493 內湖區堤頂大道二段207號 NUMBER 207, SECTION 2, TIDING BOULEVARD, TAIPEI 11493, TAIWAN

Invitation

Design
Kai Zan
Project
Alvaro Siza in Taiwan China, Architect Seminar Invitation

Pritzker Architecture Prize winner, Alvaro Siza, specializes in landscape architecture.
This Portuguese architect was invited to Taiwan China to participate in an architecture seminar.

The invitation card was inspired by landscape architecture and used the horizon, sky, and shadows as its main designs to convey the seminar's topic.

Design

Kai Zan

Project

ARCHI-GREEN

Identity and promotional materials
for Archi-green exhibition.

PART1.

[ARCHI-GREEN]

綠色建築與綠建築的對話

7.02 - 8.22

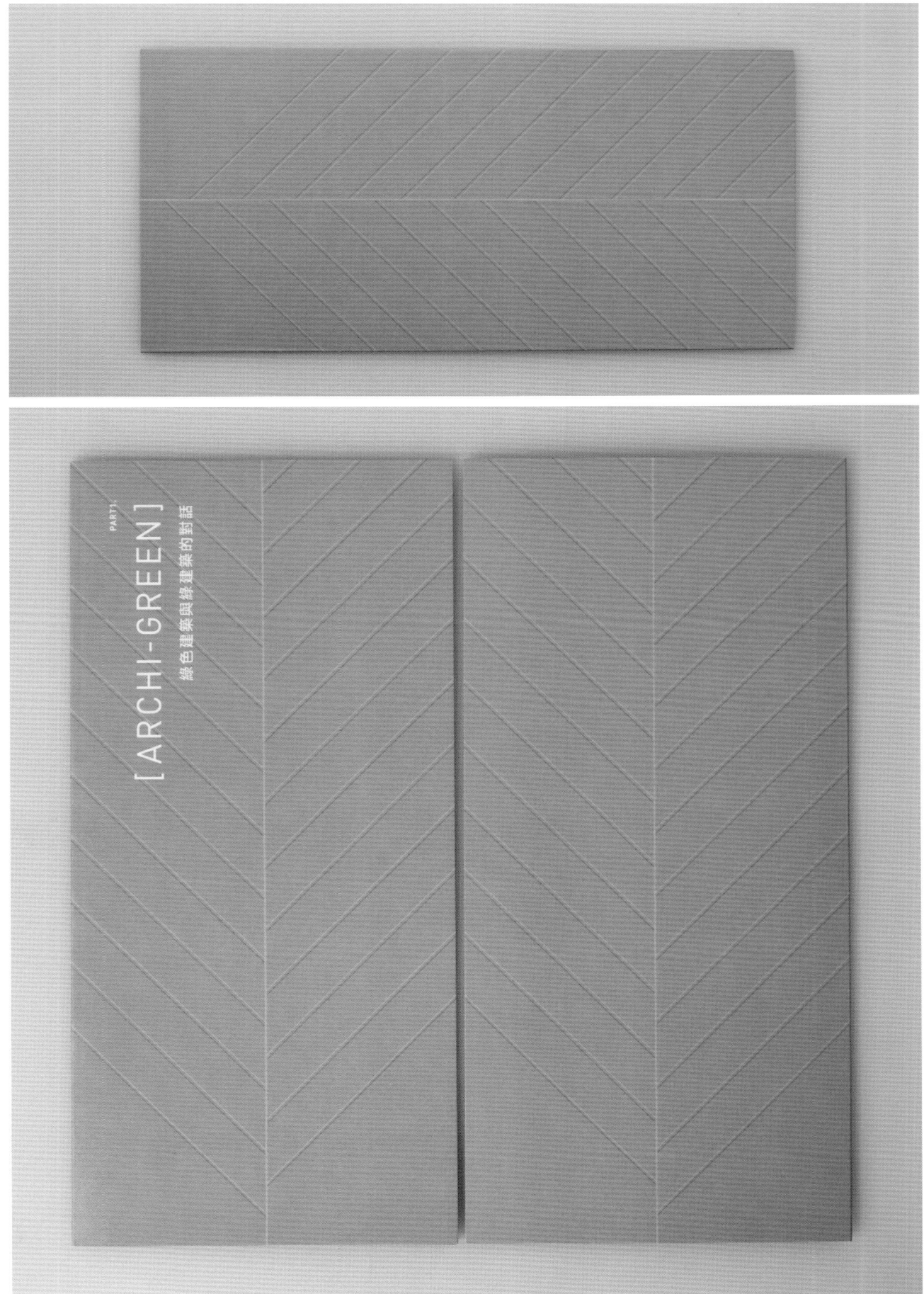

[ARCHI-GREEN]

PART1

綠色建築與綠建築的對話

Design
Kai Zan

Project
VITAMIN D+P+E

Promotional materials for the Taiwan cultural and educational institution, Xue Xue Institute, and its three types of courses: Design, Plan, and Express.

These course types are matched into three types of corresponding vitamins: D, P, and E, so that bottled vitamins are used as a visual concept to communicate with consumers.

This satisfied both the visual creativity and marketing needs for the client.

126

Design
Tadas Karpavičius
Project
Personal Identity

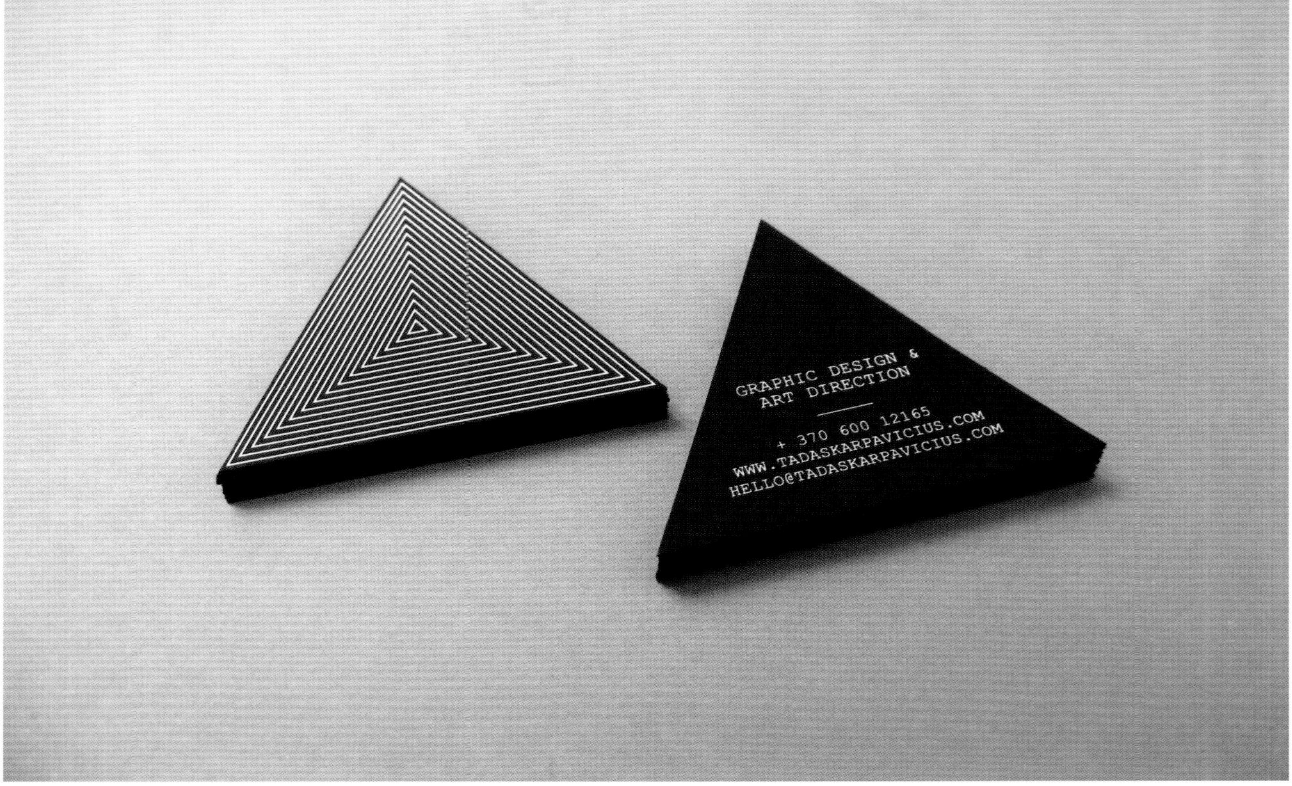

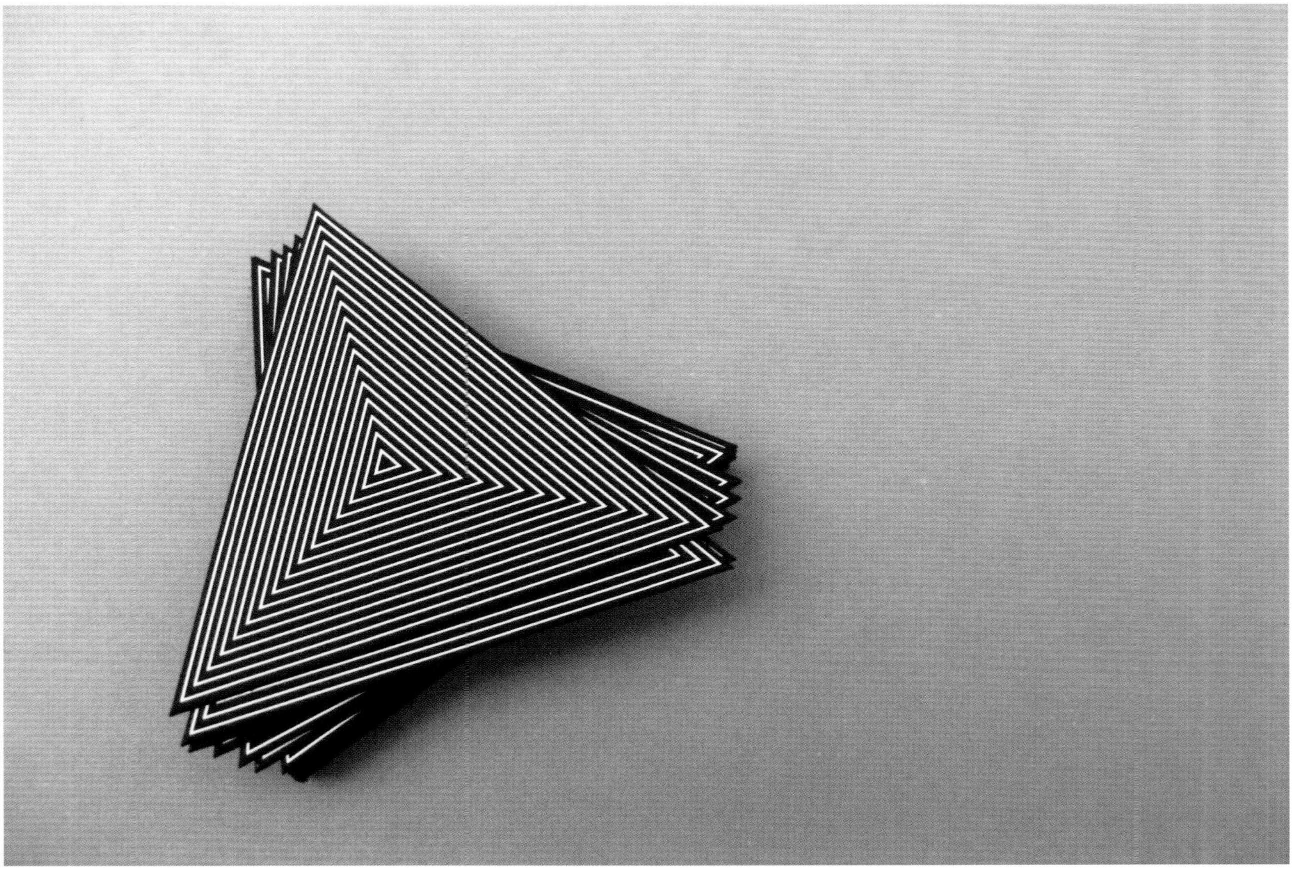

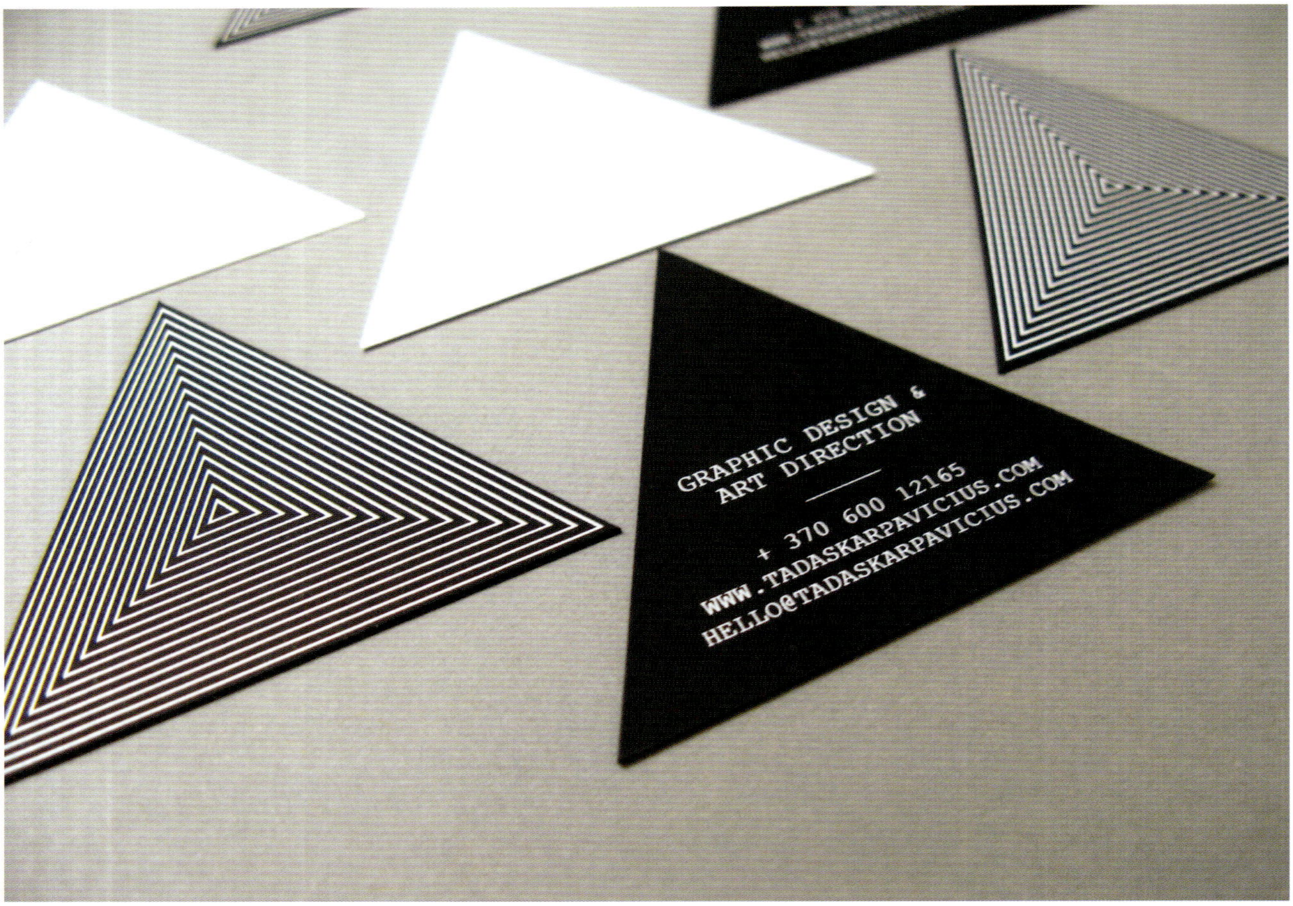

GRAPHIC DESIGN &
ART DIRECTION

+ 370 600 12165
WWW.TADASKARPAVICIUS.COM
HELLO@TADASKARPAVICIUS.COM

GRAPHIC DESIGN &
ART DIRECTION
——
+ 370 600 12165
WWW.TADASKARPAVICIUS.COM
HELLO@TADASKARPAVICIUS.COM

Publication

Design

Ken-tsai Lee

Project

'One Takes on the Colour of One's Company' gift book

The Chinese proverb 'one takes on the colour of one's company' illustrates the influence of environment has on people. It literally means 'one who stays near vermilion gets stained red, and one who stays near ink gets stained black'. It is a metaphor meaning one's habit may change or come under the influence of other people, events, objects or environments.

Given the relevance of paper, ink and colour, using this book as a media to express this proverb is quite appropriate. A book entirely of red paper and a book entirely of black paper, each with a pen-shaped cut-out in the pages to place a pen in, carry pens of corresponding colour—red book carries a red pen; black book carries a black one.

The emphasis here aims to stress that the influence of the two objects on each other is subtle and invisible.

Ask people who purchase 'One Takes on the Colour of One's Company' gift book to offer a piece of writing on their life experience to mirror 'one takes on the colour of one's company'. The collected writing will be published to become a book titled 'One Takes on the Colour of One's Company'.

Books are printed words, figures and pictures. Readers will receive messages from the words. From a different viewpoint, when you see the proverb 'one takes on the colour of one's company', though we all understand what it means, each may offer a different story to interpret this expression for each reader comes from different age group and experience.

The book does not have any word printed. When you look at this book, your story might appear in it. Although we are all holding the same book, each reading will bring out a different story from the same book.

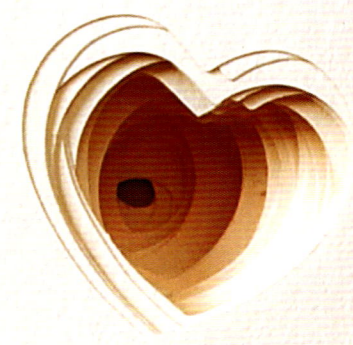

Design
Ken-tsai Lee
Project
Daily book—Time is a revealer of a man's sincerity

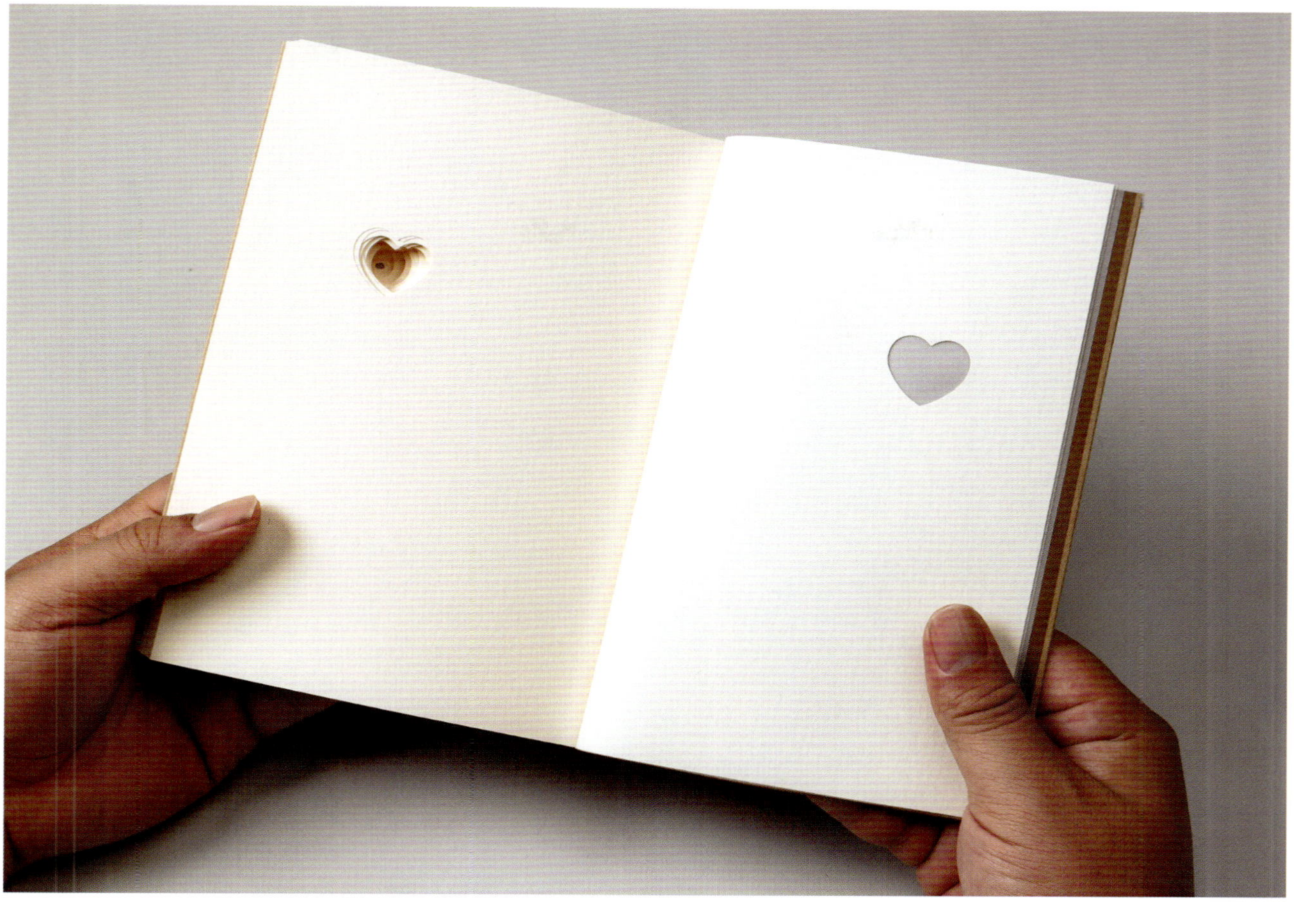

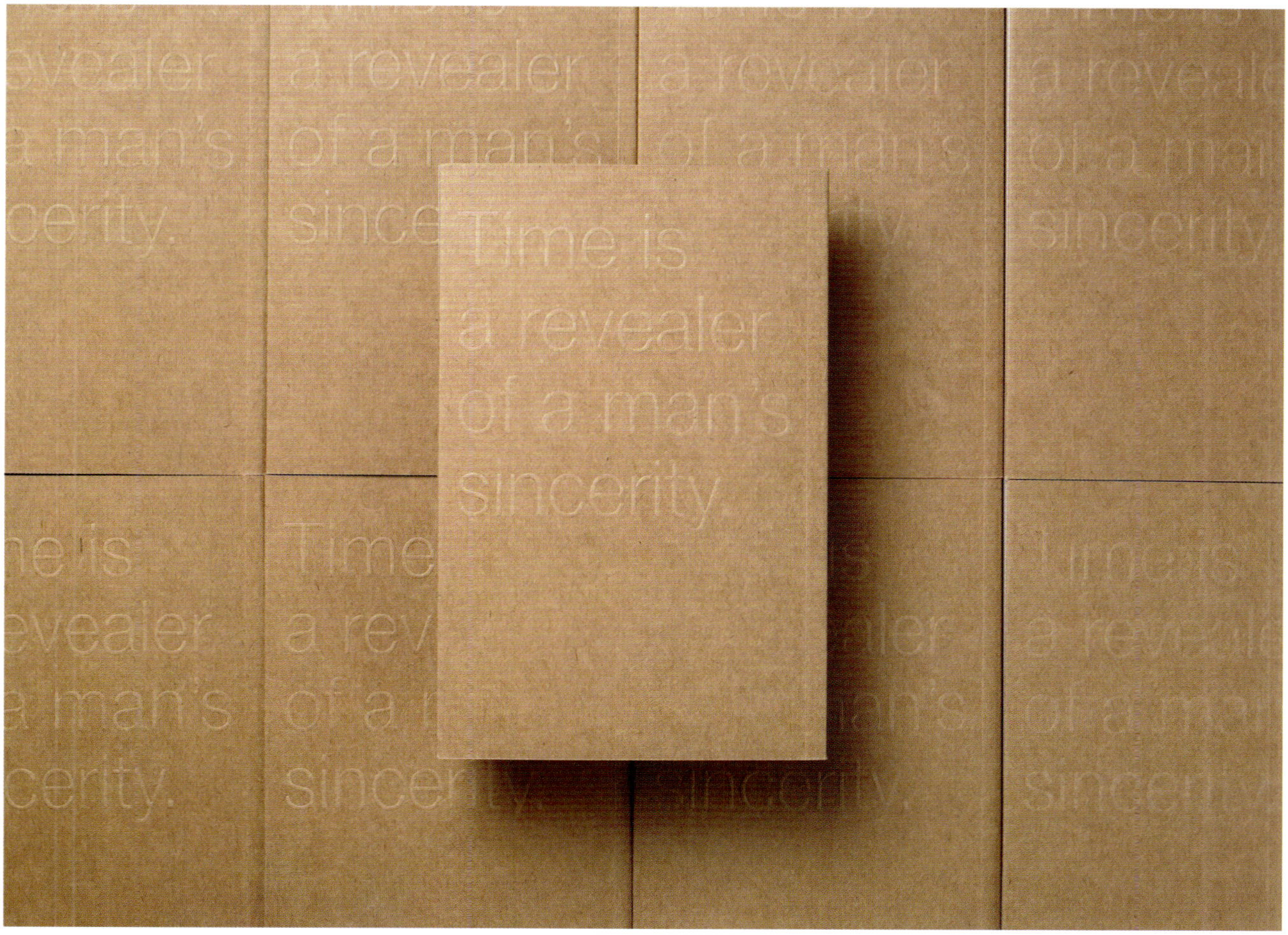
Time is
a revealer
of a man's
sincerity.

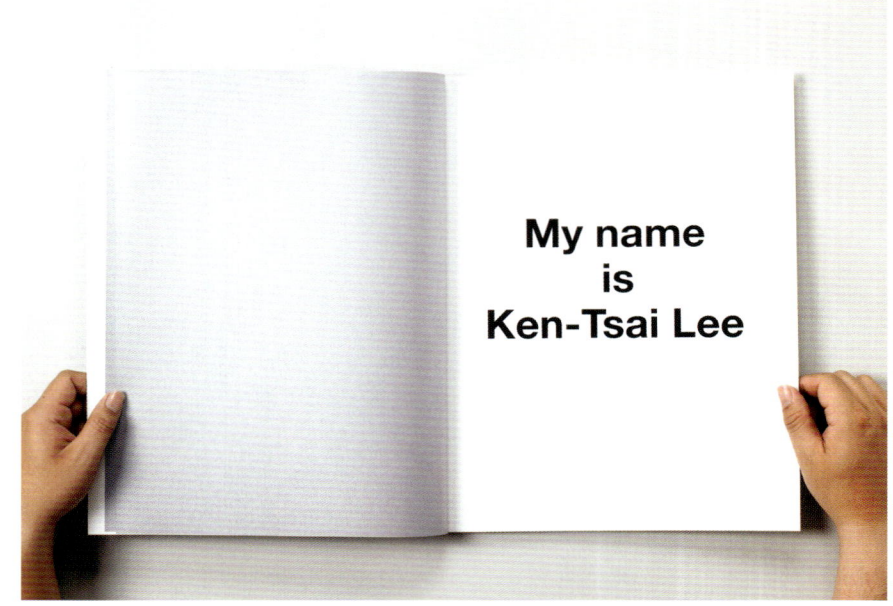

My name is Ken-Tsai Lee

我是李根在,辭掉工作來到紐約的台灣設計師.對一個即將邁進中年的東方人而言,離開自己熟悉的地方,沒有家人,朋友,想在這裡得到機會是難上加難,我必須要克服很多問題,如語言問題等...紐約是設計者最好的舞台,有人說你可以在這裡成功,你將會成功在世界上任何地方.安迪沃霍爾說,在現代社會每個人都會成名十五分鐘.而我的十五分鐘在哪裡?在語言學校,我遇到很多來自不同國家的人,他們教我用他們的母語寫我的名字.我想如果我用不同國家的文字寫我的名字,然後設計成海報張貼在紐約的街頭,那全世界不就都認識我,尤其是紐約這個舉世第一的移民都市.尋找自己的十五分鐘成了在枯燥的語言課程外的遊戲.我將會試不同的想法並張貼在紐約街頭

This is my first exposure to New York. I came from Taiwan five months ago, I have met a lot of people from different countries. They taught me how to write my name in their native languages. I think, New York is the best stage for me although I do not have any contacts here. I want to promote myself by designing posters using my name in different languages. I will put up posters in the streets of New York. By doing so I hope to develop an interest in my work. I will try out different ideas by posting them in the streets of New York.

Design
Ken-tsai Lee
Project
Fame

March,2003
I put up the posters
in streets of
New York.
Special thank
my classmates,
Hyun-jim Do
who helped me to
take the photos,
Young-woong Jang
who gave me
some suggestions
to make my idea
more perfect.

Design

Kai Zan

Project

RECHARGING Xue Xue Extension Courses

Course promotion materials for Taiwan's cultural and educational institution, Xue Xue Institute. Courses were tailored mainly for those who held jobs, but wished to continue their education.

Therefore, RECHARGING used batteries to express its concept, representing each of the five course subjects with a different battery model.

The cover was designed to be a battery package which could be hung on a rack.

This satisfied both the visual creativity and marketing needs for the client.

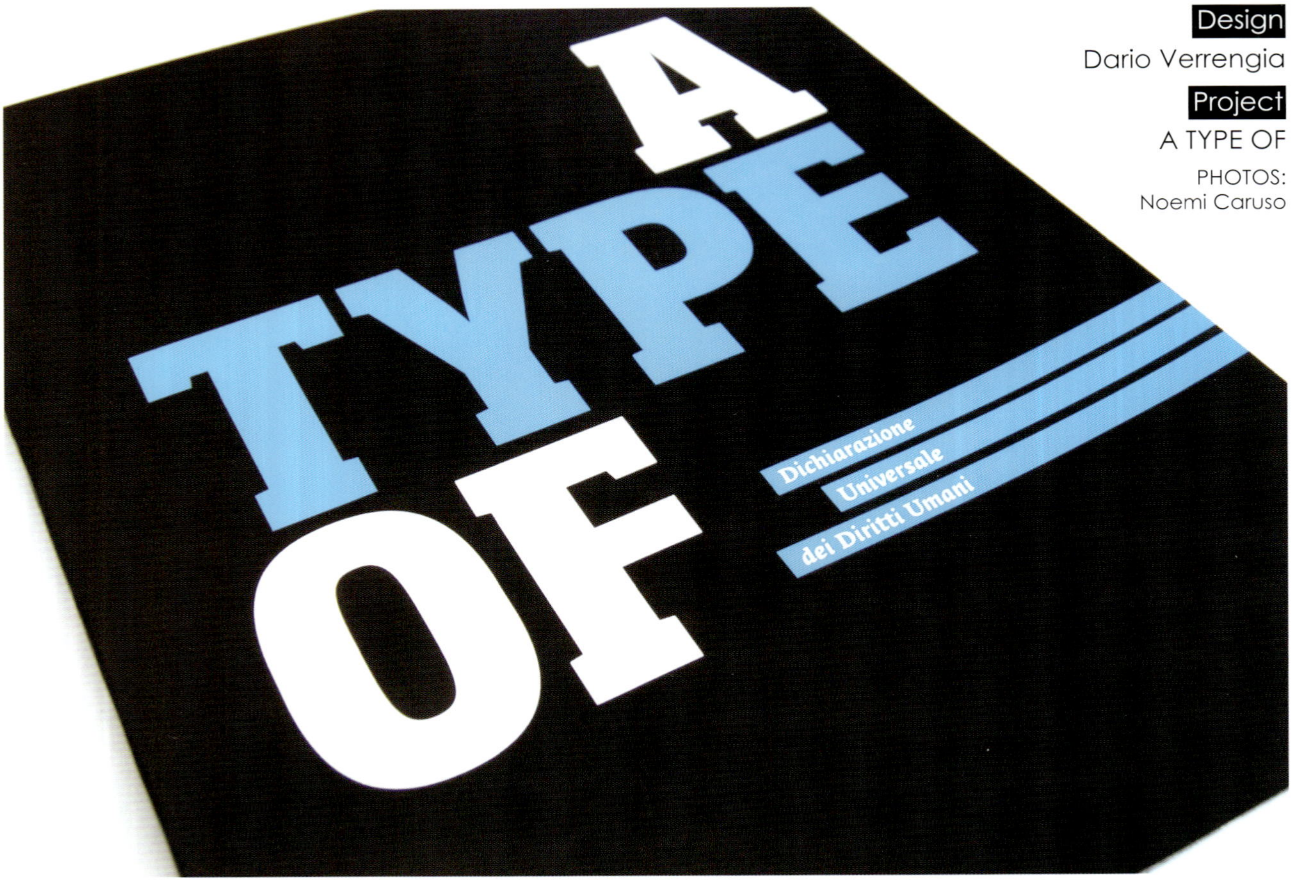

Design
Dario Verrengia
Project
A TYPE OF
PHOTOS:
Noemi Caruso

'A TYPE OF' comes from a university project of the course 'Project's theories and practices' (Communication Design, at Politecnico di Milano).

The aim of the course was to develop an editorial product enabled to communicate efficiently the content of the Universal Declaration of Human Rights.

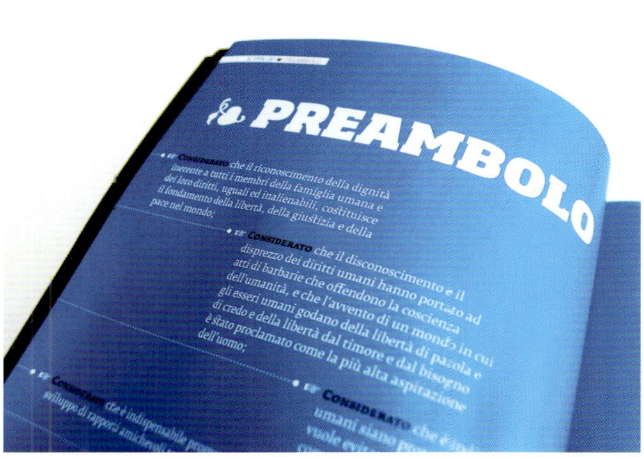

The project is based on the keywords of the Declaration, whose meaning is developed, in a typographical way, into image-words, in order to achieve a deeper and more careful meditation, instead of the superficial one that comes from a fast reading of the Declaration.

ORDINES
OCIALEE
INTERNA
ZIONALE
ORDINES
OCIALEE
INTERNA
ZIONALE

Dario **Verrengia**
matr#731677

DESIGN DELLA COMUNICAZIONE
Politecnico di Milano
A.A. 2008-09

LABORATORIO DI TEORIE E PRATICHE DEL PROGETTO
Anna Steiner, Ivana Tubaro, Giovanni Baule

"I am really interested in type that isn't perfect. Type that reflects more truly the imperfect language of *an imperfect world inhabited by imperfect beings*."

- Barry Deck

Design
KentLyons
Project
Catalyst strategy

Photography by
Richard Learoyd

Design
KentLyons

Project
Catalyst strategy

ast/Present/Future

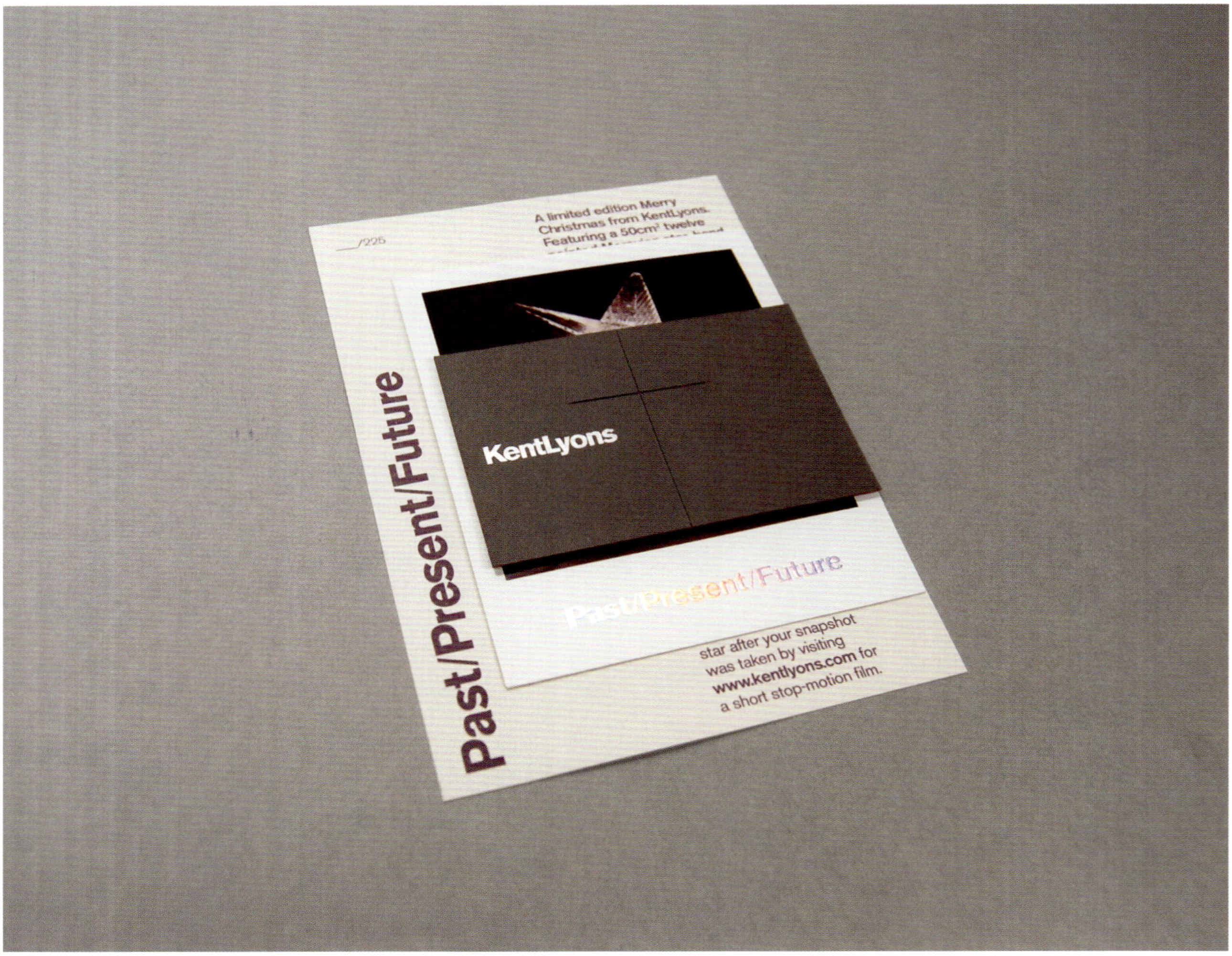
A limited edition Merry
Christmas from KentLyons.
Featuring a 50cm² twelve
225
KentLyons
Past/Present/Future
star after your snapshot
was taken by visiting
www.kentlyons.com for
a short stop-motion film.
Past/Present/Future

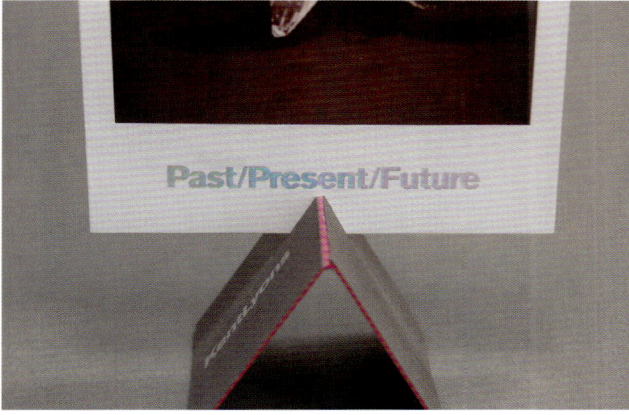

Design
KentLyors

Project
Past/Present/Future

For our 2009 Christmas card a 50cm² twelve pointed Moravian star, hand carved from ice was left to melt over 15 hours. We documented this process with Polaroid film and sent the results out as cards to our friends.

We also created a stop-frame animation of that process that can be seen here:
http://vimeo.com/7916611

Design
KentLyons

Project
Pulp—Paper

A project by KentLyons, Generation Press, GF Smith and James Cropper Paper Mill.

A book about the paper making process—from pulp to paper. Photographs in the mill and thoughts about paper from prominent designers.

We used many different print processes and stocks. The cover is made from pulp!

Photography by KentLyons

As a breed, designers tend to be naturally inquisitive (nosey), and this project started because Mark Diggins and Jon Cefai (two inquisitive designers from KentLyons) had been curious to see how paper is made. Seeing sheets of paper being transformed into printed objects is an exciting and rewarding part of a designer's job but we wanted to go back a step and see the process from tree to sheet.

GF Smith organized a trip to their mill and so we went along with Paul Hewitt and Chris Wood from Generation Press, and John Haslam, Chrys Livings and Neil Woolley from GF Smith, we set off for the James Cropper Paper Mill in the Lake District where they make Colorplan, Colorlux, Accent and Zen exclusively for GF Smith.

The mill is positioned in the small village of Burneside, near Kendal, and sits at the base of a valley on the River Kent about ten miles from Lake Windermere. The mill produces 3,800 tonnes of paper each month and seeing how it is made on that scale was a surprisingly uplifting experience. Paper can be memorable, beautiful and has a keepsake value that makes you want to collect it. It can colour our lives and become a part of our identity.

Seeing the paper changing form as you walk around each corner of the mill was an unexpected and exciting experience. At times the process is slow and you have time to examine what is going on, at others it is extremely fast and mesmerising.

Paper feels like a first hand experience, whereas you can often feel the distance between yourself and digital content. There is also an issue of ownership with digital content. You can bookmark a favourite website, but it doesn't belong to you. Websites are constantly being updated and there is no guarantee they will be the same when you return.

Paper represents an opportunity to create something. For us paper is always the beginning of any project, print or digital, but when it is also the end there is something special about it, something real, something that will never be replaced.

We asked a number of people about their relationship with paper—when was the first and last time paper made them stop, think or smile, what they would store in a time capsule for later generations to discover, and what they thought would become of paper in the future. Their responses are featured throughout this book.

Design
Purpose
Project
VIEW Magazine and Conference mailer

EFFP provides consultancy to the agricultural and food industry. They strive to build bonds between these two industries, to make both more efficient.

The resulting black and white identity is bold, pioneering, confident and revolutionary, all attributes EFFP aspire to.

Taking a step away from the industry norm, Purpose created a large format, black and white newspaper. The bold visual language reflects EFFP's ethos of expert, honest and practical advice delivered clearly and in a straight forward manner.

Alongside EFFP's quarterly magazine VIEW, Purpose have also created a full suite of stationery and marketing materials, including case studies, folders, a website and conference materials for their annual event.

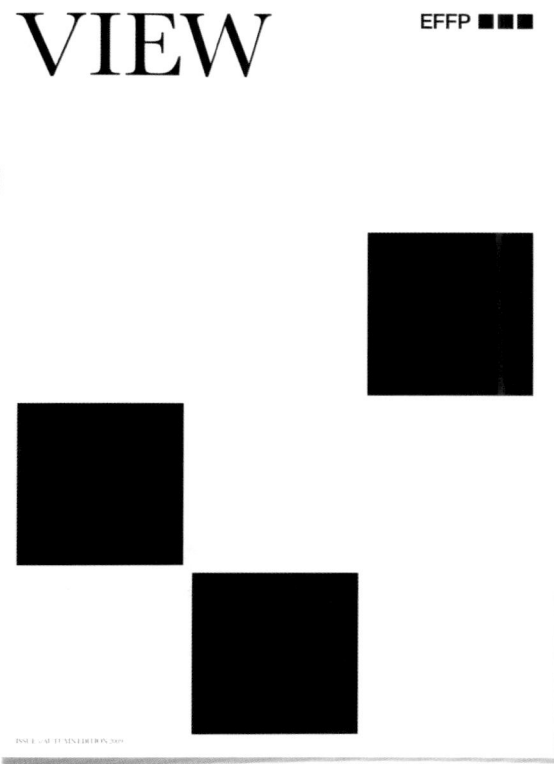

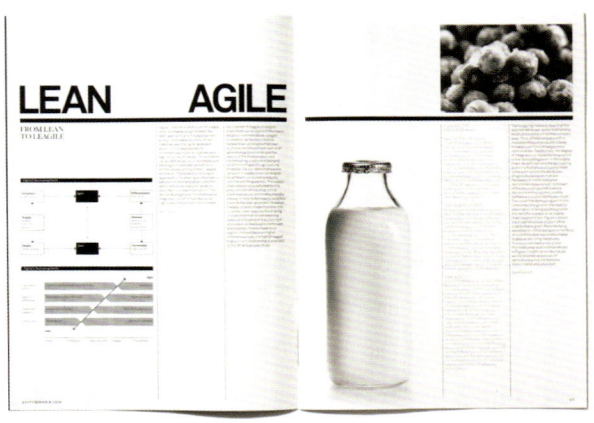

BLACK
AND
WHITE
ADVICE

EFFP'S SIXTH ANNUAL CONFERENCE

EFFP's Annual Conference continues to be one of the only events where farming and food businesses come together to discuss farm to food issues.

EFFP
RETAIL
FOOD
PRICE
FORECAST

FARM FOOD

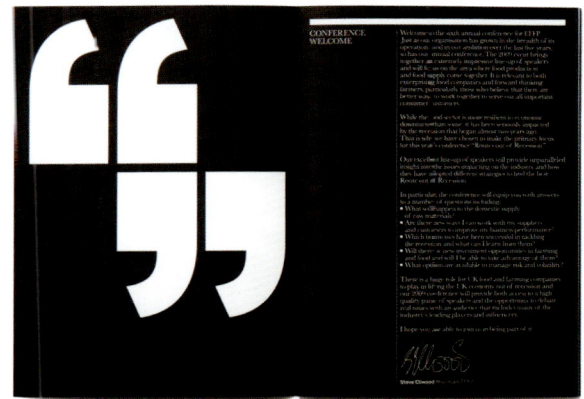

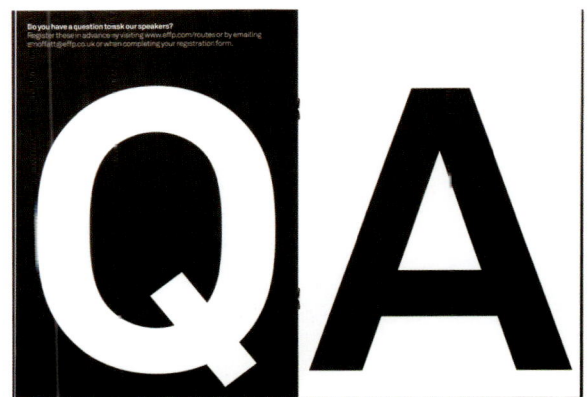

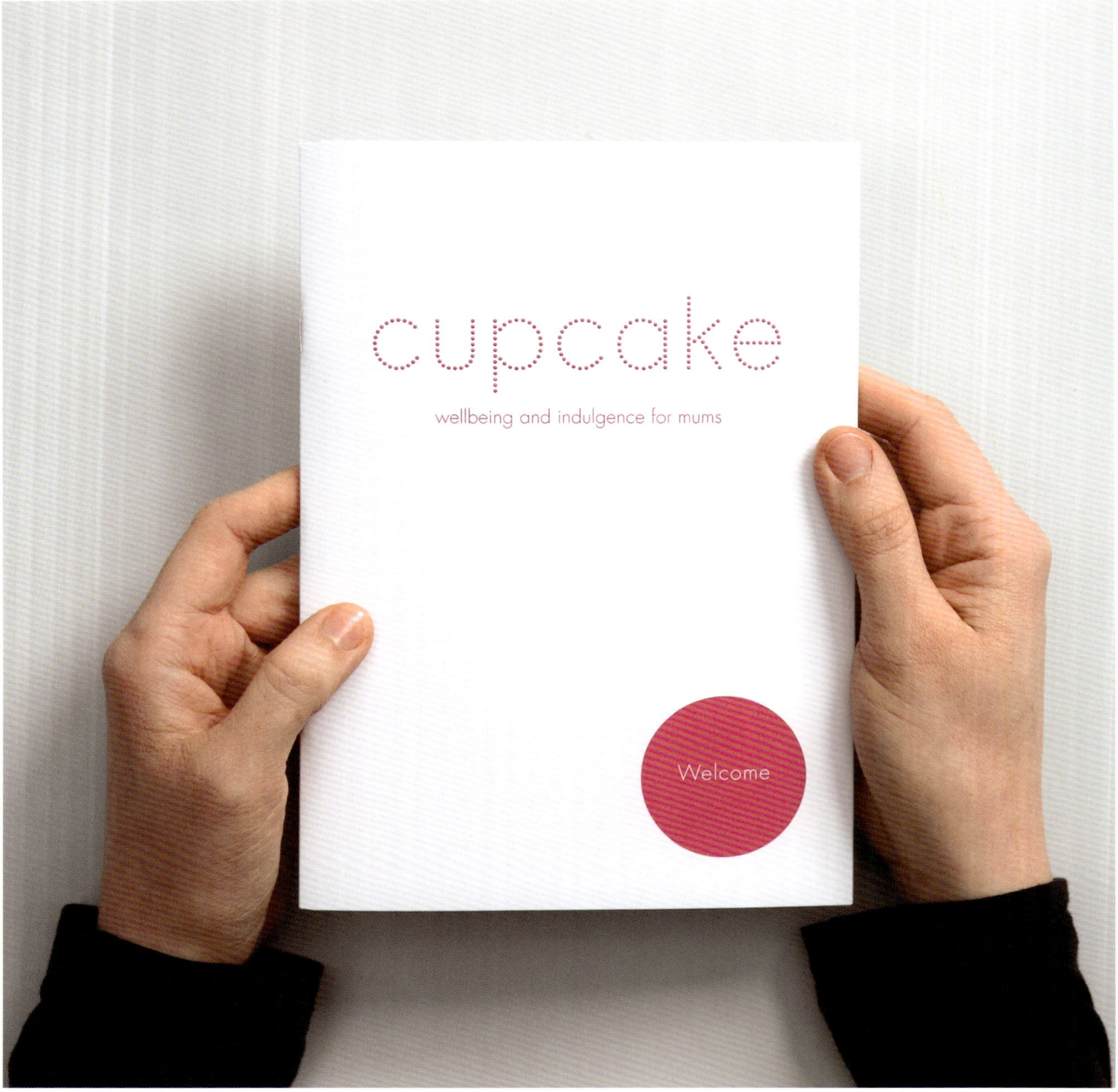

cupcake

wellbeing and indulgence for mums

Welcome

cupcake

cupcake

cupcake

Design
Mind Design
Project
Cupcake

A place for mums.
A place for wellness.
A place to connect.

Identity for Cupcake, a spa and crèche for mothers with young babies. The idea is that mothers can leave their toddlers in the crèche where they are looked after while they enjoy time in the spa, exercise in the gym or meet for a chat in the café.

Design
Mind Design
Project
Six Sites for Sound

Catalogue, flyers, poster and press adverts for an exhibition on sound art in collaboration with Resonance FM. The exhibition took place in six different locations which is symbolised by the six speaker icons in the logo.

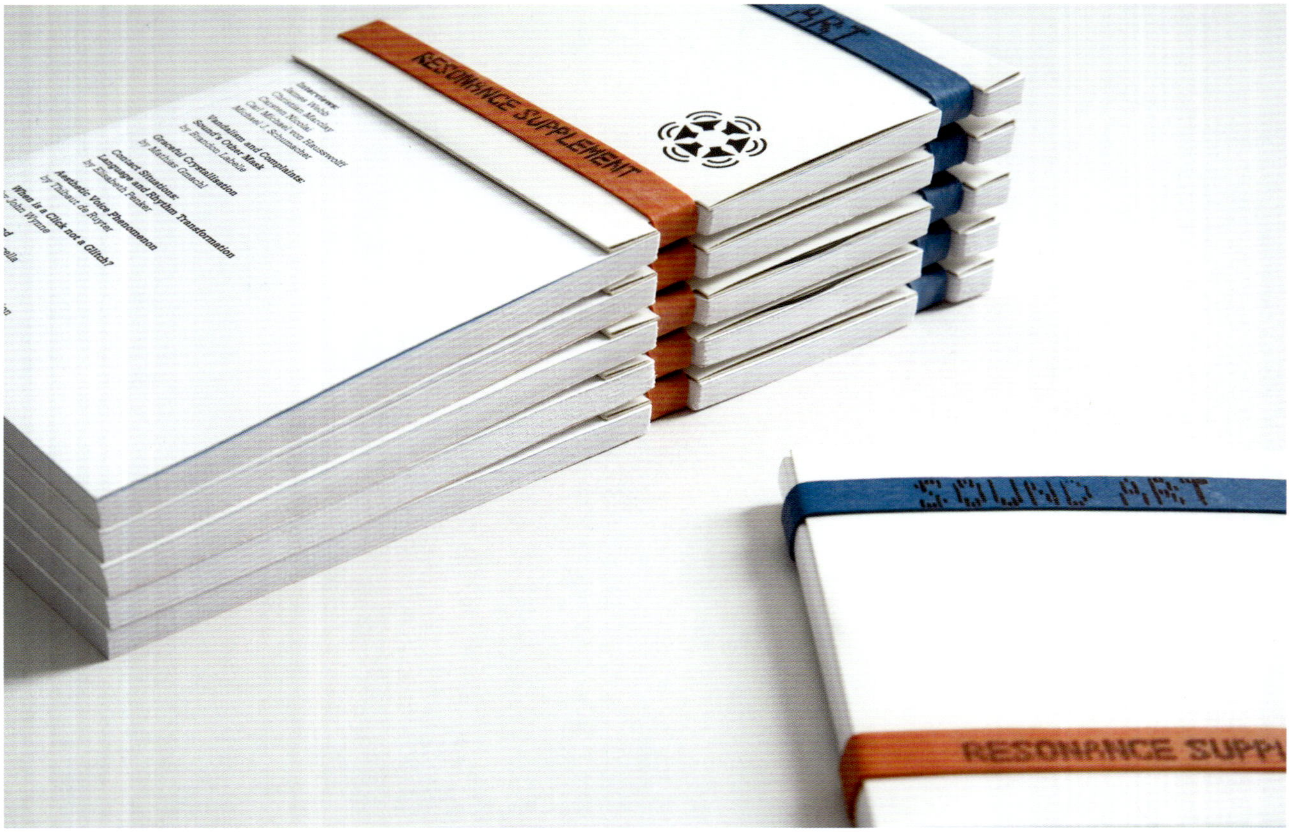

166

The catalogue consists of a book and a CD held together by two rubber bands with punched slots on each side.

The custom made font is inspired by volume scales on old stereo systems and expands when stretching the rubber bands.

Design

Fuse

Project

Fuse portfolio

The Fuse portfolio provides an insight for their new and existing clients into exactly what Fuse is all about as a design agency.

Wanting to produce a piece of marketing that says all about their creative approach to design and basing their ideas on the quote 'Good Design is Good Business', the thought process of possible ideas started. It was decided that the core audience needed to know more about Fuse as a company and the broad spectrum of creative services they offer. The solution was a simple one, a 24 page, 220mm x 310mm (oversized A4) Portfolio, with a clean design to showcase their work.

Only 100 limited edition portfolios were made and it involved 3 different companies who are specialists in their fields. The covers are white satin foiled onto ebony Colorplan from GF Smith by A14 Print Finishing in Nottingham, the text pages were printed digitally to both sides by Purely Digital in Derby. A citrine Colorplan fly sheet was added between the cover and text pages. These pages were then creased and folded and machine sewn to bind them in a cotton that matched the citrine fly sheet by a local book binders.

Overall the Portfolios were a massive success for Fuse and the plan is to produce a piece of marketing material next year to supersede this!

Design
Coppens Alberts

Project
Philharmonie – tangible contrasts

The contrast between the old 'Philharmonie' building and its newly built annex designed by Architecten Cie is closely reflected in the book by its equally distinct design and use of different types of paper per part.

The six interviews are printed on golden pages, referring to the gold used in the foyer, while Karel Martens' colourful, graphic version of a composition fills 16 pages as white as sheets, drawing attention to the musical function of the building. The styles in the book meet on the cover. Large pictures of the different spaces of the 'Philharmonie' give further metre to the book and form the upbeat for the more contemplative texts.

Design
Coppens Alberts
Project
Amsterdam

Clear direction over photography, typography
and colour and a perforation through the
heart of the leparello make the trademarks of
the new design for the monthly brochure of
Stadsschouwburg Amsterdam.

Design
Coppens Alberts

Project
Studio Piet Paris

The house style for Studio Piet Paris, fashion illustrator, consultant and art director, is a model of meticulous yet restrained design, encapsulating what the studio stands for in a simple graphic animation.

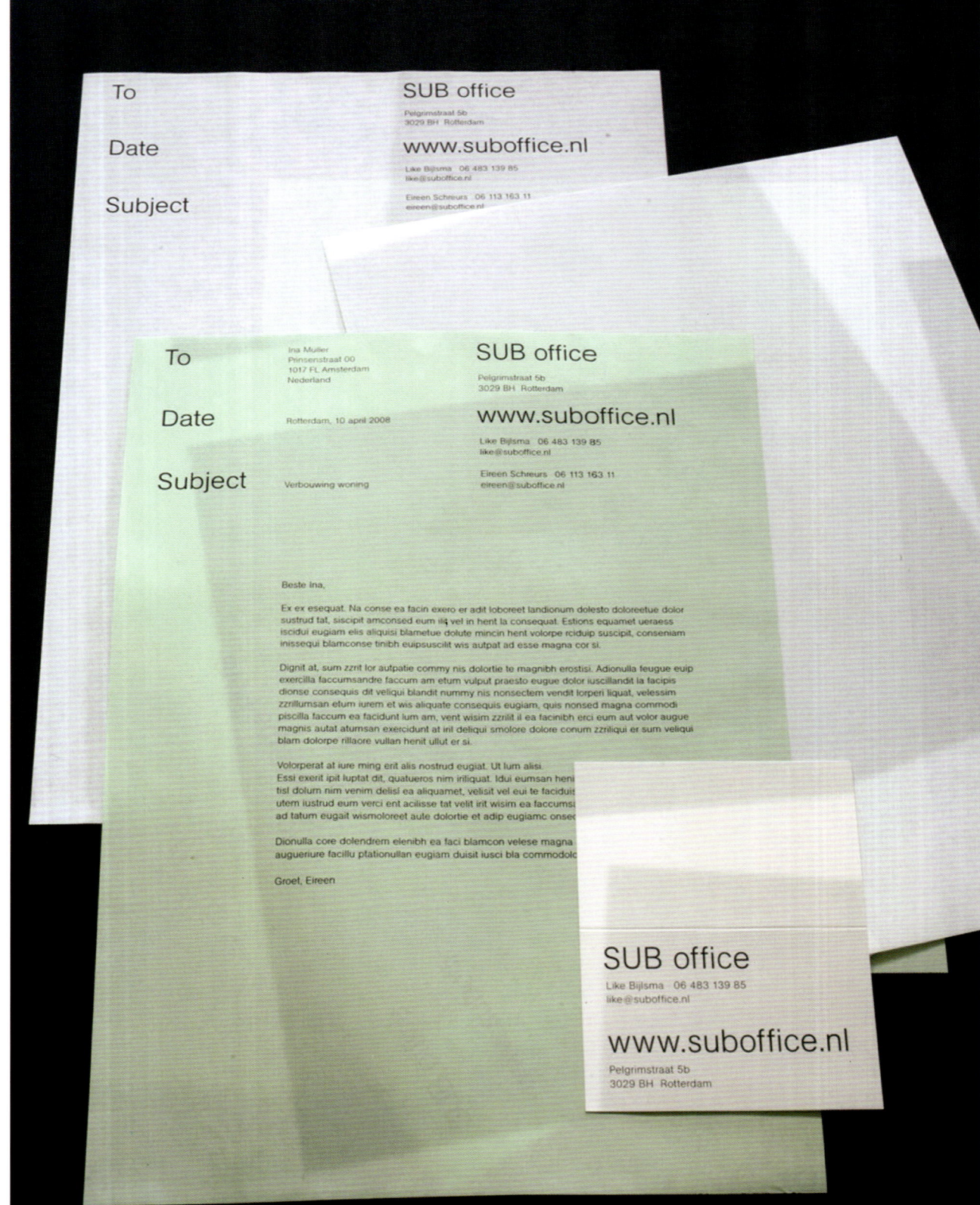

Design
Coppens Alberts
Project
SUB office

The graphic identity of SUB office, a bureau for Architecture and urban planning, is conceived of a simple yet well-defined shadow effect. Typography plays the pivotal role of clear functionality. More is not required to stand out and be recognizable.

Design
KreativeHouse
Project
Carmilla

Romantic images, as sharp as a canine. Simple and prickly colours, red pink, snow white and ink black. The young instant design of a stylish T-shirt gives life to a nowadays-gothic fairytale.

'Carmilla' brand comes from the idea of blending a teenage horror story to a series of high quality paper products (notebooks, jotters, bookmarks, pins). Design and labour are exclusively Italian and each product is realized with recycled material.

Design
KreativeHouse
Project
Pasticcini

Design
KreativeHouse
Project
Insekta

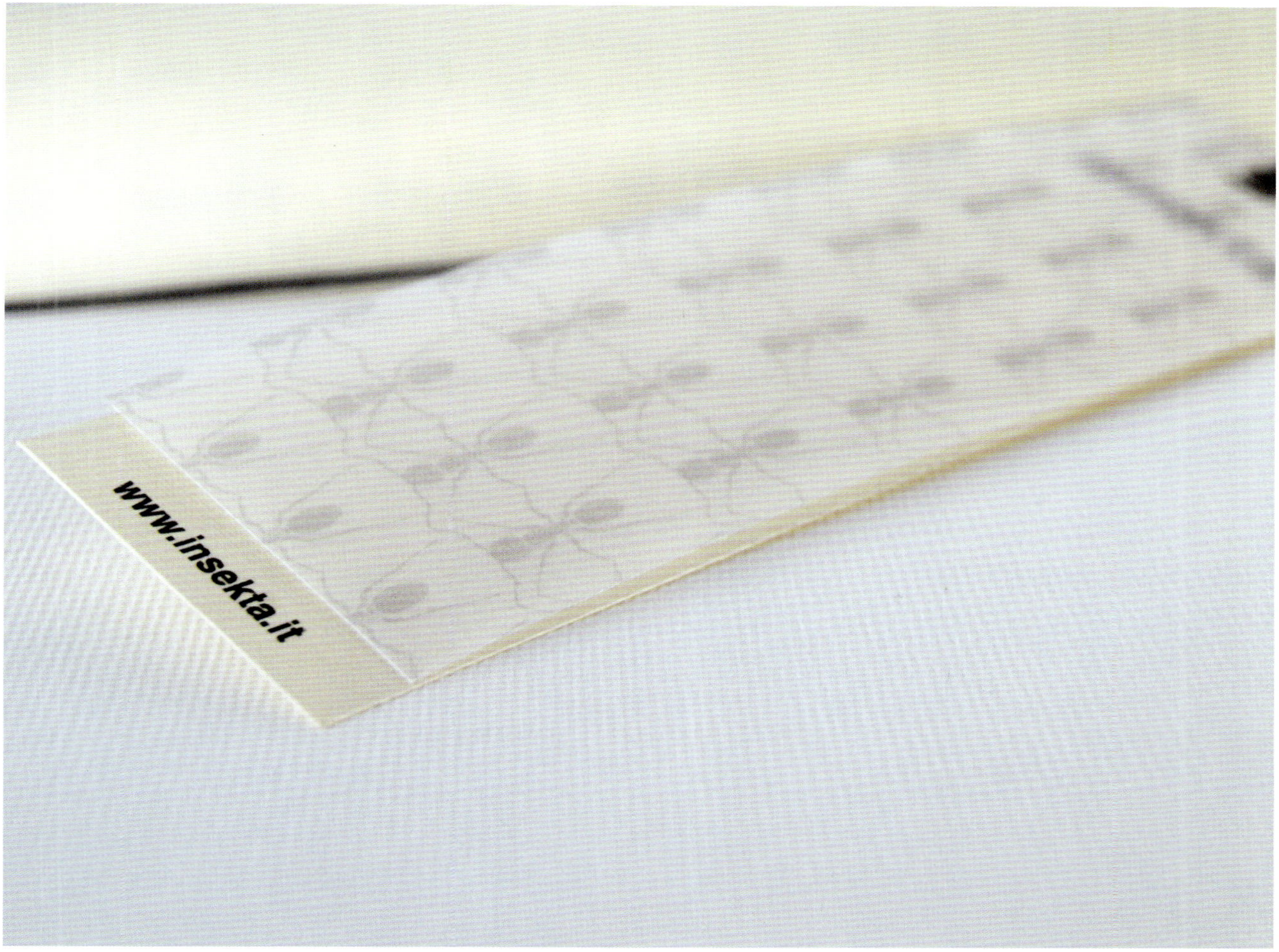

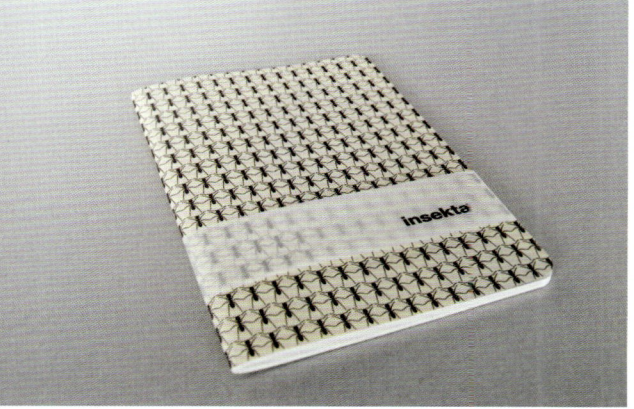

Design
Tadas Karpavičius
Project
Jazz In

Flyer design for jazz music event.

Design

Tadas Karpavičius

Project

Gatves Muzikos Naktis

Flyer & poster design for
music event.

Design

Patricio Murphy

Project

Glow

'Glow' is one of Patricio's school projects. It's an imaginary pop festival, featuring Patricio's favorite artists.
'Glow' is focused on people interested in Pop Culture, fashion and arts. The programme includes live shows, parades, exhibitions, workshops and seminars.

The project already counts with many printed pieces, such as posters, flyers, brochures and billboards.

Disclaimer: This Project, which is a school project, contains some pictures from other photographers,
that were modified and reworked. This is not a commercial work, it was never published, it is for educational purposes only. No copyright infringement is intended.

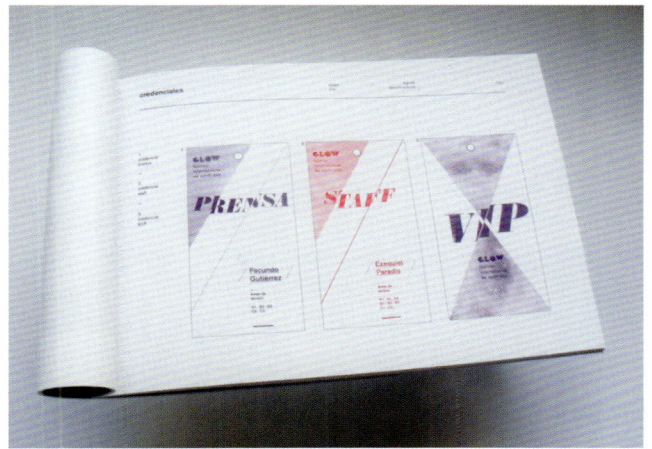

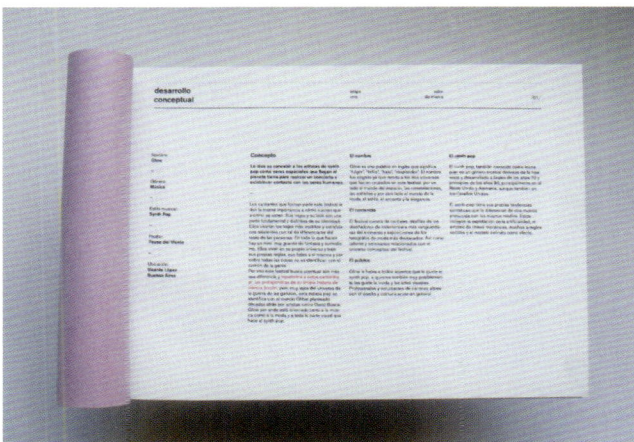

Design
Patricio Murphy

Project
Glow

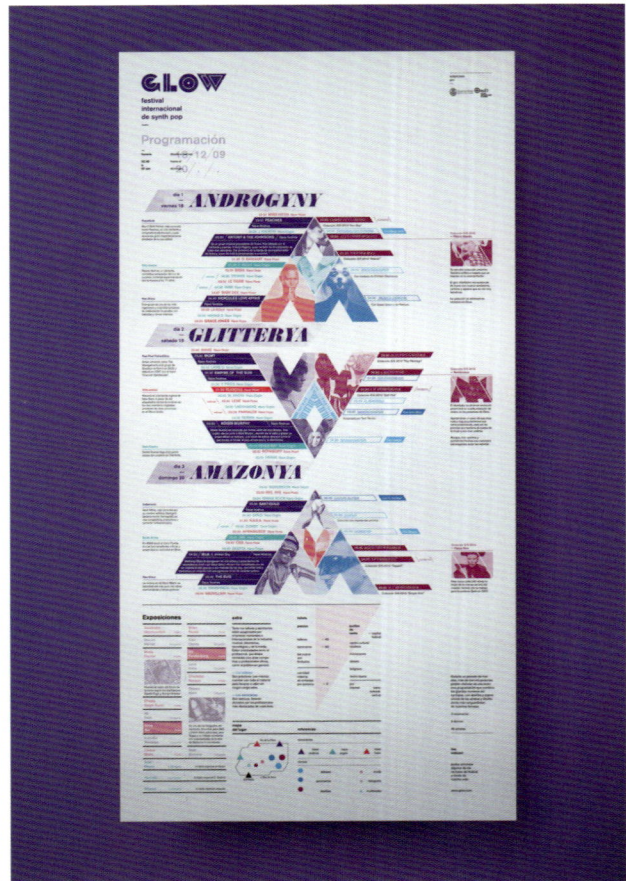

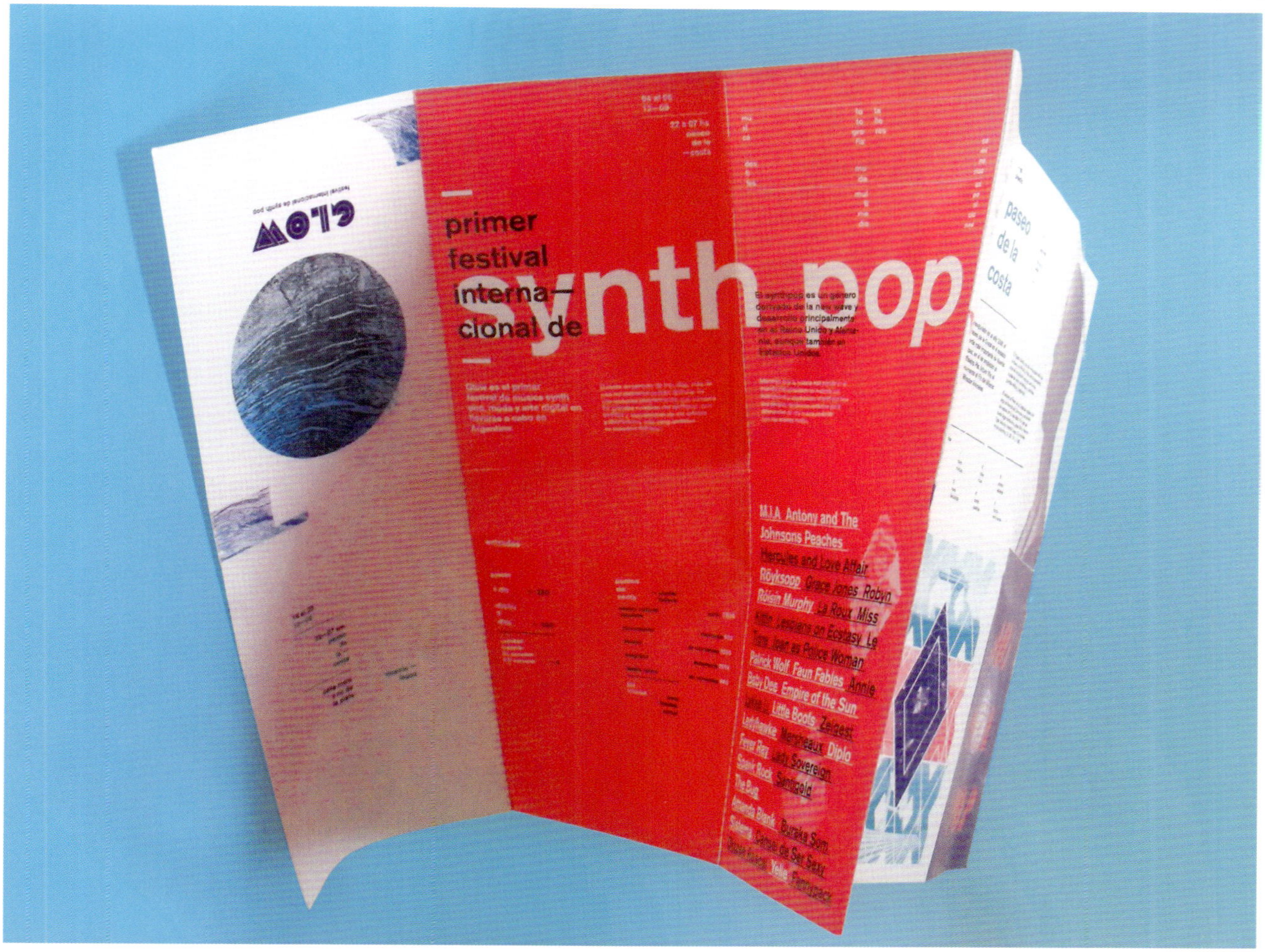

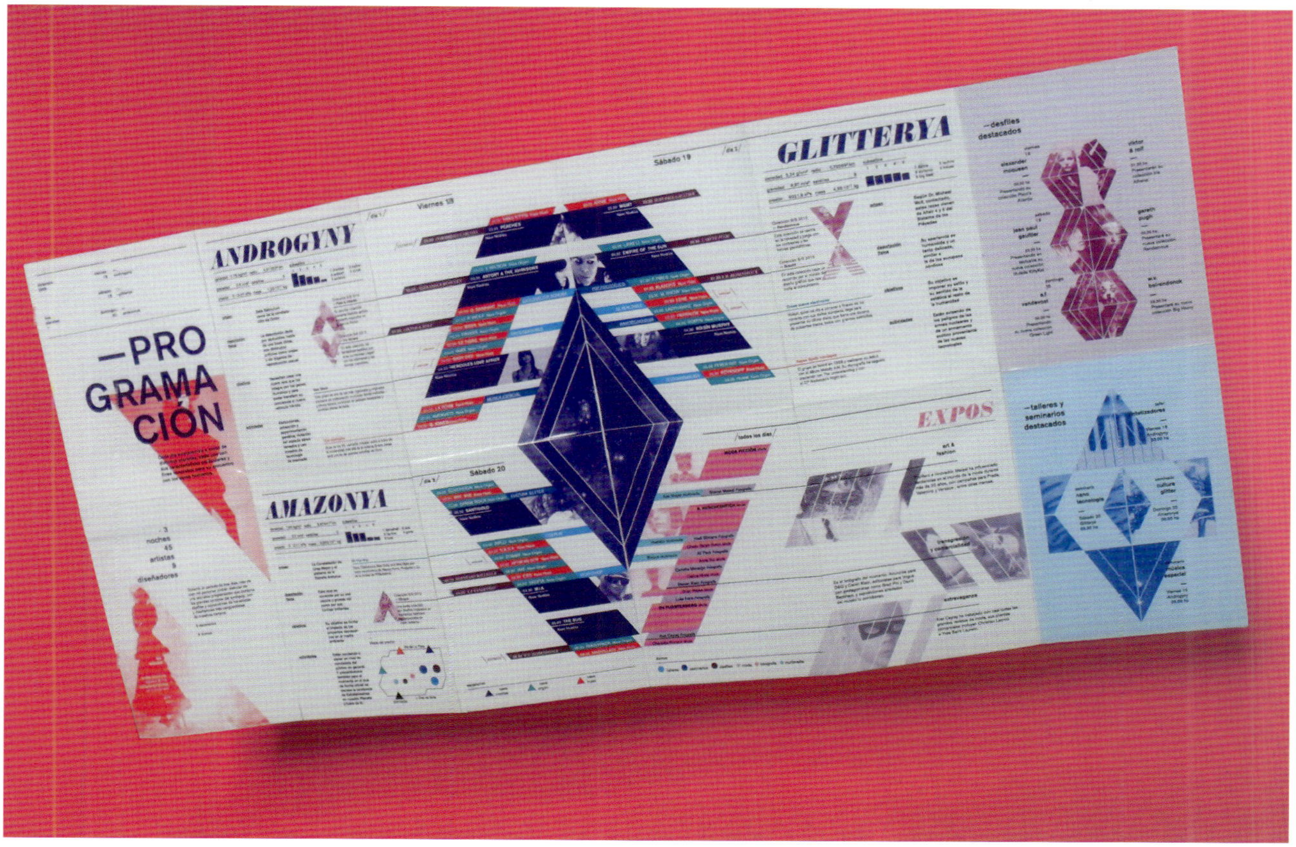

Design
Yomesuɔo
Project
BLINK 52

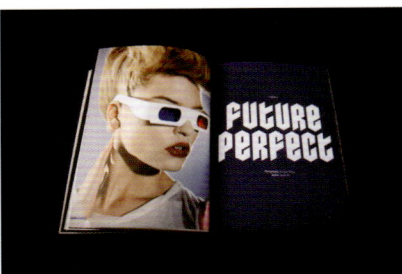

Design
Yomesubo
Project
BLINK 49

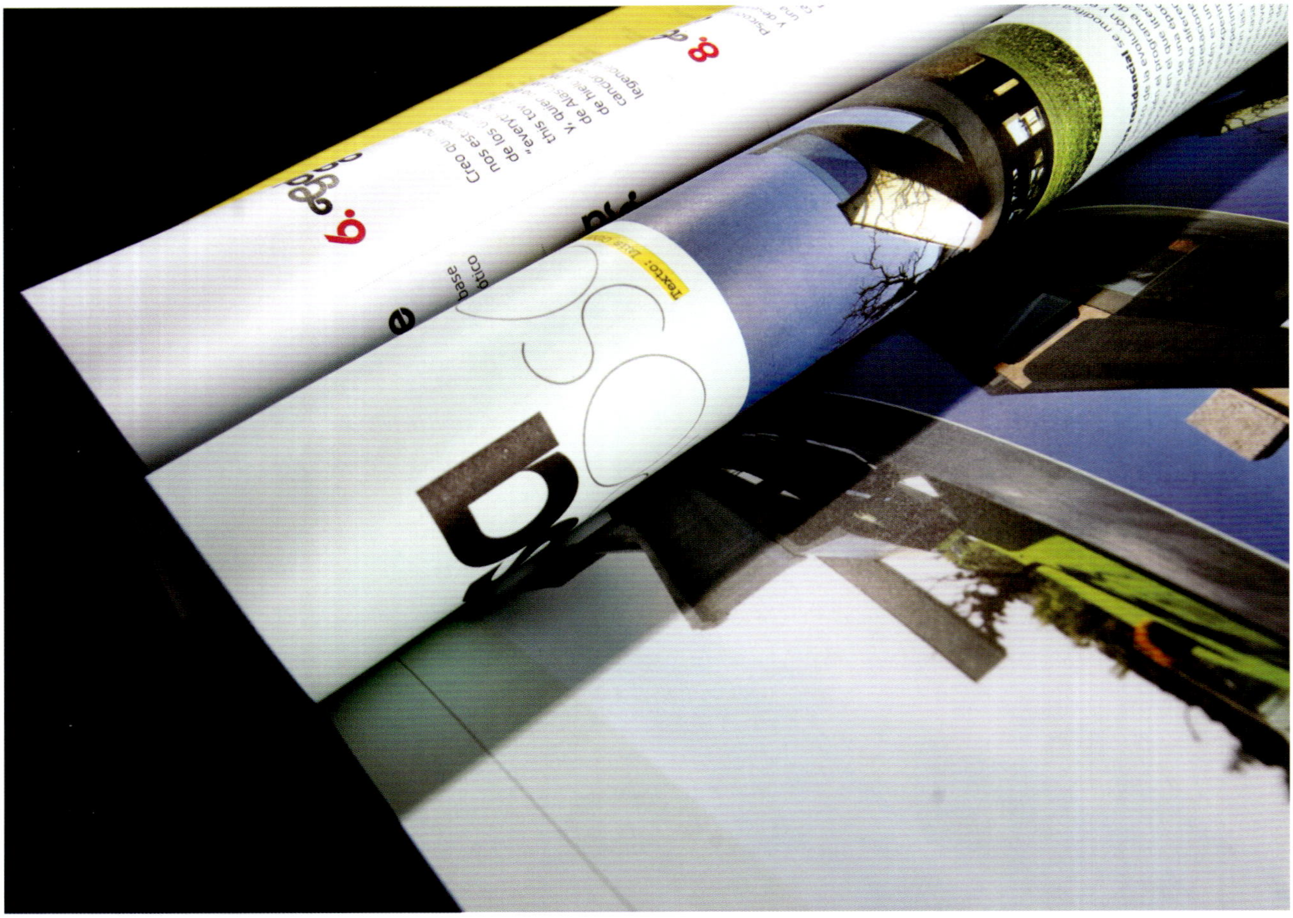

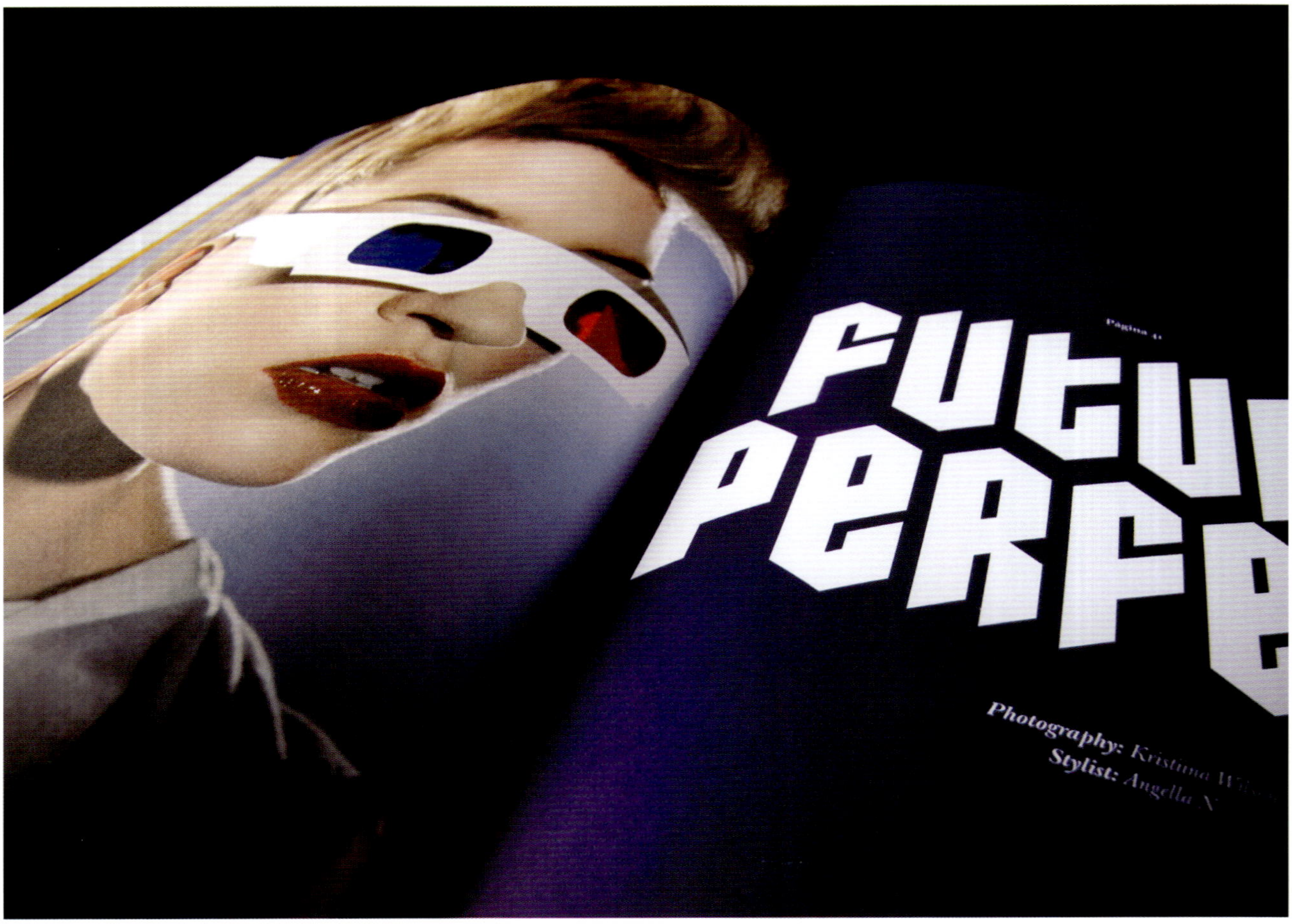
Photography: Kristina
Stylist: Angella

Design
Demian Conrad

Project
CUT&PASTE

For a personal exhibition and performance I created a visual concept based on the decomposing and reassembling of the title of the event. The idea was to anticipate the performance you would see on the show.

The exhibition itself was a set of 5 ikea's chairs which were modified into different proportions.

LA PLACETTE
RUE DES TERREAUX 8
1004 LAUSANNE
WWW.LAPLACETTE.CH

EXPOSITION 08.02.08-07.03.08
FRIDAY 8TH FEBRUARY 2008 — 18 HOURS
PERFORMANCE BY
DEMIAN CONRAD
MUSIC: FRANK SALIS

Design
Demian Conrad

Project
Instable

Instable is a community of new talented photographers who just degreed from the CEPV ESAA de Vevey. For their first public exhibition the brief was to put together 12 different artists with their own personalities and their own style.

Inspired by the Microbacteria we created several patterns that interact with each others and that express an idea of bio diversity. The posters are modular and easy to compose into bigger canvases.

198

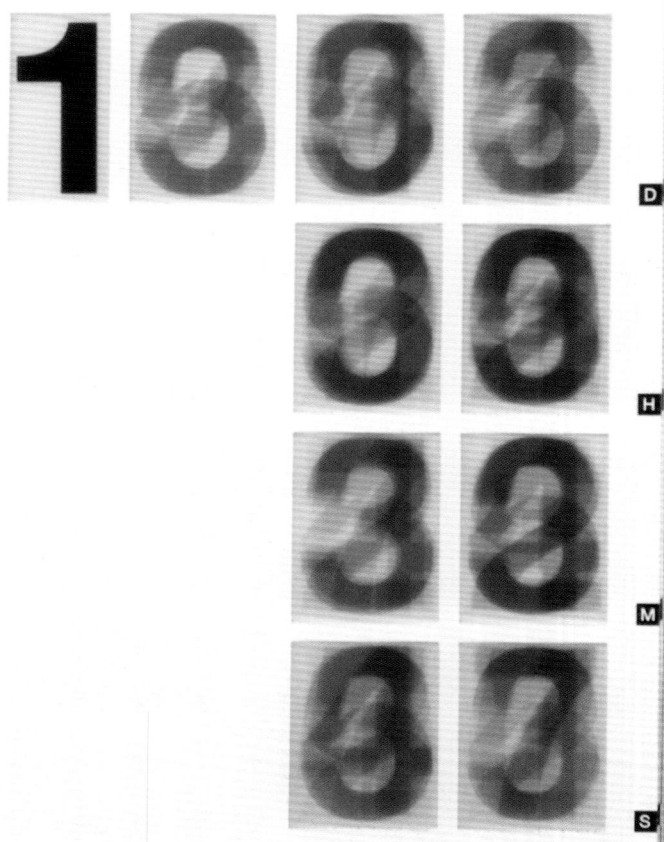

Since 6.25.2006, Gilad Shalit, an israeli soldier, has been held in the Gaza Strip by Hamas. We are still waiting for him to come home.

Design
Moshik Nadav
Project
Gilad Shalit Project

Design

Moshik Nadav

Project

Gilad Shalit Project

I attempted to show the days as they go by since Gilad Shalit's kidnapping in the span of a 1000 days. The time was split into D=days, H=hours, M=minutes and S=seconds.

Every page shows a different event that was reported on the news and the date it took place since Gilad's aduction.

Every black page represents a year gone by since Gilad's kidnapping. With the use of infographics, you can see all these events sorted by year, the specific month and the day within that month.

This project was shown a different medium such as a poster, a book and a 3D installation in my school.

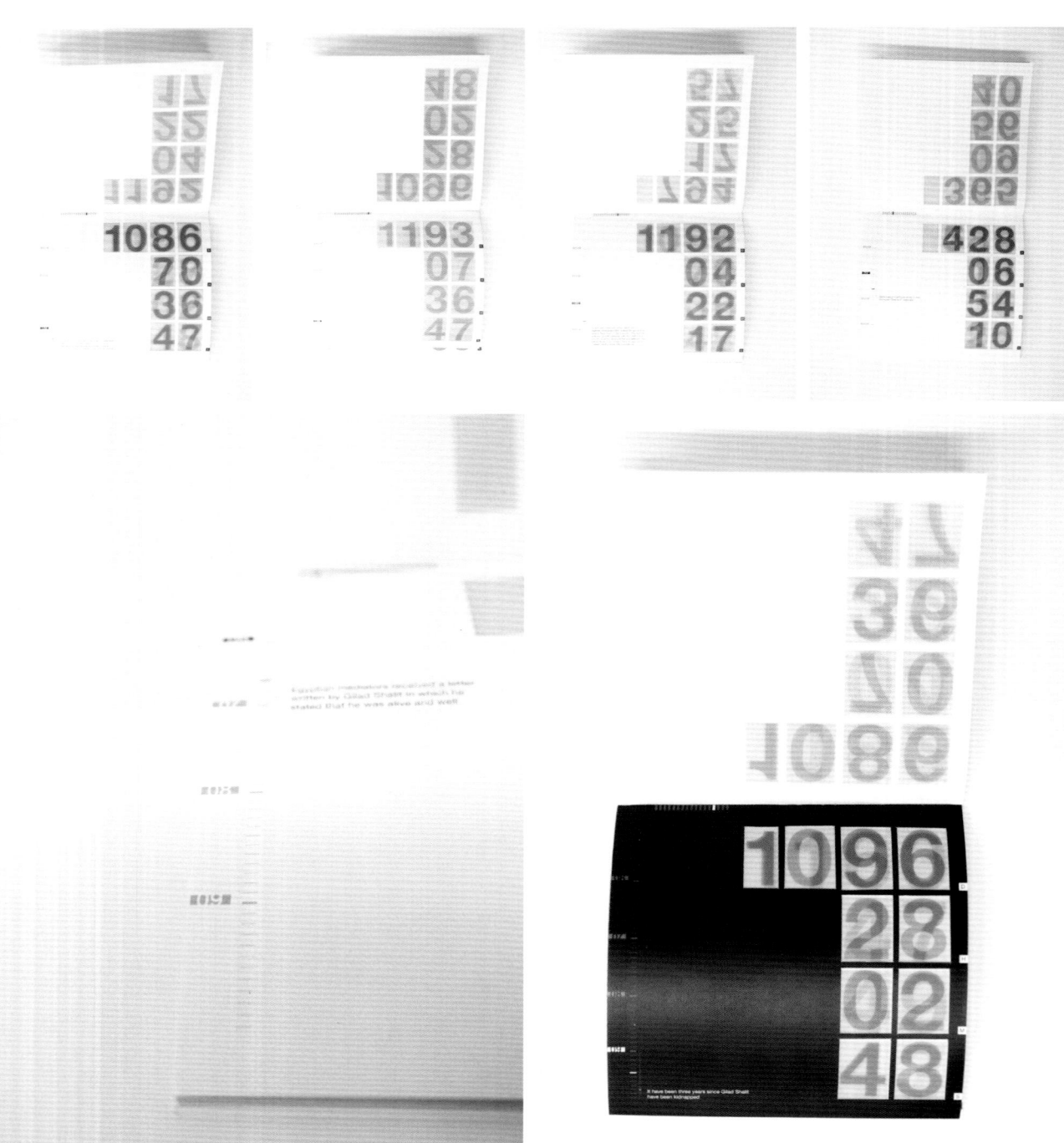

Since 6.25.2006, Gilad Shalit, an israeli soldier, has been held in the Gaza Strip by Hamas. We are still waiting for him to come home.

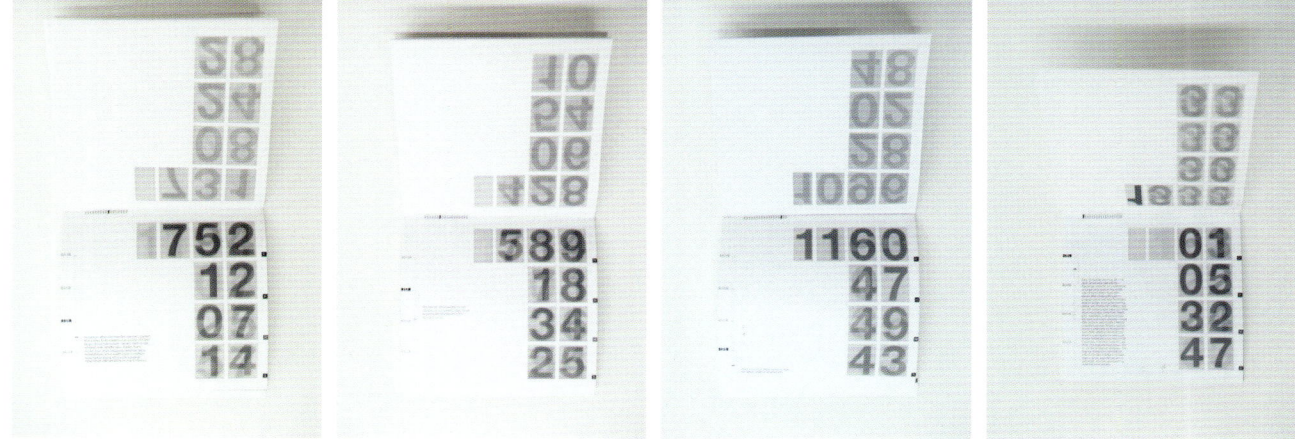

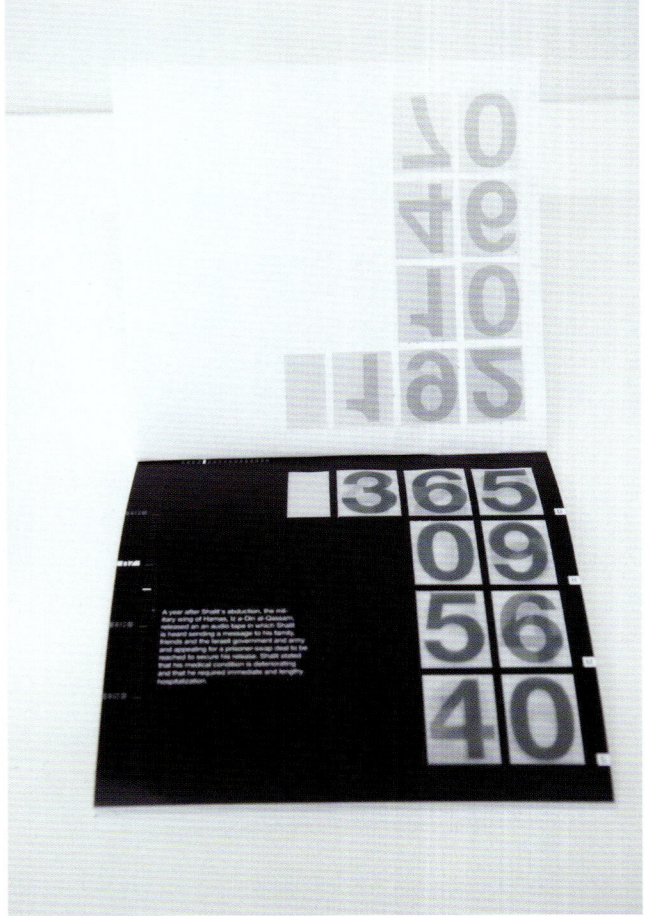

Design
Moshik Nadav

Project
Gilad Shalit Project

Christmas card design for Aalto University School of Art and Design Department of Media. Silk-screen printed.

Design
Tuukka Koivisto
Project
Joulukortti

Design
Tuukka Koivisto
Project
Joulukortti

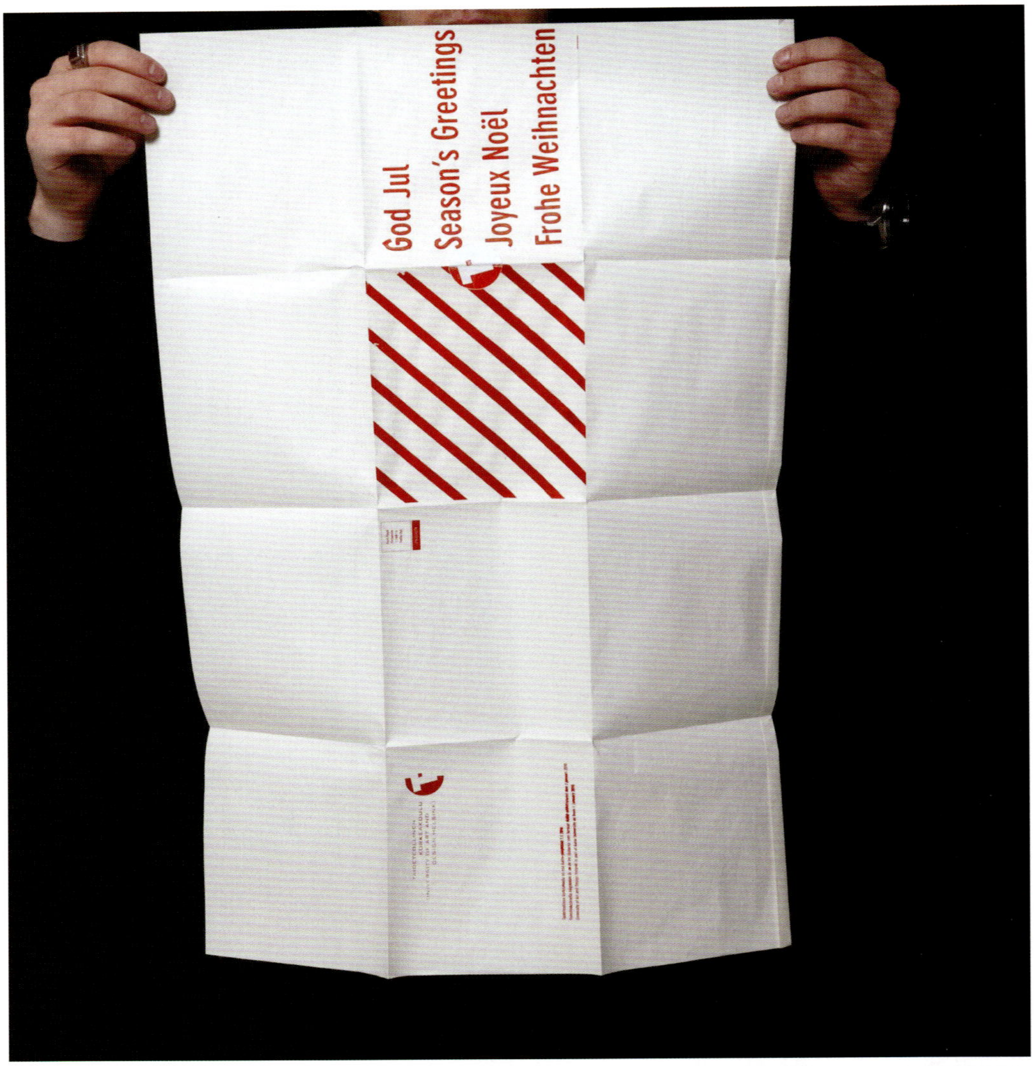

God Jul
Season's Greetings
Joyeux Noël
Frohe Weihnachten

Design
Tuukka Koivisto

Project
Media poster

Invitation for the opening party of the new Aalto University School of Art and Design Department of Media. Posters were silk-screen printed on varying sized silver foils.

The posters with the printed M-motifs were first hung around the school. Later on the title was hand written on the posters.

Design
Daniel Dittmar
Project
Dopesmoker

A custom typography and poster design based on the epic 1-hour stoner metal masterpiece 'Dopesmoker' by Sleep.

This design stemmed from an open brief that required each creative choose a song to base a visual narrative on. With religious parallels evident in the songs lyrics, this design looks to appropriate the ancient language of Sanskrit, whilst still keeping a western perspective.

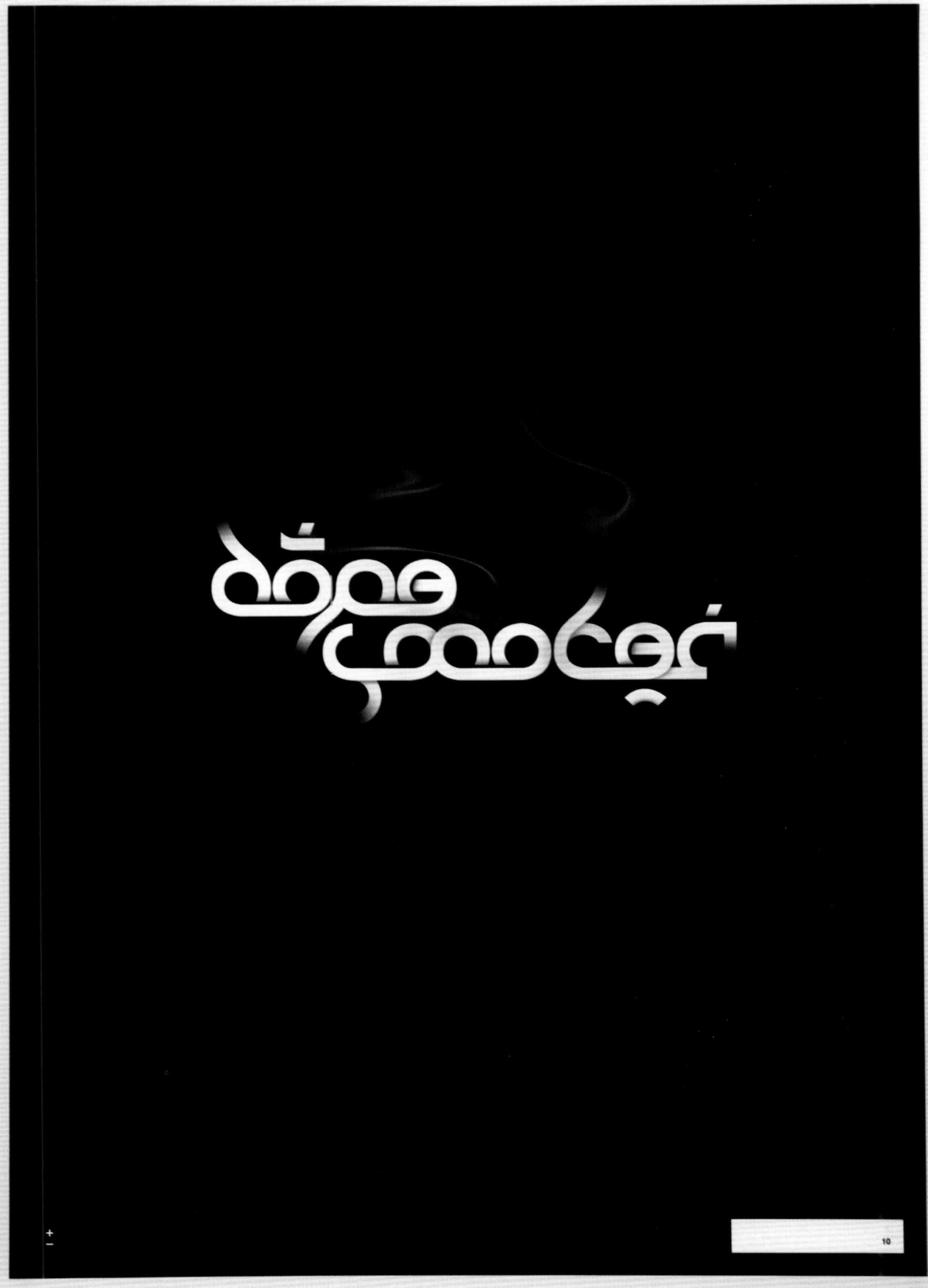
10

Design
Saffron Brand Consultants
Project
Capital Generation Partners

Capital Generation Partners (CapGen) is a London-based family office serving the investment needs of high net worth clients: individuals, trusts and foundations.

In a highly competitive market where they were competing not only against other wealth advisory firms but also with major banks, they wanted to raise their profile as a credible player.

Their communications did not convey their strong beliefs about how investing should, and should not be done. Nor did their lively, opinionated, sophisticated personality come across. Moreover, their target audience varied in their level of financial sophistication and interest in the detail of investing.

Investing is a complicated, somewhat dry subject so we asked ourselves, how could they tell their story in a compelling way?

We started by articulating their brand idea—what did they stand for, and to define their personality. Once that was agreed, we wanted to give them something to position CapGen in the minds of potential clients, referrers and even new recruits.

For this we created a limited edition book—'Notes on investing'—to capture CapGen's beliefs about the do's and don'ts of investing and designed and wrote it to reflect their distinct personality.

The book is a miscellany – a collection of writings on various subjects. Each belief is paired with a fact that illustrates the belief in an interesting and unexpected way. The miscellany draws from history, nature, science, art and even the sport of golf. The combination of belief and fact engages the reader on several different levels.

In a market where the conventional approach to wealth management communication is through glossy, aspirational 'Patek Philippe-style' imagery and copy, 'Notes on Investing' stands out.

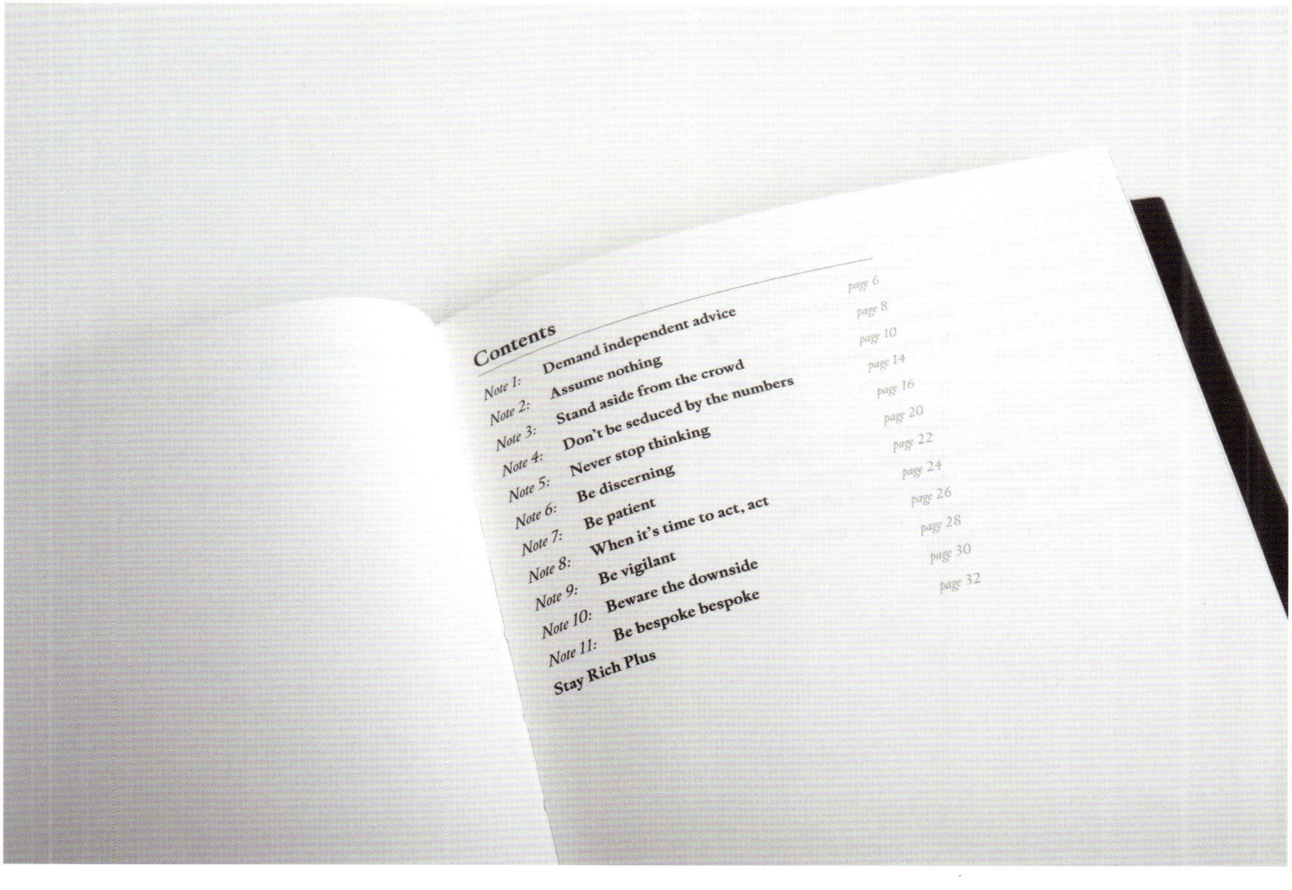

Contents

Note 1: Demand independent advice — page 6
Note 2: Assume nothing — page 8
Note 3: Stand aside from the crowd — page 10
Note 4: Don't be seduced by the numbers — page 14
Note 5: Never stop thinking — page 16
Note 6: Be discerning — page 20
Note 7: Be patient — page 22
Note 8: When it's time to act, act — page 24
Note 9: Be vigilant — page 26
Note 10: Beware the downside — page 28
Note 11: Be bespoke bespoke — page 30
Stay Rich Plus — page 32

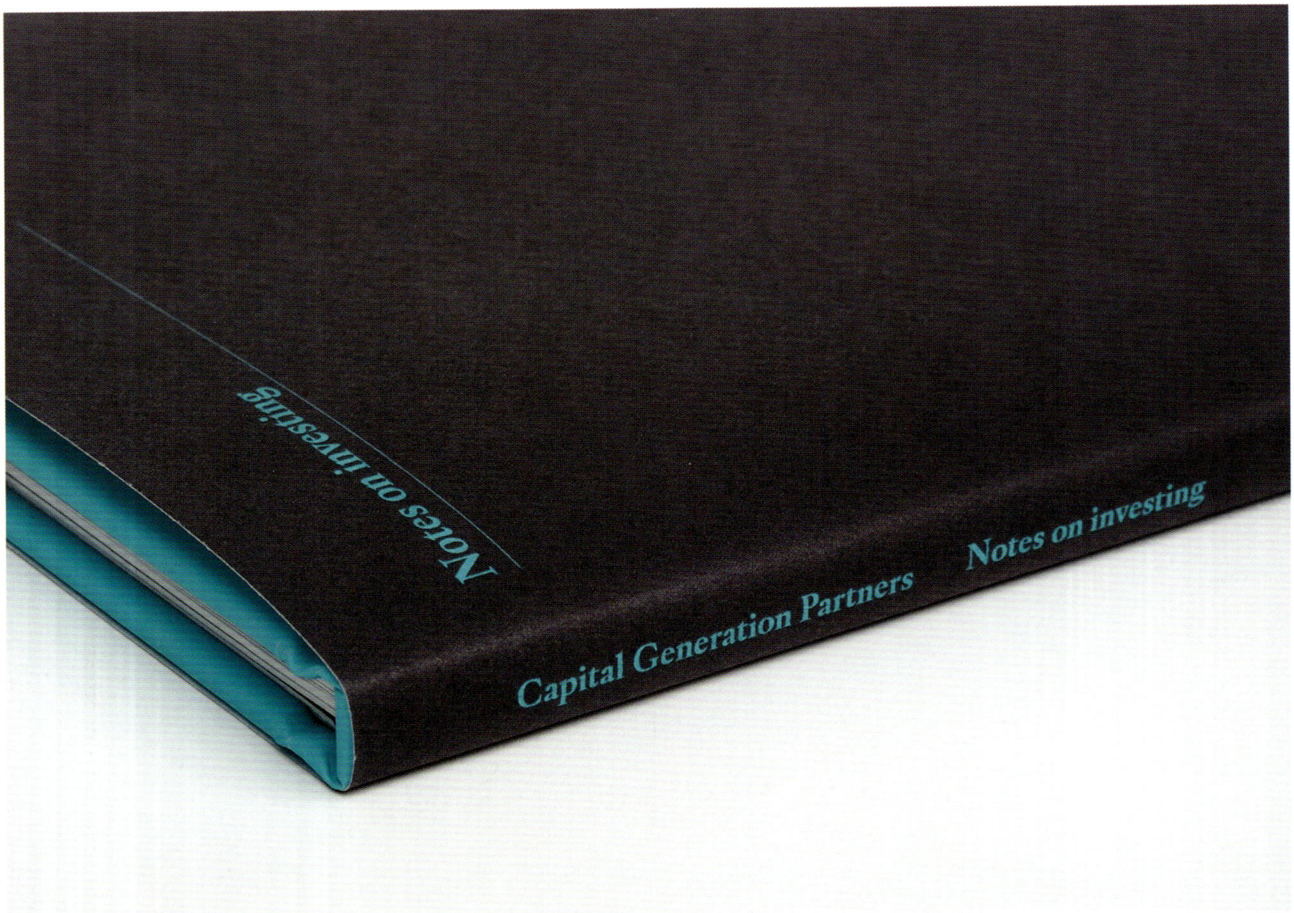

Capital Generation Partners Notes on investing

Notes on investing

Note 9: Be vigilant

'The price of freedom is eternal vigilance' and the same might be said for investing. As advisers, our role is to watch out for the unexpected – because the unexpected can be catastrophic. So we set ourselves the unpleasant task of imagining the worst outcomes and working out how we can avoid them.

This level of vigilance demands open-mindedness, breadth of vision and constructive scepticism. There are no certainties in investing but the more vigilant your approach, the less likely you are to be caught saying, "I never saw that coming."

fig 9. Keep your eyes open
The dolphin sleeps with one eye open, still swimming.

26   Capital Generation Partners   Notes on investing

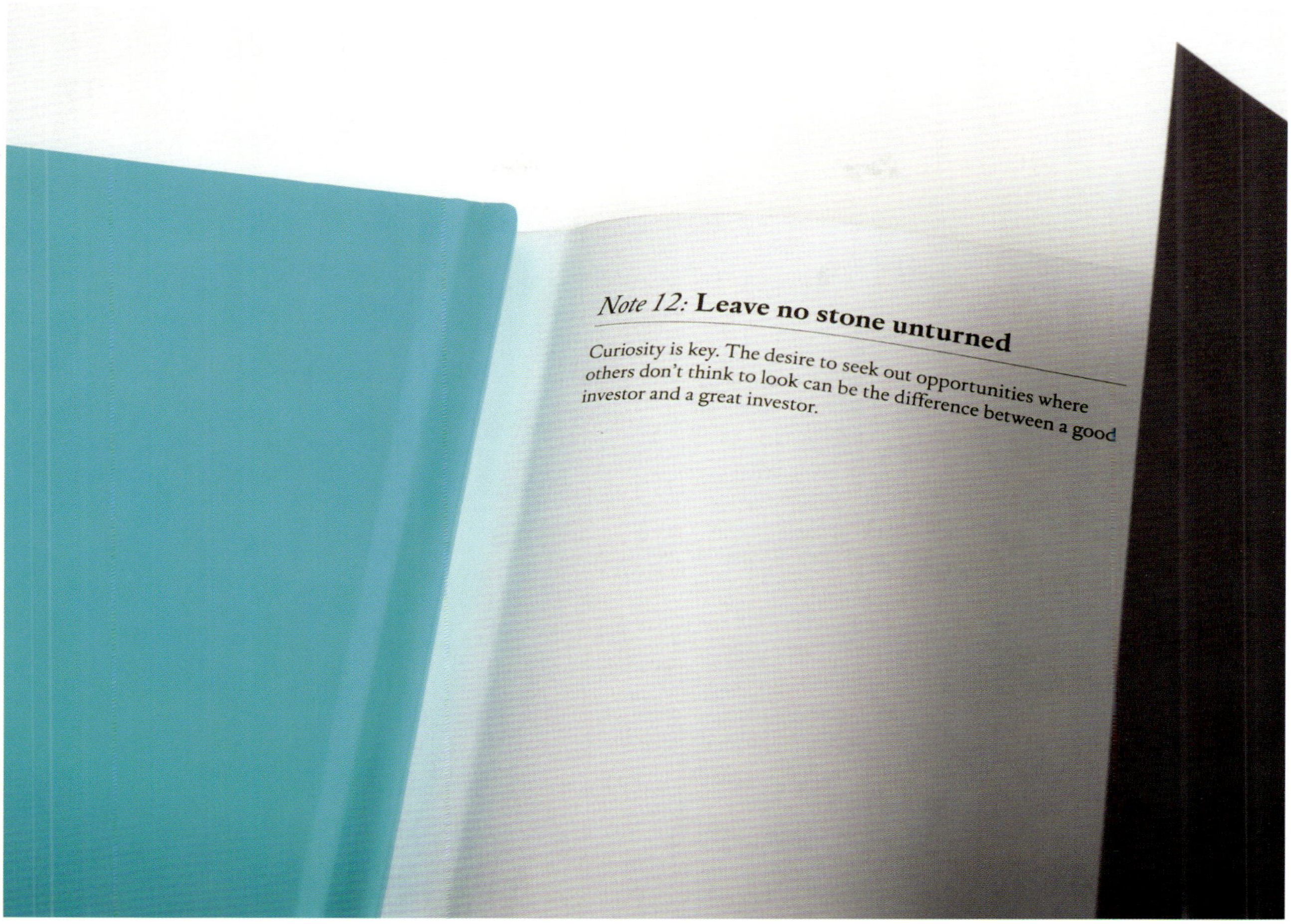

Note 12: **Leave no stone unturned**

Curiosity is key. The desire to seek out opportunities where others don't think to look can be the difference between a good investor and a great investor.

Note 4: **Don't be seduced by the numbers**

Mathematics is deductive and so, on its own terms, always right. Its patterns and symmetry beguile us, satisfying our craving for explanation, narrative and order. Mathematics, though, predicts nothing beyond its own world.

In our view, mathematics should be a supplement to, not a replacement for, thoughtful analysis and reasoning. A mathematical model of the real world is accurate until the moment that it is not.

It is more important than to understand the qualitative elements of an investment than to consider an investment in the round. Who is driving the investment? How stable is the management? At what point in their careers are they? Are the fund managers' incentives aligned? Technological innovations? What about broader economic indicators? Social indicators?

An investment is always about judgment, not just process; never about the numbers on their own, always about how you use them.

Not everything that counts can be counted, and not everything that can be counted counts.

(Albert Einstein (sign hanging in his office at Princeton University))

$$111{,}111{,}111 \times 111{,}111{,}111$$

$$12{,}345{,}678{,}987{,}654{,}321$$

Design
Saffron Brand Consultants

Project
Gorrissen Federspiel

Organisations, like individuals, have different personalities. Law firms are no exception. As one of the leading law firms in Denmark, clients have always thought highly of Gorrissen Federspiel Kierkegaard.

However, they weren't as well known among potential recruits and clients and there was a widespread misperception that they were old fashioned and dull. This is when they came to Saffron, looking for a way to help them express their true personality.

As part of our brand work, we shortened their name to Gorrissen Federspiel (the full was difficult for the Danish, and near impossible for non-Danish clients) and gave them a new symbol represents the teamwork at their heart and is derived from the names of the partners in the firm.

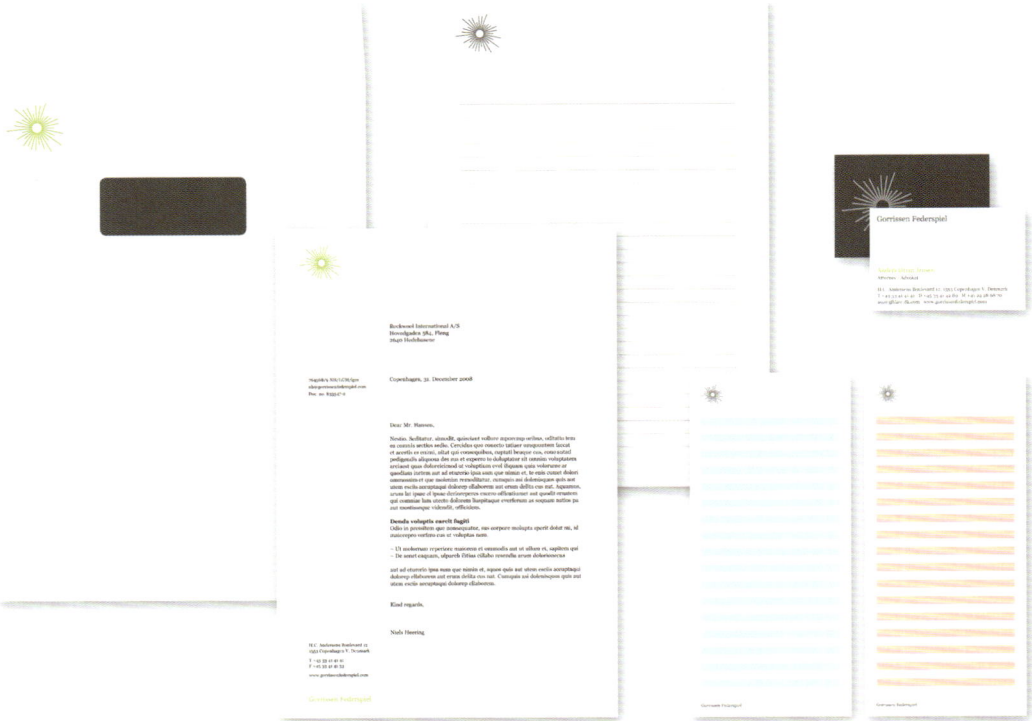

216

The new brand captures their true personality with an identity and tone of voice that is fresh and energetic and was applied to both online and offline channels. The print work included guidelines and a full set of stationery with a distinctive colour palette that definitely positioned them as the innovative firm they are.

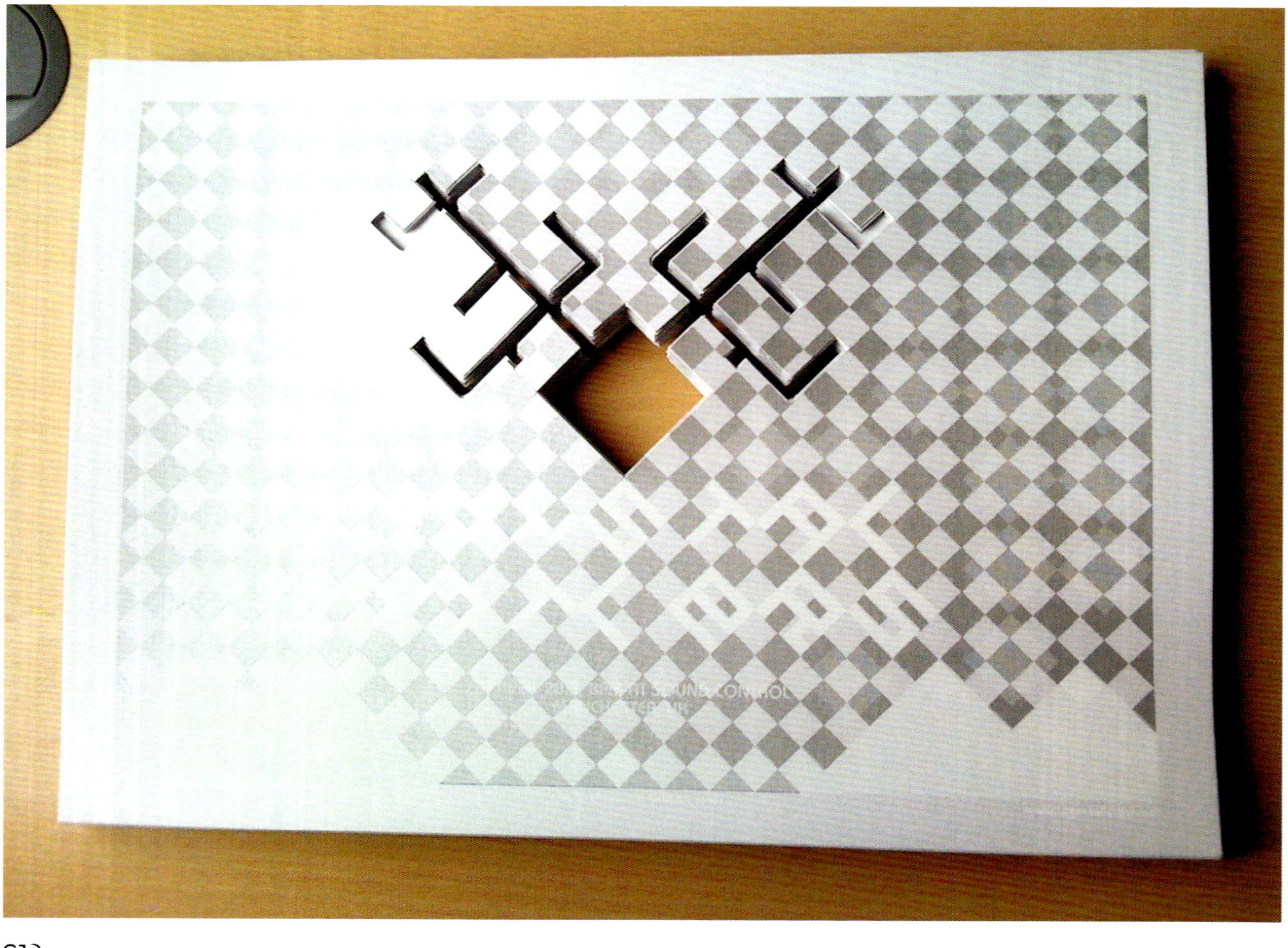

Design
G-MAN
Nick Rhodes

Project
Crystal Antlers

A design collaboration between G-MAN and designer Nick Rhodes (Switchopen) for the Californian band Crystal Antler's Manchester UK gig.

Poster style one is screen printed in silver and white on light grey Colourplan with cutout antlers. Poster style twc is screen printed in white on light grey Colourplan. Limited edition of 70.

Design

Mammal

Project

Fairy Cookbook

A promotional cookbook containing some of the nation's favourite recipes. To ensure the book would be as practical as possible, the book has a PVC removable cover which can be put in the dishwasher or washed in the sink to remove any food spills. The Fairy logo and knife, fork and plate graphic was heat embossed onto the PVC cover.

Each of the pages was also laminated so these too can be easily cleaned.

Design

Mammal

Project

Twenty
Northdown
Street

For a new residential development in Kings Cross we designed a brochure based around the number 20. The brochure is 20cm x 20cm square and all the margins are 20mm wide. The twentieth letter of the alphabet is T and so all the T's in the book are underlined creating a unique pattern across the cover and all the pages inside the brochure.

The cover was created from box board with the title foil blocked in matt white and the inner pages printed on a silk sheet with spot varnishing throughout.

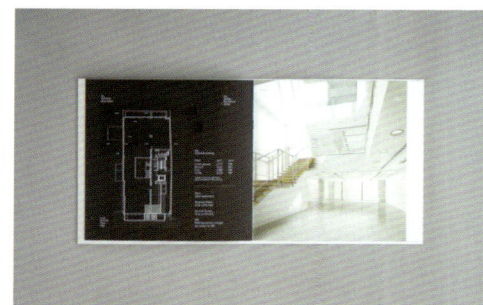

Identity for a music production company based in Camden, London. The business card was folded and die-cut so the logo can be seen through the front of the card, this referenced the multi-disciplined nature of the business and how all departments work together as one.

Design
Mammal
Project
iPressPlay

Design

Mammal

Project

Parkheath Brochure

Brochure designed for a leading estate agent in an affluent area of London. The company's strapline is 'sold on service' which was embossed on the front cover.

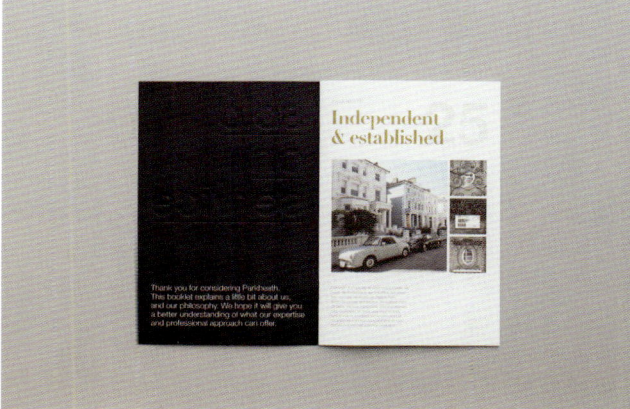

Design

Thompson Brand Partners

Project

Ispace Fruit Market

Architects ispace were responsible for a proposed bid for the regeneration of the old fruit market in Hull, Yorkshire. Their plan was to convert the old fruit market into a hub for arts and culture, and put Hull on the map.

We were asked to help them with their bid by creating a book to tell the story of the old fruit market and the journey they were proposing to take it on.

Design
Thompson Brand Partners

Project
Kingsbury Press

Kingsbury Press are a growing, ambitious print company based in the North of England. We were asked to develop a promotional piece that would showcase their extensive in-house capabilities and create new business opportunities within the design community.

A diary format was chosen, and the overarching theme was 'meticulous attention to detail—something which Kingsbury can genuinely deliver and which is vital to their key audience of world-class designers, who are always on the lookout for an execution which can meet their creative ambition for each project.

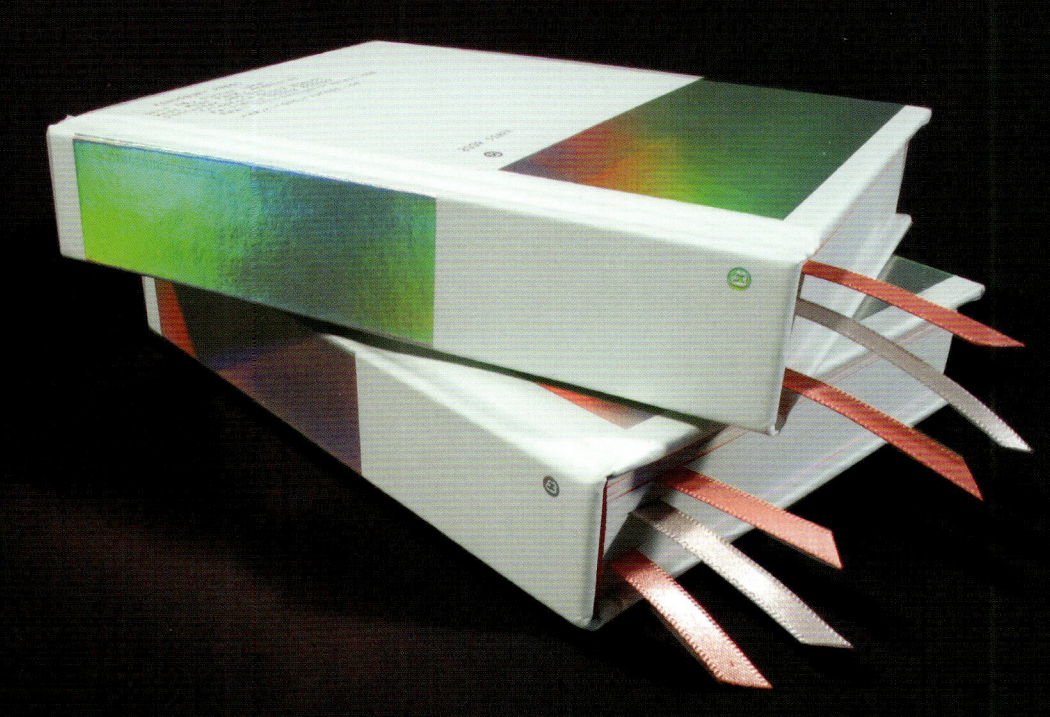

Design

Thompson Brand Partners

Project

Leeds University – LDS09

LDS09 was a diverse fine art exhibition put on by Leeds University in the Summer of 2009 and consisted of paintings, sculptures, installations and new media. We were asked to create an exhibition guide to showcase all of the fantastic works which the students had created.

We created a guide which was all about the contributing artists, each having a spread dedicated to them and featuring the works they had on show as well as some of their other works from outside the exhibition.

Metal presents

VILL AGE GRE EN.

SAT 27 SEPTEMBER

A FESTIVAL OF ARTS AND SPORT IN CHALKWELL PARK,
SOUTHEND ON SEA, IN CELEBRATION OF THE LAUNCH
OF THE CULTURAL OLYMPIAD.

11AM – 10PM
FREE ENTRY – BRING A PICNIC

ACT WATCH EAT TALK SING RIDE
DANCE IDEA MOVE MAKE RACE...

WWW.METALCULTURE.COM/VILLAGE-GREEN

Design

Thompson Brand Partners

Project

Village Green

The first Village Green was created as part of the Cultural Olympiad and took part over the Open Weekend in September 2008. Village Green was awarded the London 2012 Inspire mark—part of the Olympic Games brand family, making it one of only 33 events out of 600 to successfully gain the mark.

In 2008 we created a visual identity to bring to life the contributions of 263 artists and 46 local arts and community groups in a day which was about fun, intrigue, talent, and participation.

After the success of the 2008 festival we were asked to refresh the identity and collateral for 2009 and in response 20,000 people flocked to the event, representing another resounding success. In line with Metal's exceptional approach to sustainability and environmental innovation, all of the collateral created for the event was made from 100% recycled materials. Even the events team's T-shirts were old ones brought along on the day and screen printed on the day with the new identity.

technical guide
material by
robert horne
samples
colour chips

creative
material by
robert horne
www.roberthorne.co.uk
08457 44 33 22
creative
material by
robert horne
samples

Design

Thompson Brand Partners

Project

Robert Horne

As part of the 'Material by Robert Horne' brand identity campaign we needed to create a new paper specification guide for the design industry – 'The Creative Guide'. We were briefed to develop a new iteration of 'The Creative Guide' that would be the dream specification tool for designers – with the simple aim of getting designers to specify more paper and to choose Robert Horne every time.

The Guide contained a chip chart that included a piece of every material that RH held in stock, as well as a 'sample book', which contained an A5 piece of every type of RH material. We also produced a technical guide with extensive information on every product available. Building on our own experience of working in print and specifying materials, we created the ultimate tool for Robert Horne, which we knew was guaranteed to fit the bill for the creative industry.

We utilised a range of different print finishes to deliver design impact and credibility to specifiers – a range of foil blocking, screen printing and matt lamination, as well as litho printing on wide rage of substrates.

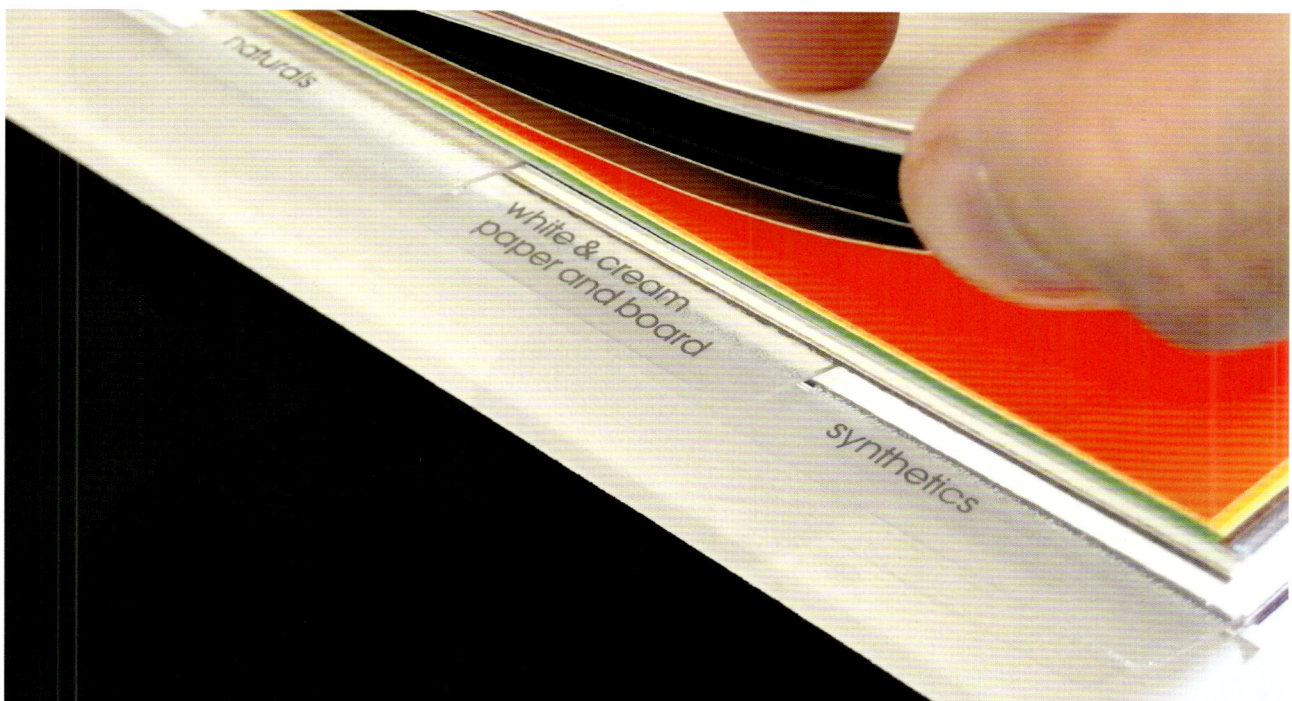

Package

Design
Anagrama
Project
Theurel & Thomas

Theurel & Thomas is the first patisserie in Mexico specializing in French macarons, the most popular dessert of the French pastries.

For this project it was very important to create an imposing brand that would emphasize the unique value, elegance and detail of this delicate dessert.

One of the most important extensions of a brand, which has a business based in store selling, is the design and ambiance of the stores. The patisserie of Theurel & Thomas has an enlighten space with an exclusivity and elegance atmosphere.

The store location is found in San Pedro, Mx. Latin America's most affluent suburb.

White is a central part of the design and it plays as a contrast with the colours of the French macarons.

THEUREL & THOMAS
Maison du Macaron

HEUREL & THOMAS

THEUREL & THOMAS

EUREL & THOMAS

Theurel & Thomas

CHRISTMAS
RE-IMAGINED
FOURUM

Short item or long,
an extra knot gets you covered.
THE GIFT OF ART
Turn a special gift into an extraordinary one! With this Japanese style furoshiki wrap, no item is too difficult, no shape too unusual. See our examples for inspiration!
One bottle or two,
good wine always wraps up nicely.
FOURUM

Design

&Larry

Project

iFourum—
The Gift of Art

This Christmas campaign for iFourum is centred on the colourfu graphics we developed for a Japanese style 'furoshiki' fabric wrap giveaway. Each fabric wrapper was presented in an attractive package sealed with a foil-stamped sticker. Unfolding the package revealed instructions inside for wrapping fcr gift items of all shapes and sizes.

CHRISTMAS RE-IMAGINED
iFOURUM
LEVEL 4 · TOWER B · TAKASHIMAYA S.C.

This Christmas, surprise and delight your loved ones with a selection of thoughtful and expressive gifts, many lovingly crafted by hand from around the world. Come up to iFourum at Takashimaya Shopping Centre L4 and discover gifts of art that everyone can enjoy.

THE GIFT OF ART

- ART FRIEND
- BOOKBINDERS DESIGN
- CREATIVE HANDS
- L'ESCALIER
- MERLIN FRAME MAKER & ART GALLERY
- STUDIO MIU
- THE BETTER GIFT STORE
- THE BETTER TOY STORE

Design

&Larry

Project

iFourum—Start Imagining Things

This creative workshop promotion for iFOURUM gives a twist to the phrase 'Stop imagining things'. In this case, the ellipsis in the headline stands for whatever you can imagine. By joining the dots you can make anything you like, just like using the products and services at iFOURUM to make your ideas a reality.

A complimentary notepad for workshop attendees features die-cut holes on the cover to form the yellow dots. The concept was extended to gift vouchers and ceiling banners to show interesting line-art while highlighting the joy of creativity.

Design
&Larry

Project
iFourum – Imagination Is Your Greatest Gift

This Christmas campaign for iFOURUM focuses on the 'gift of imagination' with graphics inspired by thought bubbles to represent gift ideas. Products were photographed in their natural state to encourage readers to imagine creative ways of personalizing them.

Store brochures were presented as a pack of postcards resembling a gift box and a specially designed tarpaulin bag was produced as a promotional gift, along with two-tone metallic gift wrappers featuring the thought bubble motif

A golden-edged gift card served as a final touch to the premium feel of the whole campaign.

Christmas at
FOURUM
LEVEL 4 · TOWER B · TAKASHIMAYA S.C.

Imag
Is Yo
Grea
Gift.

Whether you are le
or designing your
lets your imaginat
boutiques that ful

STUDIO MIU ART

Imagine, a place where you could...
- master the skill of painting.
- leave your kids to learn while you go shopping.
- meet your new best friend.
- de-stress
- let your imagination run wild.
- find an inspiring work of Art.

ART FRIEND

Imagine, this posing figure could...
- be your muse for your painting.
- be dressed up as Santa Claus.
- be a scarecrow in your garden.
- be the security guard in your house.
- be the crowning glory of a Christmas tree.
- be an original MAAD creation.

CREATIVE HANDS

Imagine, this glass bottle could...
- be a bottled garden.
- be a snow globe.
- contain the sands from your Maldives honeymoon.
- house your hopes and dreams.
- be a musical instrument.

Outfit from Massimo Dutti (as shown) Jewellery from Chopard (as on)

THE MOST SERIOUSLY FUN PLAY-THINGS

Created To Engage Kids & Grown-Ups As Few Other Toys Can.

THE BETTER TOY STORE

iFOURUM LEVEL 4 TOWER B ART FRIEND • BOOKBINDERS DESIGN • CREATIVE HANDS • CREATIVE HANDS – FINE ARTS
L'ESCALIER • MERLIN FRAME MAKER & ART GALLERY • STUDIO MIU ART • THE BETTER TOY STORE

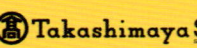

Design
&Larry

Project
iFourum—Imagination Is Your Greatest Gift

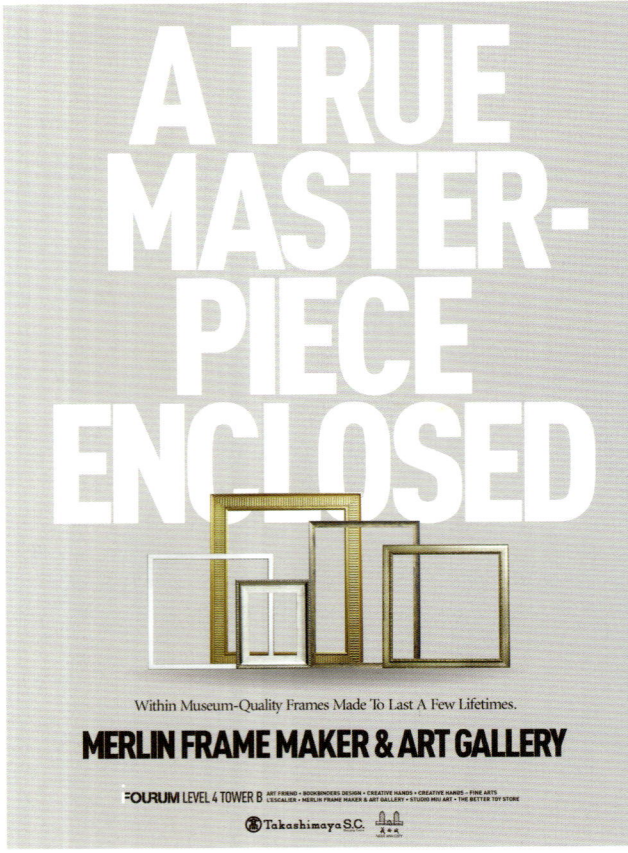

This Christmas campaign is inspired by the natural attraction for exclusivity and unique gift ideas. The twist is that uniqueness comes from the individual. Thus each bold claim in the campaign is cheekily qualified by an accompanying down-to-earth statement.

250

SUPER LIMITED EDITION GIFTS

SHIMAYA S.C. LEVEL 4 TOWER B   ART FRIEND • BOOKBINDERS DESIGN • CREATIVE HANDS • CREATIVE HANDS – FINE ARTS
L'ESCALIER • MERLIN FRAME MAKER & ART GALLERY • STUDIO MIU ART • THE BETTER TOY STORE

To complete the package, thematic gift wrappers were designed in two festive colours, with an elegant foil-stamped gift tag and ribbon combo to top-off each present. A calendar was also produced as a store gift, aptly called 'The Most Happening Calendar... As only you could have put together in 2008.'

Design
&Larry

Project
Eye Place

The exclusive Eye Place optical boutique is represented by a stylised illustration of the workings of the human eye. The logotype depicts the inversion of light rays through the lens, and also reflects the boutique's collection of unusual eyewear designs.

The name card features reverse clear foil blocking so that the brandmark appears debossed out of the shimmering card surface. The play of light and tactile feedback adds to the branding and serves as a subtle test: If you can't make out the logo, it's time to have your eyes checked.

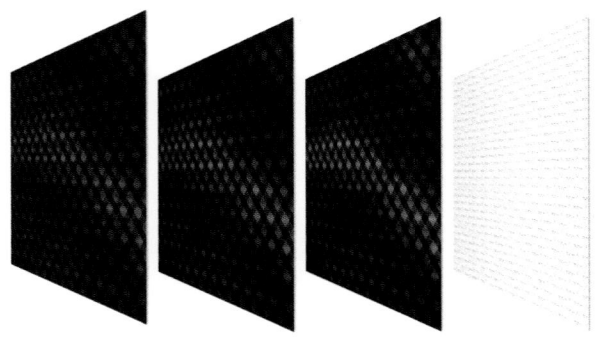

Collin Teo
B OPTOM (UNSW)

39 Stamford Road
01-06 Stamford House
Singapore 178885

T: 65 6338 3240
F: 65 6338 5791

the.eyeplace@pacific.net.sg
www.eye-place.com

Operating Hours
Mon, Wed to Sat: 11:30am to 8pm
Sun: 11:30am to 6pm
Closed on Tues & Public Holidays

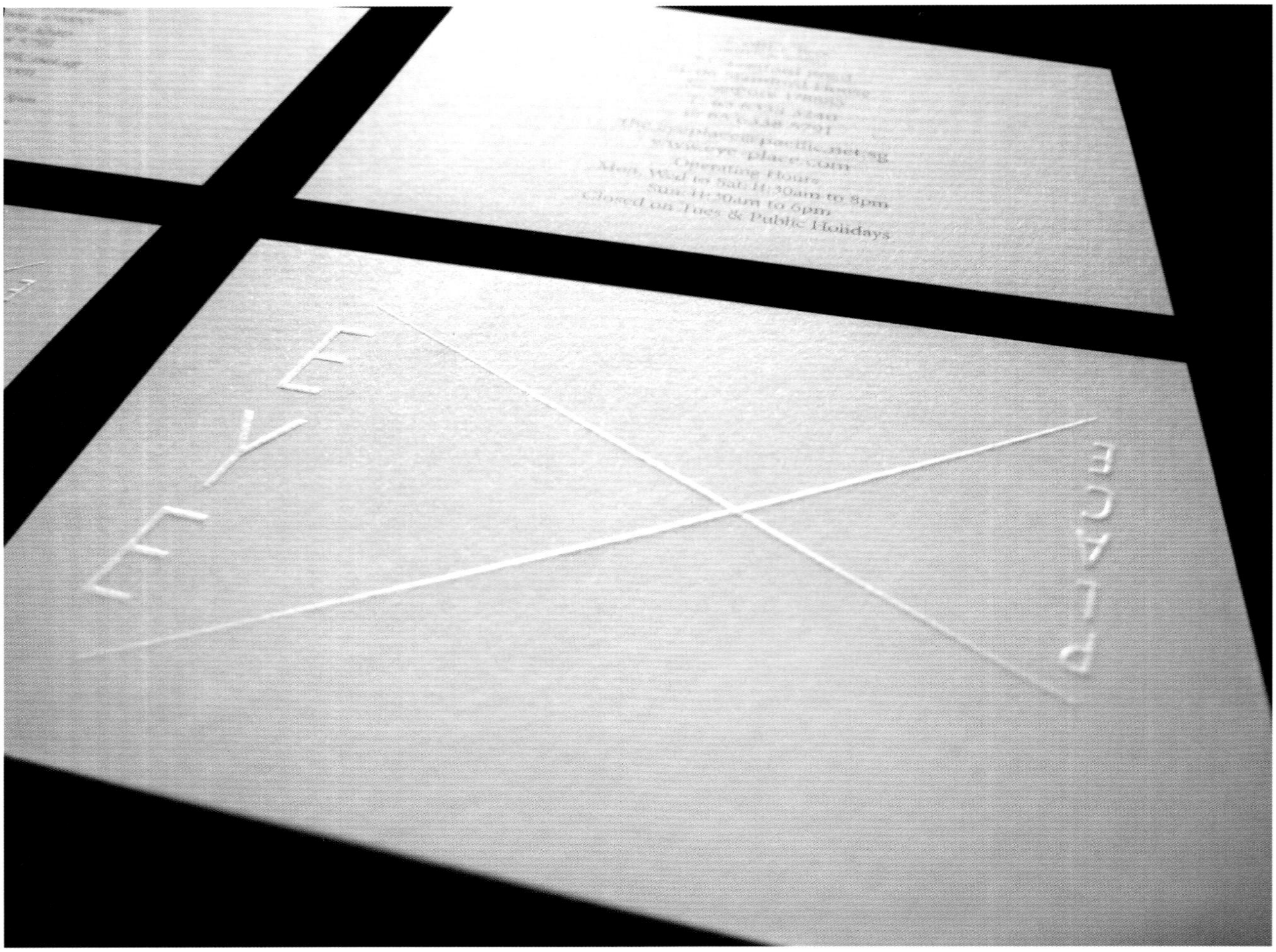

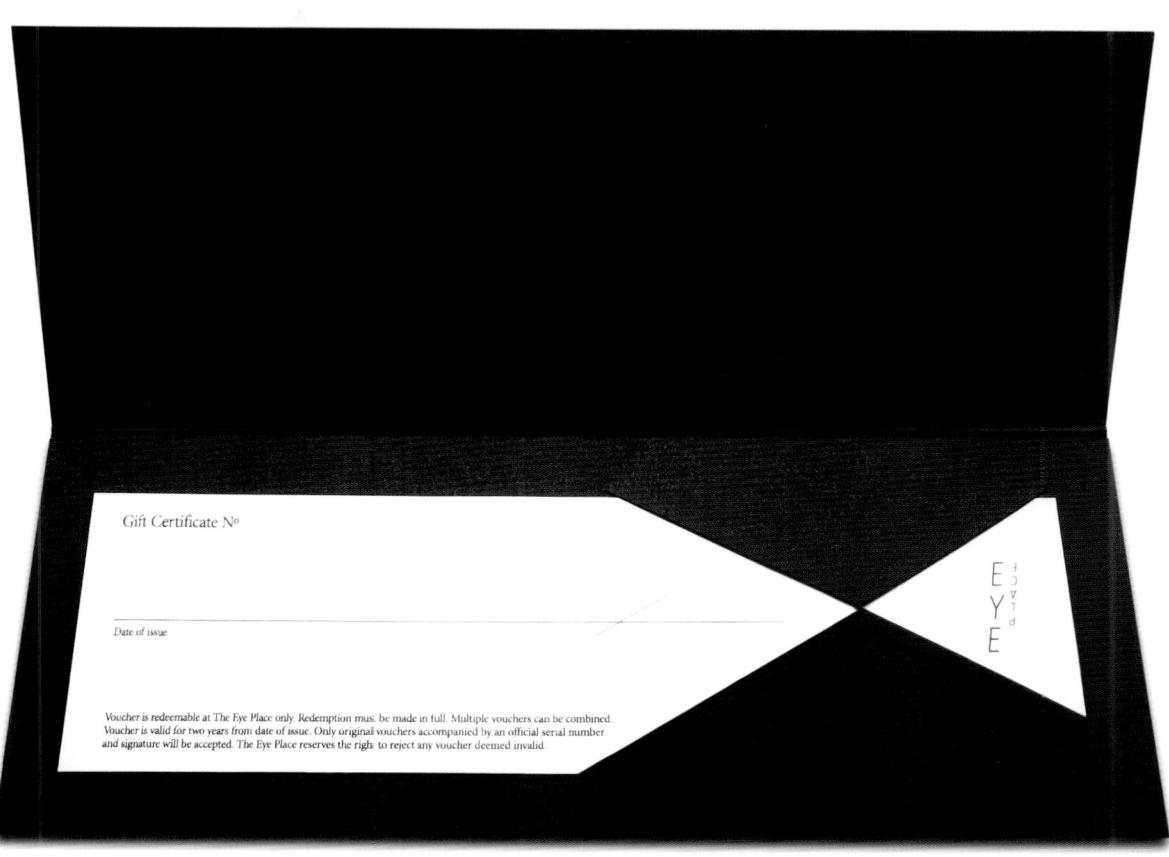

Gift Certificate No

_____
Date of issue

Voucher is redeemable at The Eye Place only. Redemption must be made in full. Multiple vouchers can be combined.
Voucher is valid for two years from date of issue. Only original vouchers accompanied by an official serial number
and signature will be accepted. The Eye Place reserves the right to reject any voucher deemed invalid.

EYE

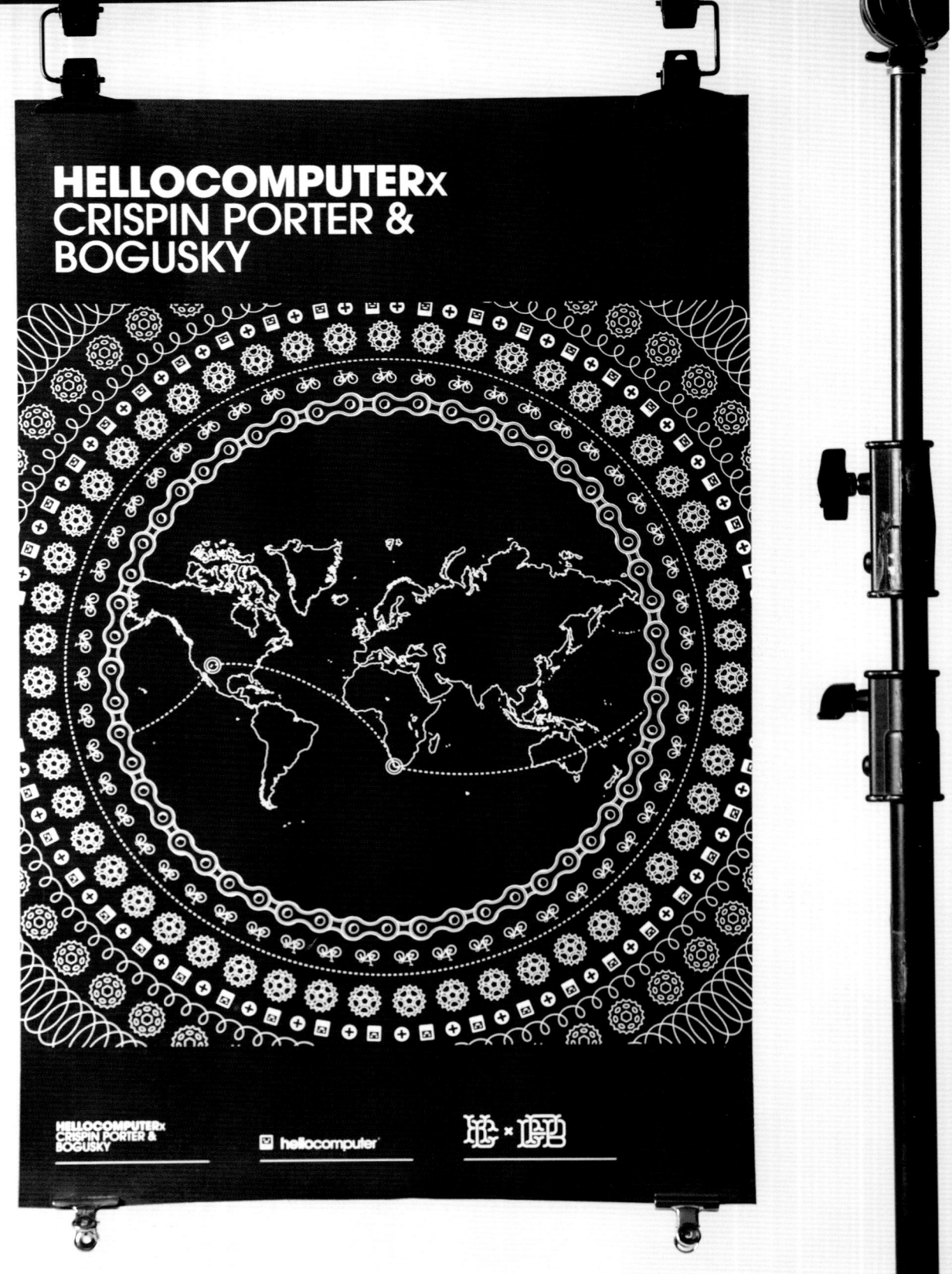

Design

Si Maclennan for HelloComputer

Project

HelloComputer x CP+B

Packaging design and collateral for a unique corporate gift. Hellocomputer commissioned Danielle Clough to create a one-of-a-kind plush toy. The toy was based on HelloComputer's mascot, Hal, and his new friend Al (after Alex Bogusky)—an extrusion of the Crispin Porter & Bogusky logo. Si Maclennan art-directed the project and illustrated the packaging.

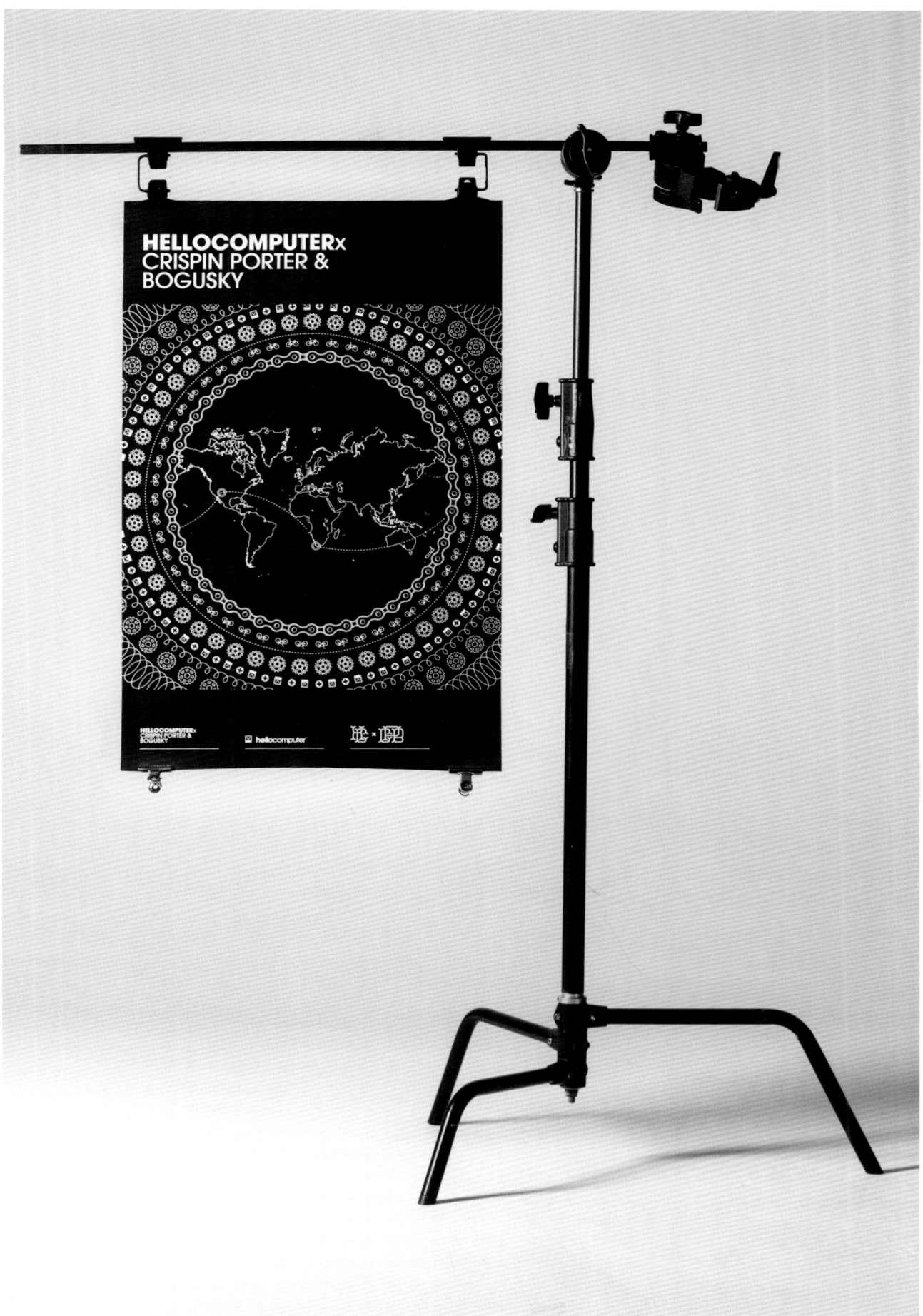

The gift, complete with hardcover story book, and commemorative poster was shipped to Crispin Porter & Bogusky in Colorado as a gesture of goodwill after the completion of a large online project by HelloComputer.

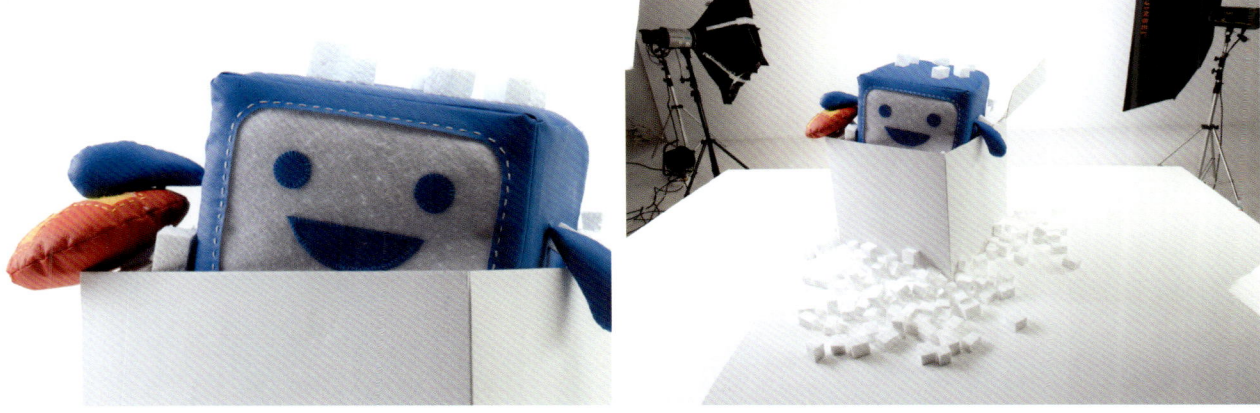

Design
Si Maclennan for HelloComputer

Project
Hellocomputer x CP+B

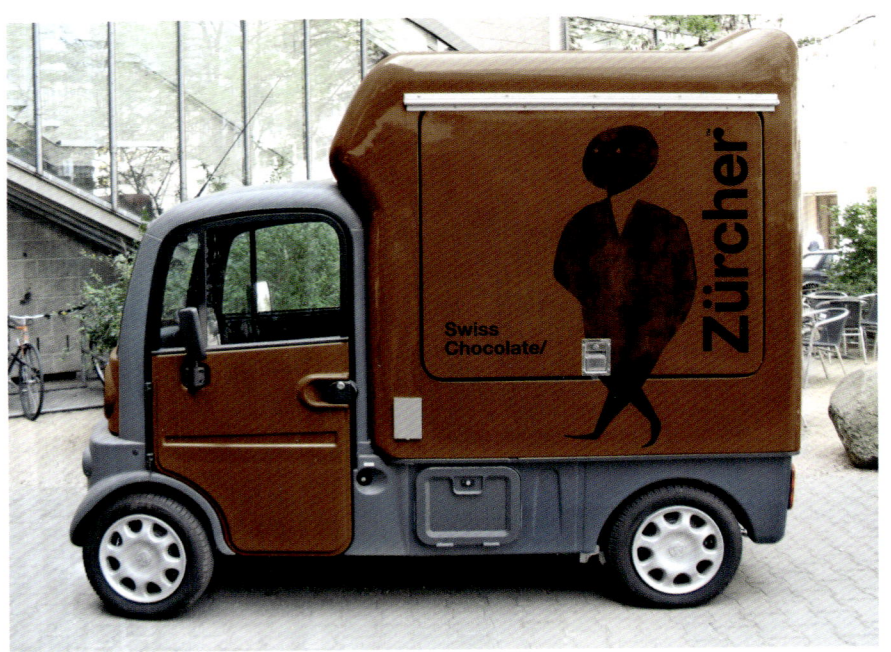

Design
Stas Sipovich

Project
Zurcher

Brand identity, logo, character & packaging design concept for Swiss family chocolate producer and takeaway confectionery based in Zurich.

Design
Stas Sipovich

Project
With Fashion Forever

Design
Stas Sipovich
Project
Postfutur

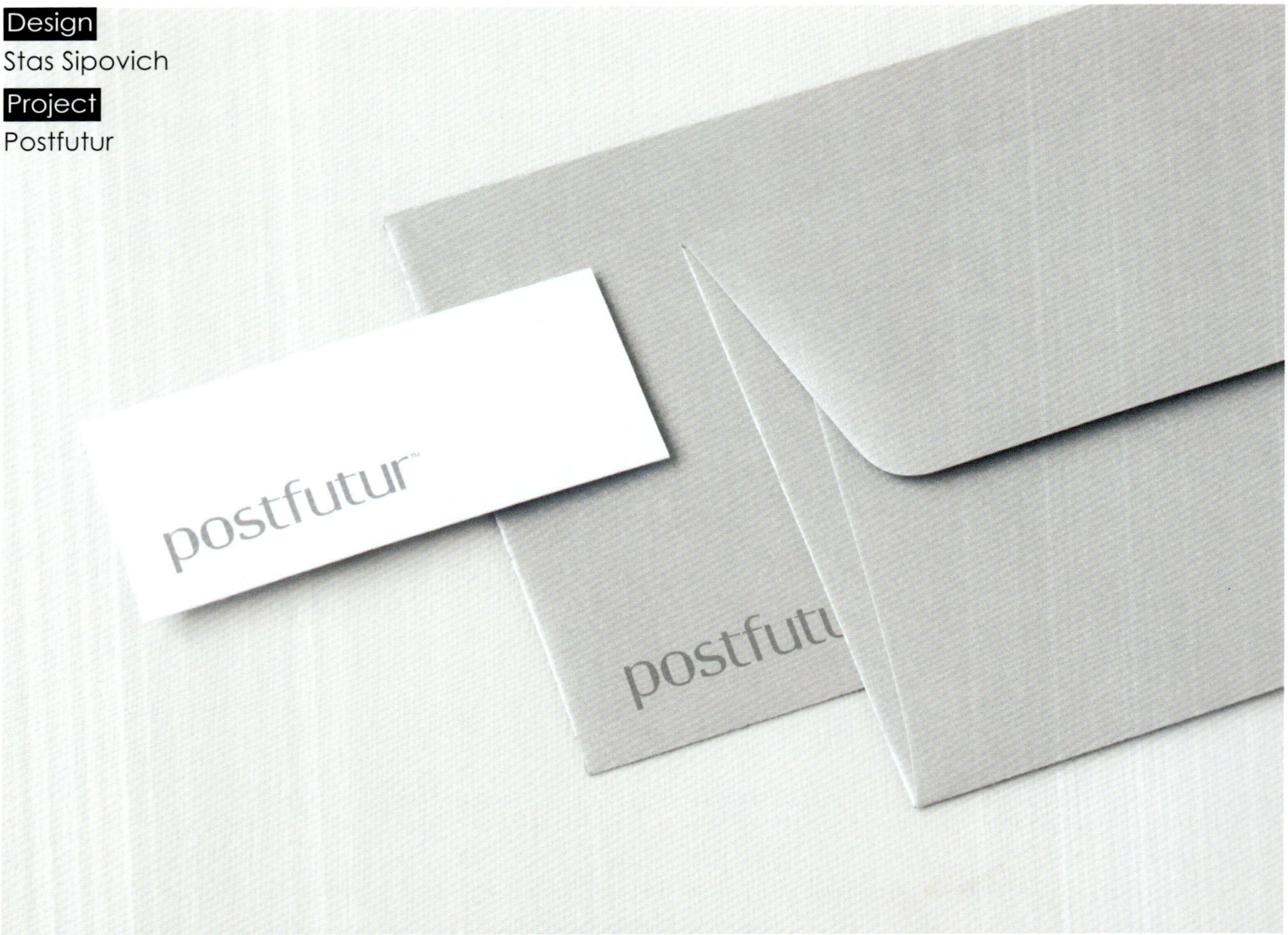

Design

Yasuko Ikeda

Project

4TH FLOOR Gift Packaging

Packaging design for hair salon. Building on the technical, monospaced identity for premier east London hair salon, 4TH FLOOR, the design of this special edition gift set extends the hard grid of characters to recreate brand elements in a flurry of halftone patterns, wrapping around the outside of the box. Just a touch of Christmas is hinted through the use of seasonal red for the sticker. Developed with North Design.

Design
Yasuko Ikeda

Project
Neyn Akasaka

Brand identity, packaging, promotional materials, and interiors for flagship store of boutique doughnut shop.

Eschewing traditional brand for a more irreverent approach, the identity for Tokyo-based shop 'Neyn' tells a story of cottage kitchen cooking, garden picnics, and countryside nature. Gingham-check and animal footprints motifs play across the packaging and shop interiors, mingling with butterflies and birds. Although the packaging is only printed in single colours a range of different papers makes each item feel distinct. Developed in collaboration with Hester Fell.

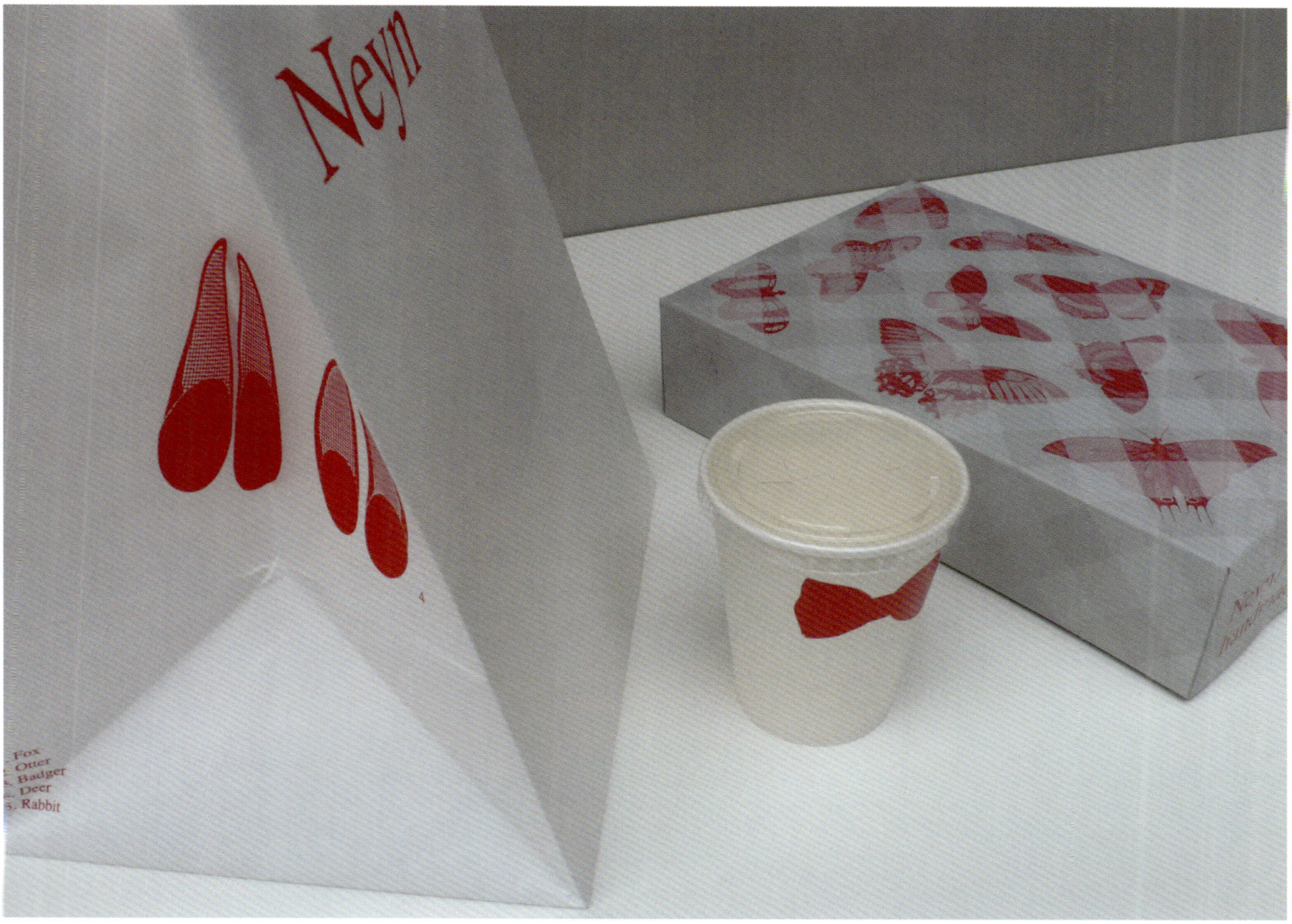

Biscuits
8 oz Plain Flour
1 Egg (beaten)
1 1/2 tablespoons Milk
1 teaspoonful Caraway Seeds
3 oz Butter
1/2 teaspoonful Baking Powder
3 oz Caster Sugar

Sieve the flour and rub in the
sugar, baking powder and car
Mix together the beaten egg
into the dry ingredients. Tu
lightly-floured pastry board
cut into small rounds. Bak
buttered baking-sheets in

Neyn /
handmade

Neyn /
handmade

Spoonful Bak
3 oz Caster Sugar

Sieve the flour and rub
sugar, baking powder a
Mix together the beaten
into the dry ingredients.
lightly-floured pastry boa
cut into small rounds. Bak
buttered baking-sheets in a

Neyn /
handmade

Design
Yasuko Ikeda

Project
Neyn Tokyo Midtown

Packaging, promotional materials, and interiors for second store of doughnut shop.

Rather than repurpose the original Neyn shop identity the branding for this second branch took the 'handmade' ethos and created new story. Reflecting the temporary, pop-up nature of the store, the interior is raw and unpolished.

The packaging and display materials – printed on stickers to echo the craft spirit – detail the hand construction of the store's custom furniture in juxtaposition with their handmade doughnuts. Likewise the utilitarian use of black and white for the branding contrasts with the colourful sweets on sale. Developed in collaboration with Hester Fell.

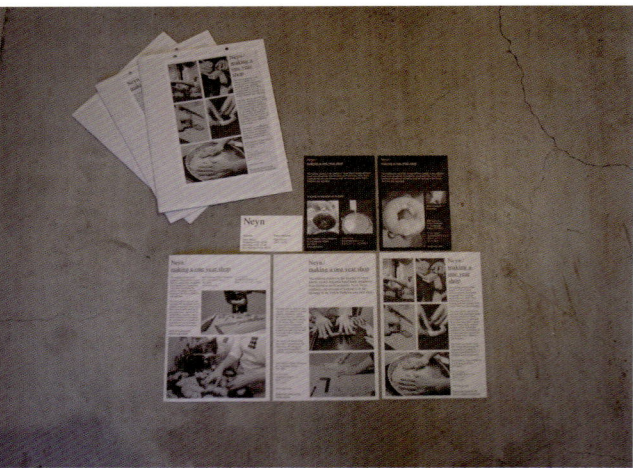

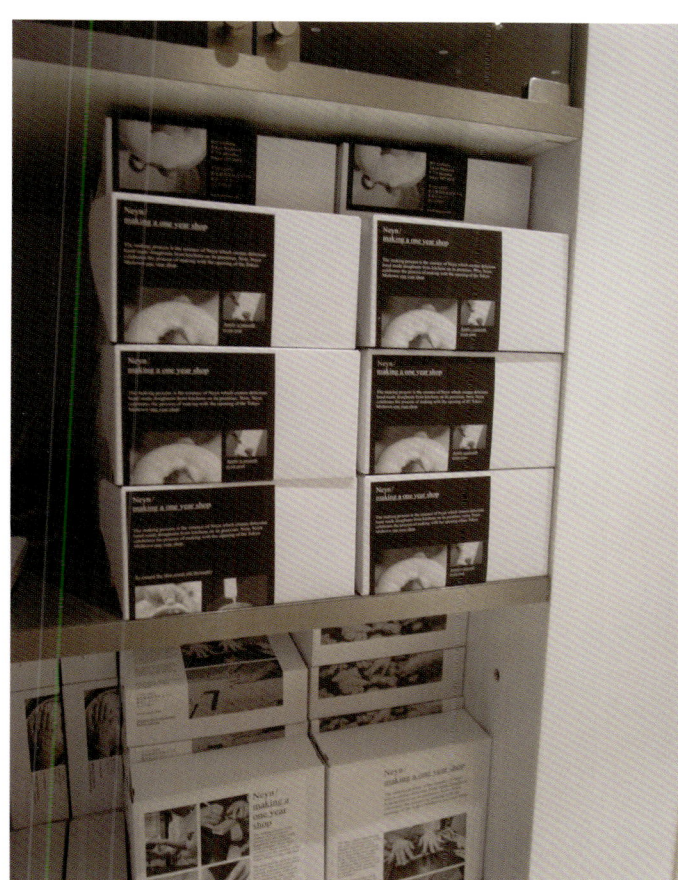

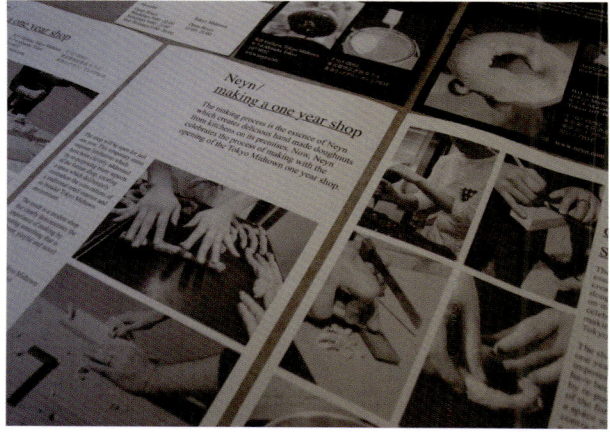

Neyn /
making a one year shop
March 2009 – February 2010

230
260
260
260
270
270
270
280
300
260
everyday
ドリンク / Drinks

Design

Moshik Nadav

Project

CD Package

Made for promoting a
student credit card.

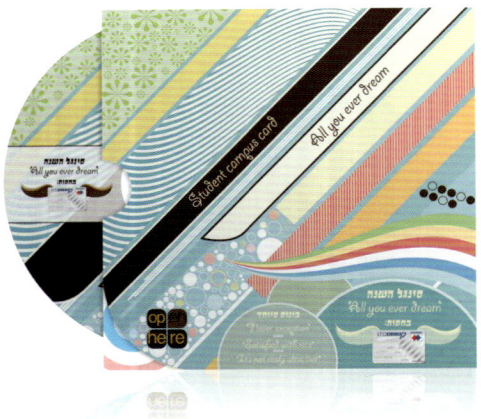

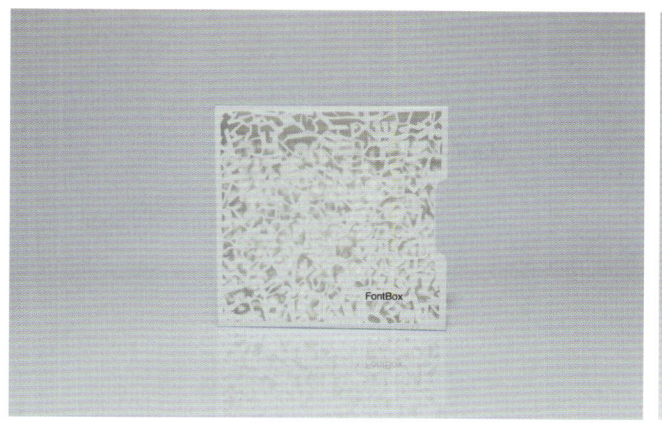

Design
Moshik Nadav
Project
Fon-Box

Design

Moshik Nadav

Project

FontBox

Made for promoting a student credit card. Small, Medium, Large & Extra Large Fonts packages.

Technique: Hand made Hebrew letter paper cuts.

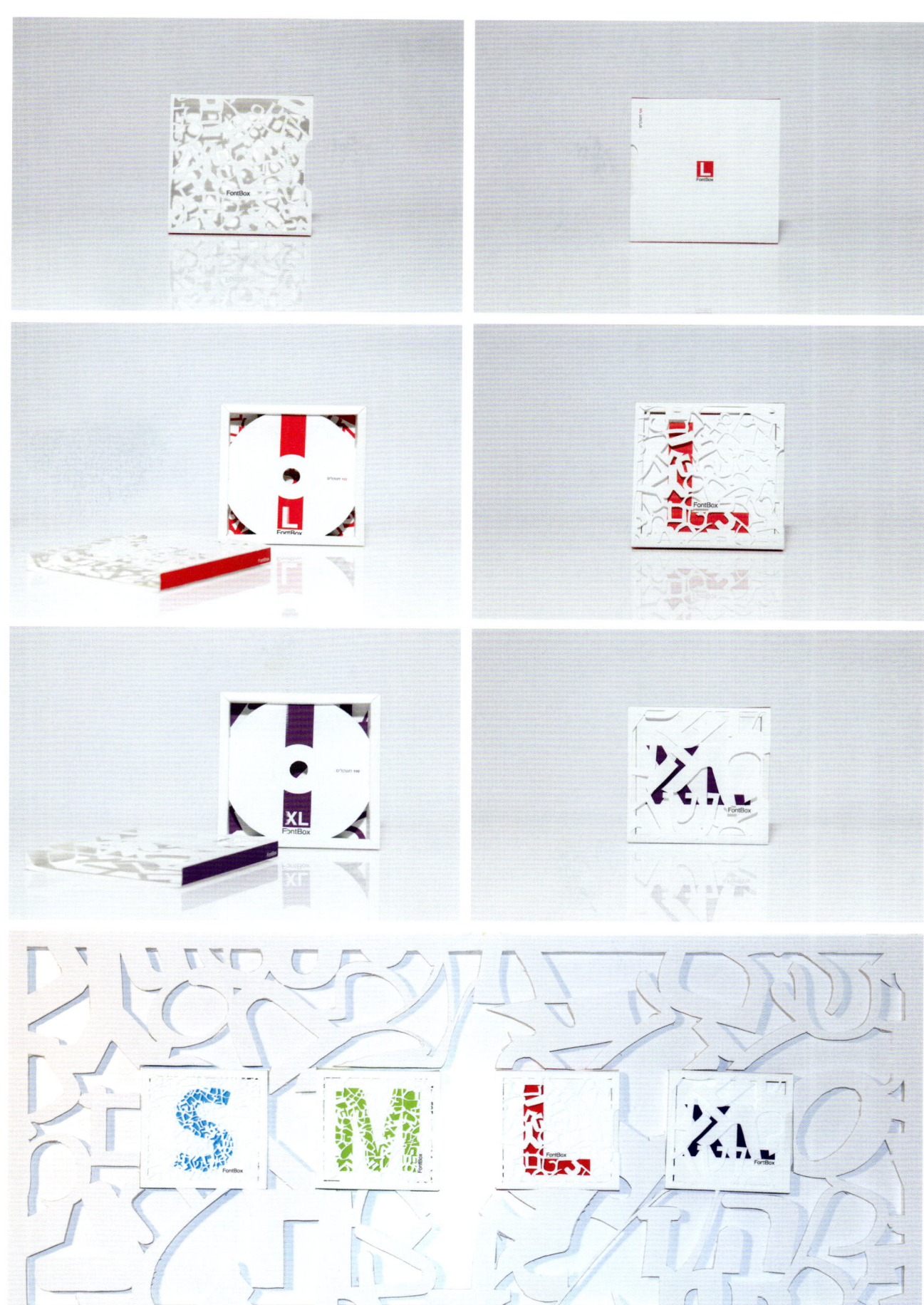

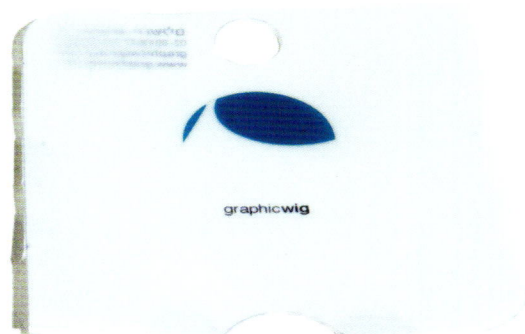

Design
Moshik Nadav

Project
GraphicWig

The brief was to choose any object that you want. Draw it, rotate it, reflect it, duplicate it and do what ever you want to it. Step two was to choose one shape from what you got, and use it as a logo for your imaginary company. Then, I needed to present a logo, in 3 different kinds of patterns based on the shapes that you got in a cold / warm and b&w colours, design a package for your object. The presentation will be in your store.

Design
Moshik Nadav

Project
GraphicWig

I choose to work with a table lamp. I got a cool shape that looks to me like a wig. I decided to open an imaginary company —'GraphicWig'.

GraphicWig is a company that designs graphic wigs for cartoon characters.

I designed 2 catalogs, one men's and one women's, along with a little bag for every wig purchased. 3 different pattern papers and a package for lamp—creative lamp—a lamp that will help you get creativity when ever you turn it on. I presented the project as mini store in my class.

Design
Moshik Nadav
Project
GraphicWig

Design
Moshik Nadav
Project
GraphicWig

Design
Fluotype

Project
Pablo Paez

Pablo Paez is a new soap and cosmetics brand. A small startup company with a strong identity, the product is unique in the cosmetic market as it features a masculine name; the company is run by a man.

The brand offers intense scented soaps for men and women of a medium high socioeconomic level. This goes hand in hand with the previous characteristic, and adds value to its identity.

We created the brand identity, from the logo to the labels. To create a link between the customers and the brand, we decided to follow the owner's passion for art and create an artistic design. To achieve this we decided on a revaluation of antique labels for cosmetics. We reinterpreted them using typography and ornaments.

Organic forms were created to identify each scent. They represent sensations created by each fruit, which in combination with geometric forms developed into a unisex styled label. These forms led to a variety of patterns to achieve an identity system with a versatile future.

The result was a powerful and edgy design for it to stand out from competitors in display racks.

Design
Ken-tsai Lee
Project
Taiwan Uni of Arts

Design
Scott Lambert
Project
Wildlife at Risk

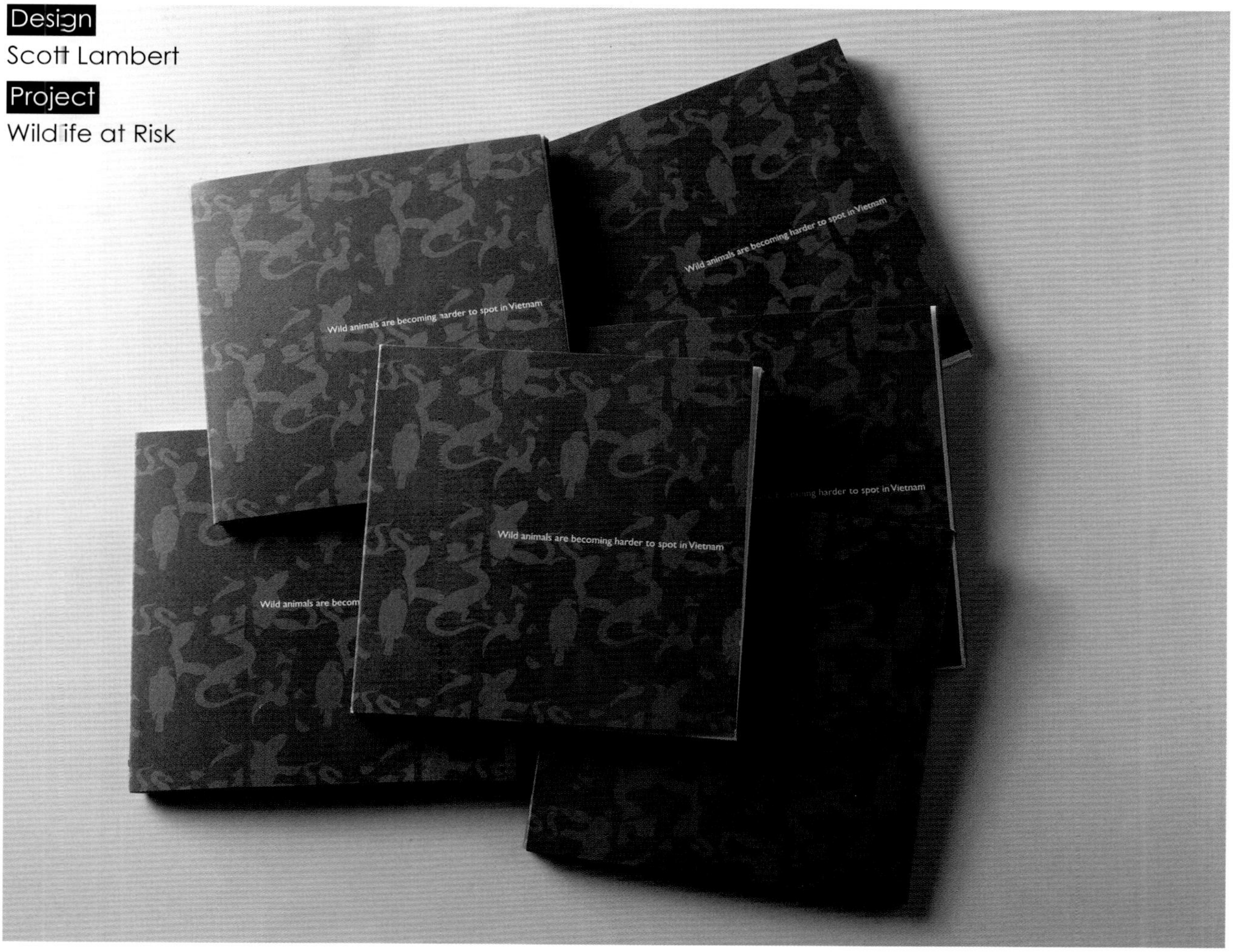

Design

Scott Lambert

Project

Mekong Red Dragon Rice

The rice is Eco friendly and Fair Trade. Furthermore husking, sifting and packaging are done by local villagers creating additional employment. It is also healthier Rice; during the husking process, the bran layer is only partly removed, as it is within the bran layer that the majority of beneficial nutrients are stored.

Design
Scott Lambert
Project
Britishisms

There are certain preferences, quirks, idiosyncrasies, ways of doing things and of having things done, manners and mannerisms that are singularly British. Britishisms. This folio of greeting cards uniquely celebrates some of those proclivities. Britishisms is a collaboration with Joanna Gregores.

Design
Scott Lambert
Project
Britishisms

Britishisms™

Certain habits, preferences, quirks, idiosyncrasies, orders of conduct, manners and mannerisms are singularly British. In a word: Britishisms. Some are better known to the casual observer, than are others. This selection of greeting cards uniquely portrays a sampling of those penchants.

Britishisms is a collaboration between Scott Lambert and Joanna Gregores.

www.greatbritishisms.com

Britishisms™

Britishisms™

Britishisms™

The Cup Final

Remembrance

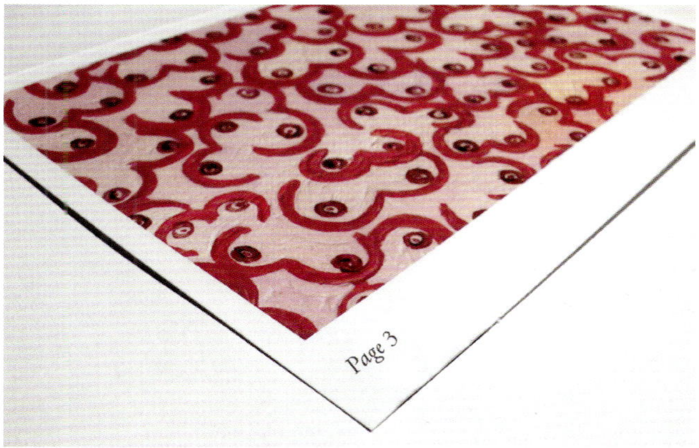

Page 3

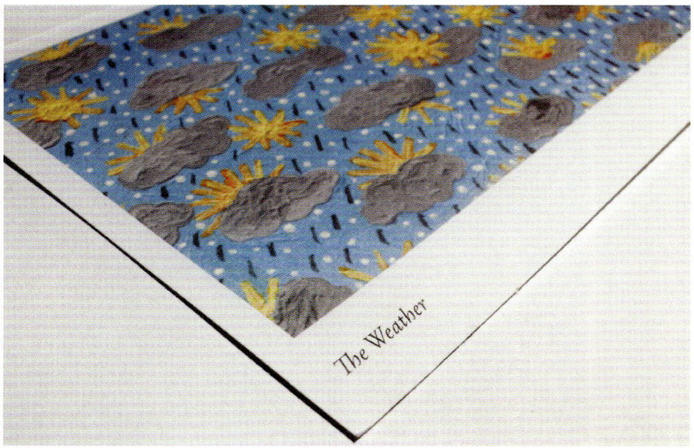

The Weather

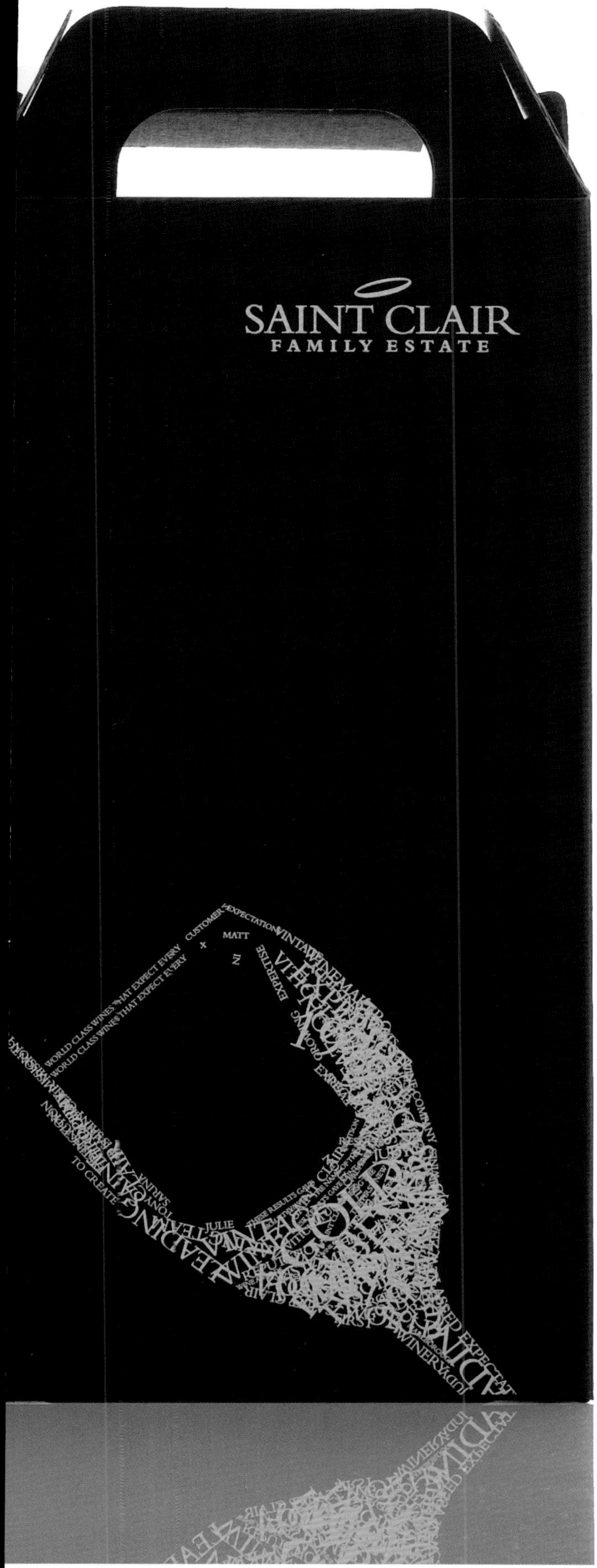

Design

The Creative Method

Project

Saint Clair Gift Box

A grape leaf, a bottle and a glass are recreated using comments, quotes and awards from Saint Clair's recent PR. The typographic solution creates impact, interest and dimension to the finished pack.

The pack works on many different levels. The first being on a single face where the consumer can read small amounts of copy and the text takes on a wrapping paper type effect.

Secondly when the boxes are lined up in the correct order the full image of the leaf is revealed. This is particularly useful for in-store displays gaining the brand more stand-out and cut-through.

Design
The Creative Method
Project
Guzman Y Gomez

The main markers for success in developing the identity were to firstly create a credible but approachable step-up fast food brand. It needed to have immediate personality, standout and begin to tell the story of Guzman Y Gomez.

We did a lot of research and deconstruction of existing fast food restaurant brands, their colours and how they worked. This gave us some initial rough guidelines including:
• The colour needed to have impact and standout.
• It also needed to reflect some aspect of the offer and if possible assist in telling a story.

The black and white imagery used throughout the packaging was chosen for a couple of reasons. Firstly it creates immediate contrast and fits with the yellow for optimum standout. The B&W colouring allows the imagery to look more premium and gives the brand a historical feel in the sense that it won't date.

It is cheap to re-produce and is ideal for use when everyday people are used instead of models—generally black and white imagery makes the everyday person look a little more attractive.

Design
The Creative Method

Project
Imaginitol

The brief was to create an interesting and engaging invitation to The Creative Method Xmas party.

It needed to illustrate what we do but also create a high level of Interest and anticipation for the party. It needed to be humorous and memorable. It was also required to work as a new business piece outside of the Christmas invitation.

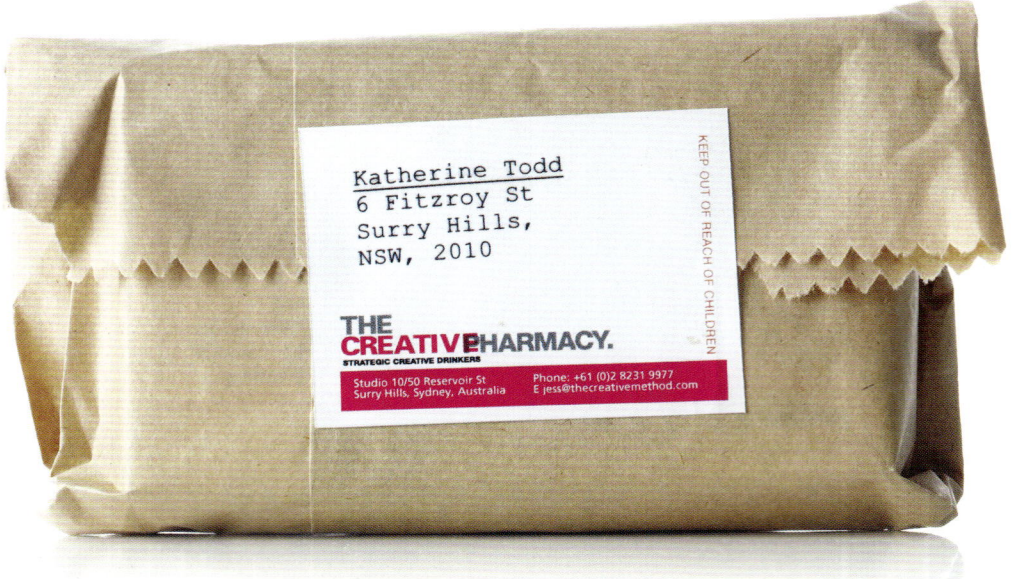

We based the idea on an imaginary pharmaceutical tablet that would solve their creative issues. Initially they were emailed a doctor's prescription, followed by the package in a discrete paper bag.

The invitation and the tablets were located inside. Tha party included staff dressed as doctors & medicinal shots administered by transvestites. The box and invitation are used as a new business teaser.

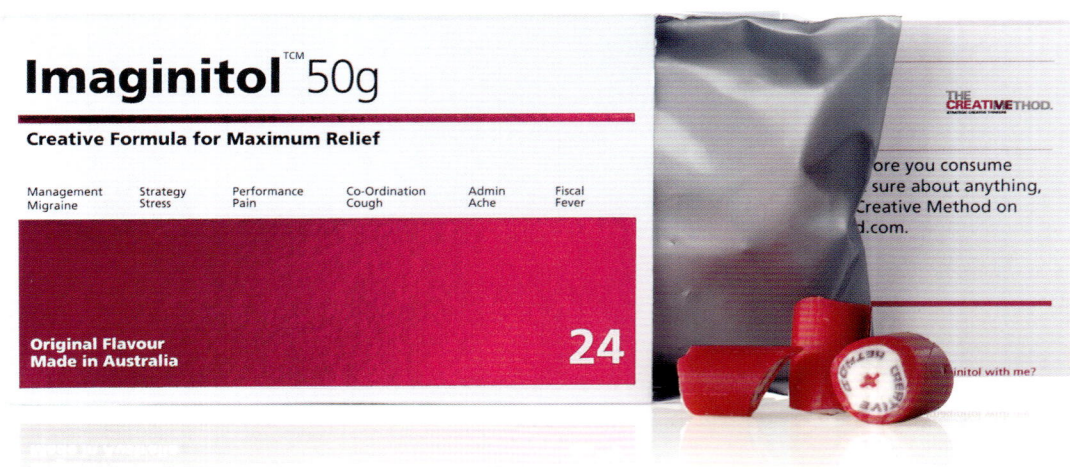

Design

The Creative Method

Project

Build Your Own

The aim was to create a unique gift to give our clients at Christmas and to act as a new business introduction. It needed to remind them of who we are and the long hours that we put into our work. It needed to feature all of our staff, reflect our creativity and sense of humour. The print run was 5000 labels.

We obtained high quality cleanskin wines and created our own labels. Each label was based on one staff member. It included a number of facial features and the client is encouraged to BYO (Build Your Own). The wine and the label is the perfect substitute for when the real thing cannot be there.

Design
The Creative Method

Project
Over The Moon

Directory

&Larry
Singapore

www.andlarry.com
info@andlarry.com

Bart van Delft
The Netherlands

www.bartvandelft.nl
info@web-farm.nl

&Larry begins every project by putting the name of their client or creative partner before their own. This spirit of collaboration and mutual respect is reflected in the thinking that goes into each piece of work.

&Larry believes that art and design shouldn't exist in separate vacuums. Be it commercial or experimental, &Larry always seeks to create works that are honest, functional and expressive beyond aesthetics.

The studio has adopted the Eames motto of 'Take your pleasure seriously' and examples of this philosophy can be seen in a diverse body of work from posters and print campaigns to our series of Singapore-inspired art objects.

Bart van Delft is a Dutch Designer who started designing at the age of 16. He calls himself Mediadesigner, he even is the initiator of the original Dutch term 'Mediaontwerper'.

He has worked for Philips Design and Dedato Designers and Architects. And currently Bart is working for B-total Hot Creative Concepts.

As a Mediadesigner he is interested in all sorts of media, from print to web, from video to audio. Typography is his biggest fascination. This is visible in every project of his hand.

Daniel Dittmar
Australia

http://d-dittmar.com
dittmar@floodstudio.net

Edwin Tan
Singapore

www.bravo-company.info
info@bravo-company.info

During the discourse of delving into the depths of design, Daniel Dittmar developed a disdain for dignitaries and dilettantes alike, displaying detrimental, destructive, and dispiriting deeds. Despite damply dilating such doings with directional dynamism through detailed doctrines and decadent drudgery, depravity doesn't die.

Desecration of dames, drugs and Drambuie provided decent dosage during the dusk till dawn days, but Dittmar discovered this developed a disharmony with his design and a deviation of his disciplines and demeanour. He duly deterred. The discotheque of discord still despicably dwells despondently (sometimes dormant) so the duel for design decency isn't done!

Dittmar's decree is a desire to desegregate different design disciplines, and diffuse the local district through distinctive, deluxe and dexterous design.

During his 4 year stint in Asylum Creative under the creative direction of Christopher Lee, Bravo Company`s founder/art director Edwin Tan has worked on projects ranging from interactive and environmental design to branding and graphic design.

Conceptualising Frolick, Loof and The White Rabbit from the very start and working with clients such as Club21 and Levi's, he has won numerous international awards from Communication Arts, One Show, ADC and also the local CCA.

His works have been featured in many design books and magazines.

Homework
Danmark

homework.dk
info@homework.dk

Kai Zan
Taiwan
China

www.themm.info
Kaizan@themm.info

Homework is an independent graphic design studio and consultancy that focuses on art direction, visual identity and communication for lifestyle, fashion and cultural clients.

Jack Dahl established homework in 2002. Jack Dahl was responsible for kick starting a visual presence and direction for international men's fashion publication HE magazine and Cover magazine (Copenhagen).

Among others Jack has worked with Self Service magazine and Work in Progress advertising design studio (Paris) on some of today's leading fashion references including Jil Sander, Prada, Pucci, Chloé, Celine, Colette, Sophia Kokosalaki and Veronique Branquinho.

Born on May 21, 1984, Taiwanese designer Zan Bokai (Kai Zan) was originally trained in the fine arts.

His work later branched out into the areas of graphic design, interactive design, and digital art.

His style and thinking are deeply influenced by the idea of minimalism. He believes that the designer's job is to simplify complexity by using the clearest and most powerful images to communicate effectively.

He once held position within Taiwan's culture and creative institution, Xue Xue Institute.

Currently, he is a graphic designer working in such fields as branding, brand identity, print design, packaging design, website construction, and art direction.

Ken-tsai Lee
Taiwan
China

www.kentsailee.com
leekentsai1@yahoo.com

KreativeHouse
Italy

www.kreativehouse.it
info@kreativehouse.it

Ken-tsai Lee was born in Taipei, currently living in New York. Established Ken-tsai Lee design studio since 1996, 2002 he moved to New York to continue his career. His partner Chou Yao-Fong keeps the studio still working in Taipei.

After coming to New York, Lee's worked in different media and cooperated with professionals in other fields, such as photography, animation, in order to explore new methods of design.

Since Lee established his own studio in 1996, he's won numerous design awards and participated many design exhibitions worldwide, such as D&AD Award, AIGA 365 Annual Award, Communication Arts Design Annual Award, New York Type Director Club Annual Award, Graphis Platinum, Gold Awards in Design, Poster Brochures Annuals, One Show Design Award, Red-Dot Award —Communication Design, How magazine—International Design Competition, Self-Promotion Design Competition, Step inside 100 Awards, Tokyo Type Directors Club Annual Award, Two Gold Awards form Hong Kong Designers Association Award, Best Printed Graphic Design Award from IDN Magazine—

KreativeHouse is a laboratory of images, ideas, projects and words. Founded in the 2008 in Italy from two creatives to spread creativity graphic and communication in a sustainable way.

KH study promotional strategies which have low ecological impact and high emotional impact to draw attention, to stimulate and make people reflect.

La caja de tipos
Spain

www.lacajadetipos.com
estudio@lacajadetipos.com

Mind Design
UK

www.minddesign.co.uk
info@minddesign.co.uk

La caja de tipos is a graphic design studio formed by María Sáez and Ander Sánchez and bases in Leioa (Bizkaia, SPAIN). On February 25, 2008 they began working for the first time in La caja de tipos.

Both love what they do and what matters most in each of their works is to convey concepts through a correct choice of colours, fonts, compositions and graphic resources. They understand that all 'means', so they always try to make what they do respond to this premise.

Among other things, La caja de tipos made visual identity projects for companies, posters for music festivals, wedding invitations, websites and editorial projects. They like to take care of every detail and all of their works are considered important no matter how small they are. Both María and Ander are involved in each project by providing ideas and solutions.

They love everything that is done from the heart. And occasionally also they leave aside the computer and stain their hands while they work because they think that what really matters are the ideas and not the tools.

Mind Design is an independent graphic design studio based in East London. The studio has been founded by Holger Jacobs in 1998 after graduating from the Royal College of Art.

Mind Design believes in practical, engaging and friendly design solutions. The studio's approach is design led, not marketing driven. Content and form are seen as equally important and inseparable from each other.

Beside a passion for typography the studio is interested in integrated design solutions that combine corporate identity, print, web and interior design. Working in close collaboration with clients is important as it allows being involved in projects right from the start. Every project is treated as a new challenge and the studio never imposes an already established graphic house style.

Ministry of Design
Singapore

www.modonline.com
studio@modonline.com

Moshik Nadav
Israel

www.moshik.net
moshik@moshik.net

Ministry of Design was created by Colin Seah to Question, Disturb & Redefine the spaces and forms that surround us and add meaning to our world.

An integrated spatial-design practice, MOD's explorations are created amidst a democratic 'studio-like' atmosphere and progress seamlessly between form, site, object and space. Ministry of Design love to question where the inherent potential in contemporary design lies, and then to disturb the ways they are created or perceived—redefining the world around us in relevant and innovative ways, project by project!

This, Ministry of Design declares, is real change, not change for the sake of novelty.

Fortified with these aspirations, Ministry of Design begins each distinct project anew by seeking to do 2 things—to draw deeply from the context surrounding each project, but also to dream freely so that they might transcend mere reality. Each MOD project endeavours to be delightfully surprising but yet relevant, distinctly local but still globally appealing.

Moshik Nadav was born in Febuary 21th, 1983 in Israel. During 2007-2011 he studied Visual Communication in Bezalel—Academy of Art & Design, Jerusalem, Israel.

On December 2009 he completed a student exchange program in Toronto, Canada where he had the opportunity to study at OCAD for one semester.

Moshik has worked for two years at a prominent advertising firm in Israel as a graphic artist and since 2005 he is working as a freelancer. Moshik`s true love is making Typefaces and working with Typography.

Moshik sees typography as a distilled form of graphic design. When Moshik is working on a new Project, he is taking inspiration from everything that surrounding him, his view about inspiration is that it can be very close to you, but if you won`t keep your eyes open enough, you can lose it.

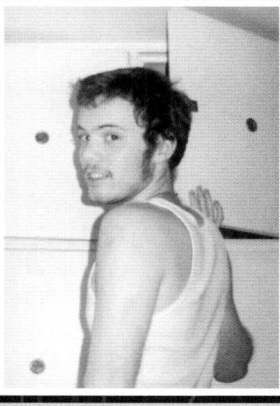

Patricio Murphy
Argentina

behance.net/patriciomurphy
pmurphy1987@hotmail.com

Research Studios
UK

www.researchstudios.com
info@researchstudios.com

Patricio Murphy is an Argentine graphic designer, born in 1987. He recently graduated from the University of Buenos Aires (UBA). After his first internship in a graphic design studio, he started to work as a professional designer, taking some freelance works as well as working at the studio.

He's passionate about illustration, editorial design, typography and branding. One of his professional goals is to travel around the World, working in different studios, in order to earn knowledge as well as different experiences.

RS London was launched in 1994 by Neville Brody. For the past 15 years the studio has collaborated with a diverse range of international clients on a spectrum of projects. Research Studios London has become the hub of their network and office base for Neville Brody.

The studio is located in a Georgian town house in Angel Islington close to the famous Camden Passage antiques market, boutiques and small restaurants.

Scott Lambert
UK

www.design-positive.com
scott@design-positive.com

Stas Sipovich
Czech Republic

www.stassipovich.com
contact@stassipovich.com

Scott Lambert was born and raised in Southampton, England. He pursued his early studies, as most boys do, drawing on toilet walls, beginning with squeakers, then graduating to the flexibility of aerosol spray cans—anatomy being his coup d'oeil. His passion for graphic design grew with fine art studies at Winchester School of Art, going on to further his studies at Middlesex University, London, graduating with a BA Degree in Illustration.

After a two years working in London Scott joined the university of life and travelled the world. Since then he has worked for several agencies applying his touch to many well known brands and organisations across the globe. But some of his most acclaimed projects have been for small Charities, boutique brands and Non Government Organisations.

Stas Sipovich lives and works in Prague, Czech Republic. As far back as he can remember he draws since childhood. He grew in the environment among markers, pencils and paints.

He specialises in graphic design, visual communications and also he travels. Sometimes he participates in exhibitions and different non-commercial projects.

Switchopen
UK

www.switchopen.com
switchopen@gmail.com

Tadas Karpavičius
Lithuania

www.tadaskarpavicius.com
hello@tadaskarpavicius.com

Nick Rhodes (Switchopen) is the Illustration and design company run by Nick Rhodes. Nick has been involved within the rock poster scene since 2000.

He has designed and illustrated posters for many bands within the UK and United States. Creating hand screen printed limited edition posters for bands including Queens of the Stone age, The Decemberists, Elbow and Ian Brown to name but a few.

Switchopen is a fully functioning art studio, housing a range of print machines (screen/lino/digital), all primed ready for action to handle a full spectrum of design projects.

Tadas Karpavičius is a graphic designer from Lithuania currently living in London. He is working in the fields of illustration, motion graphics, print design, art direction and design for music industry.

Tadas is experimenting with mixed media like collages, shapes, type and believes in design that touches the viewer. He is dedicated to simplicity and thinks that the most important in design are clarity, form and function. The idea of how design shapes visual environment is always influencing him and inspiration usually comes from daily life, music, people watching or those tiny details.

Thorbjørn Ankerstjerne
UK

www.ankerstjerne.co.uk
thorbjorn@ankerstjerne.co.uk

Tuukka Koivisto
Finland

www.tuukkakoivisto.com
tuukkakoi@gmail.com

Danish Thorbjørn Ankerstjerne, 29 years old, graduated in 2007 from Central Saint Martins with a BA in graphic Design.

He has lived in London for 7 years and is currently working as a freelance designer as well as an editor and art director for FILE Magazine.

He enjoys working across a broad range of media from moving image, installations to conventional graphic design.

Tuukka Koivisto is a Helsinki-based graphic designer. He has learnt more by doing than by paying attention at school. He does anything he gets his hands on. And he does it without hesitating and he does it big.

If Tuukka was wine, he would be vinegar. If Tuukka was a woman, he would be a man. If Tuukka was a vegetarian, he would feast on meat. If Tuukka was an animal, he would be a lion. He is more extreme than you are.

He is a nightmare to work with because you do not know what he does next, but you love to work with him for the same reason. And what he does next is something that helps you out of the trap.

VONSUNG
UK

VONSUNG.COM
info@vonsung.com

VONSUNG is a branding design studio. They provide design services across the full spectrum of total identity, print and screen graphics, internet, product, space and interiors.

They believe unequivocally that creative design is a different beast—a flexible commerce and communication channel that requires specialised knowledge across a broad range of disciplines. They synthesise strategy, creativity, function, value and technology seamlessly to deliver winning solutions that exceed the rigorous standards of the world's top marketers.

They think that while visual identity tends to refer to literal identification specifically to the characteristic way a company or institution writes its name and the rules that govern that characteristic signature, branding now includes all of the above but extends its experience further and deeper—into environments, sounds, smells and attitudes.

Above all, they believe simple design equals power.

www.anagrama.com
hello@anagrama.com

Mexico
Anagrama

Brown&White

www.brownandwhitecreative.com
rich@richbrown.info

UK
Brown & White
Creative

www.coppensalberts.nl
info@coppensalberts.nl

The Netherlands
Coppens Alberts

Anagrama is a specialised brand development and positioning agency providing creative solutions for any type of project. Besides their history and experience with brand development, they are also experts in the design and development of objects, spaces and multimedia projects.

Anagrama create the perfect balance between a design boutique, focusing on the development of creative pieces paying attention to the smallest of details, and a business consultancy providing solutions based on the analysis of tangible data to generate best fit applications.

Their services reach all of the branding spectrum from strategic consulting to fine tune brand objectives for the company to logotype, peripherals and captivating illustration design.

Brown & White Creative Ltd was setup by Rich Brown and Susannah White.

Brown & White Creative Ltd offering interaction design, branding and creative solutions in both digital and print.

They will work independently or as a creative team.

Coppens Alberts is an Amsterdam-based design studio focusing on editorial design for web and print, graphic identities and custom fit type design.

Coppens Alberts is fascinated by the uniqueness of each individual project and the ongoing process of designing. Every new project is a new question with a new answer. The bureau stands for outspoken solutions that convey the content in the clearest as possible way.

A designing attitude that holds a straight eye on typographical detail, materialisation and visual statement.

www.cargocollective.com
/darioverrengia
dario.verrengia@gmail.com

Italy
Dario Verrengia

Dario Verrengia is a 21 years old student and freelance graphic designer based in Milan.

He studies Communication Design at Politecnico di Milano. He collaborated with magazines, blogs, museums and events.

His works have been published in books, magazines and blogs, in Italy, England, Spain and out of Europe, in China and USA.

He has a particular interest in editorial design, typography and information design.

www.demianconrad.com
contact@demianconrad.com

Switzerland
Demian Conrad

Demian Conrad Design is a creative studio based in Lausanne and Bellinzona. They create graphic design for paper, and design product and interiors for companies, artistic institutions, international organisations.

Their goal is to create works with commercial aim, to innovate and to find new path to the best solution for their clients.

www.fluotype.com.ar
info@fluotype.com.ar

Argentina
Fluotype

Based in Buenos Aires, Argentina, Fluotype is a small team of great people that work together at a young company providing high-quality services for branding, graphic design, illustration and packaging.

Innovative ideas, original concepts and customized work are commitments delivered with passion by Florencia Lopez and Agustina de Tullio, partners and co-founders at Fluotype.

www.fuse-design.co.uk
studio@fuse-design.co.uk

UK
Fuse

Fuse Design is a creative, passionate and friendly multi-disciplinary design agency based in Nottingham. Who excel in original, creative and effective design solutions.

They have vast experience and a knowledge base that covers a large area within the graphic design realm. Their portfolio showcases works from a range of clients, from small start up businesses to large prestigious names, all from a variety of business sectors. These offer different challenges, but each and every project shares Fuse's underlying belief in originality and creativity.

www.loosecollective.net
gman@loosecollective.net

UK
G-MAN

Graham Jones (G-MAN) is a graphic designer in Manchester England with over 10 years' experience. Recent clients have included Candy Studios, Steranko Clothing, Interval, music label The Lab, the BBC, and interactive media company Bellyfeel.

On top of that G-MAN is a founding member and designer/art director of Loose Collective that comprises of creative people from different walks of life who come together to collaborate on projects. G-MAN is also a Senior Lecturer on the BA(Hons) Graphic Design degree at the Manchester Metropolitan University.

www.jameskape.com
mail@jameskape.com

Australia
James Kape

James Kape is a designer from Sydney, Australia who does a little bit of everything, but has so far specialized in a variety of print-media, some web and branding.

Within his design life so far, he has worked for names such as 'Ksubi' (An Australian fashion collective) and 'Ben Frost' (An Australian street artist). In addition to this he studied at the 'Hogskolan for Design and Crafts' (HDK) Gothenburg, Sweden and much of his current design workings reflect a strong influence from his time spent there.

KentLyons

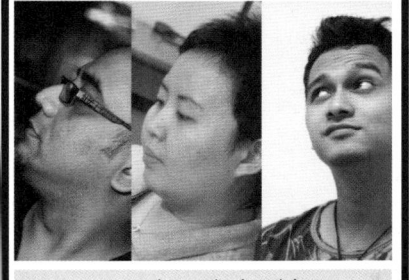

www.kentlyons.com
info@kentlyons.com

UK
KentLyons

KentLyons is an award-winning London-based graphic design agency. They work on a wide variety of creative projects, including branding, print, interactive and environmental design. Their design service caters to many high profile clients and produces print that is visually stunning and highly engaging.

Formed in 2003, KentLyons creates dynamic and effective graphic communications that engage and entertain. Online, a KentLyons site is instantly recognisable by its ease of navigation and accessibility, combined with a rich and engaging online experience.

---

www.leapdesign.biz
info@leapdesign.biz

Indonesia
LEAP Design

LEAP Design Associates started as an in-house design team in 2003 for one of the biggest financial advisory firm in Asia and Middle East. Managed by Cynthia Mononutu, who started as a one-woman team and grew the department to 20 plus personnel handling a broad range of services from branding, print design, publication to interactive projects.

In 2007, having started to offer its services to external clients, the team moved to become an independent design studio under the brand of LEAP and is now well established in Jakarta, Indonesia and Hong Kong,China, working with clients from a variety of industries throughout the region.

www.lundgrenlindqvist.se
hello@lundgrenlindqvist.se

Sweden
Lundgren+Lindqvist

Lundgren+Lindqvist is a design bureau based in Gothenburg, Sweden working with a wide spectra of clients in different business fields and parts of the world. Print work, branding as well as web design and development are handled with the same care and attention to detail.

www.mammaldesign.com
info@mammaldesign.com

UK
Mammal

Mammal is a small creative led design agency based in central London, which was founded 4 years ago by MD and Creative Director Joe Hosp.

They're a team of skilled designers from diverse backgrounds including graphic design, advertising, typography and web design which means they can ensure that each job gets the care and attention it deserves.

Purpose

www.purpose.co.uk
info@purpose.co.uk

UK
Purpose

Purpose is a brand consultancy, specialising in brand identity and marketing communications.
Their work helps clients to stand out, to connect, and to prosper.

Purpose is 25 strong, independent and listed in the Design.Week league table of Top 50 UK Creative Award winning agencies.

Saffron

www.saffron-consultants.com
hello@saffron-consultants.com

UK
Saffron Brand Consultants

Saffron is an independent consulting firm working for companies, countries, cities and other enterprises in branding and identity issues.

Founded by Wally Olins and Jacob Benbunan in 2001, they work globally from their offices in London, Madrid, New York, Vienna, Dubai and Mumbai.

www.ohhi.co.za
ssmaclennan@gmail.com

South Africa
Si Maclennan

www.thecreativemethod.com
mail@thecreativemethod.com

Australia
The Creative Method

www.thompsonbrandpartnmers.com
info@thompsonbrandpartners.com

UK
Thompson Brand Partners

Si Maclennan is a young and passionate South African illustrator and designer. He lives in Cape Town, and works for leading digital agency, HelloComputer. His work is striking, decorative and often abstract, leaning towards a mostly digital method in production.

The Creative Method was established in October of 2005 and was built from the desire to create a world class design studio out of Sydney.

The philosophy is simple, to produce the greatest ideas with the best possible execution. It's an ongoing work in progress and involves constantly pushing ourselves, our clients, the mediums we work within and ultimately the consumers.

The Creative Method has won a number of awards both nationally and internationally and has featured in a mountain of publications globally. Whilst recognition of our design peers is great, we will only judge ourselves on the success of our clients.

Thompson Brand Partners partner brands at many different stages in their development. They create new brands from the vision up. They rebrand and roll-out, managing the change that comes with it.

When the key elements of a brand are in place, their role can be to stretch or reposition a brand. And often they're creating communications for a brand that's already well established. At every stage, they work from the very essence of what makes a brand different—its true commercial advantage.

www.flicca.com
yasuko@flicca.com

Japan
Yasuko Ikeda

www.yomesubo.com
info@yomesubo.com

Mexico
Yomesubo

Yasuko Ikeda is a Japanese graphic designer. In the late nineties she moved from her hometown of Osaka to the UK to study graphic design at Central St. Martins College Of Art.

After graduating she stayed in London and continued to develop her approach towards design while working with a number of well-known smaller studios, including Value and Service and North Design.

Now working between Japan and Europe her focus varies between brand identity, illustration, fashion textile, and print design—all linked by simple, bold use of graphics and a love of fluorescent colours.

Her most recent projects include branding work for Tombow and Coca Cola, and fashion design for Helly Hansen and Adidas.

In 2004 in Mexico City, Benjamin Aceves, with the idea of a creative boutique, inspired by the work of great designers and design firms decide to open Yomesubo.

With the philosophy of working under a scheme of specific clients, Yomesubo focuses on branding projects, editorial design and art direction, working with a small team but functional with solutions for great brands.

Specializing in the editorial area, Yomesubo has carried out the design and redesign of newspapers and magazines, art books and music. For more than a year he has made the art direction and design of the fashion magazine: Blink.

Acknowledgement

We would like to thank all the designers and design companies who made significant contributions to the compilation of this book. Without them, this project would not have been possible.

The previous pages show the profile and contact details for the designers.

Thanks also to many others whose names do not appear on the credits but also made specific input and support for the project from beginning to end.

Special thanks to Ken-tsai Lee, who wrote the preface for this book.

Futureditions

If you would like to contribute to the next book by Artpower, please email us your details to: info@artpower.com.cn.